THE COMPLETE GUIDE TO PREVENTING AND RESOLVING BROKERAGE DISPUTES

THE COMPLETE GUIDE TO PREVENTING AND RESOLVING BROKERAGE DISPUTES

Richard J. Teweles
Edward S. Bradley
Cedric Choi

WILEY

JOHN WILEY & SONS
New York   Chichester   Brisbane   Toronto   Singapore

This publication is designed to provide accurate and
authoritative information in regard to the subject
matter covered. It is sold with the understanding that
the publisher is not engaged in rendering legal, accounting,
or other professional service. If legal advice or other
expert assistance is required, the services of a competent
professional person should be sought. *From a Declaration
of Principles jointly adopted by a Committee of the
American Bar Association and a Committee of Publishers.*

Library of Congress Cataloging in Publication Data:

Teweles, Richard Jack, 1924–
    The Complete Guide to Preventing and Resolving Brokerage
    Disputes / Richard J. Teweles, Edward S. Bradley, Cedric Choi.
        p.   cm.
    Bibliography: p.
    Includes index.
    ISBN 0-471-85712-2
        1. Stockbrokers—Legal status, laws, etc.—United States.
    2. Stockbrokers—United States. I. Bradley, Edward S. II. Choi,
    Cedric. III. Title.
    KF1071.T85 1988
    346.73'0926—dc19
    [347.306926]   88-20532
                                                                CIP

Printed in the United States of America

10 9 8 7 6 5 4 3 2 1

DEDICATED TO

Ruth Teweles Joan Bradley Patricia Grady Choi
Kari Teweles   Wilbert H. S. Choi
              Flora K. Choi

Preface

This is a book about disputes between customers who acquire financial interests and brokers who provide them. When a customer loses money or makes less than was expected, disputes often arise between the customer and the broker. The problem may involve the chosen investment instrument, the size of the position taken, or the strategy employed. Sometimes brokers are negligent or guilty of wrongdoing. Brokers should not, however, be blamed for being wrong about the direction of the market as long as their recommendations were reasonably based and offered in good faith.

Part One of this book offers descriptions of the parties involved in a customer-broker relationship and includes a description of brokerage houses, the exchanges, advisors, and regulators. The various types of products offered by brokers are also discussed. Part Two, consisting of Chapters 4 through 10, covers solicitation of accounts and the opening of accounts, and the accompanying documentation, as well as the problems associated with these activities. Suitability, which is the basis for many disputes, is covered in Chapter 6. The handling of accounts, including discretion, different types of orders, time stamping, commissions and sales credits, and checks as payment for securities, is the subject of Chapter 7. A discussion of margin accounts is found in Chapter 8. The chapter on supervision specifies the duties of management personnel at all levels and the implications of any failures to perform those duties properly. Churning is a frequent allegation against brokers, and a complete discussion is included in Chapter 10. Finally, Part Two describes the customer's responsibilities and how customers can help avoid problems that could otherwise lead to costly disputes.

Part Three covers the rules, regulations, and legal duties of brokers and their customers. Chapters 11 through 18 emphasize avoidance of disputes through knowledge and common sense. Court decisions, exchange rules, statutes, custom and trade practice, and internal policies and procedures of brokerage houses are discussed. Although legal compliance is the topic under consideration, this section is written for customers and brokers, not just their attorneys. Attorneys will, however, find the case discussions and legal citations helpful as a starting point for research.

Part Three also covers arbitration and litigation, including discovery, and provides a helpful discussion of the types of documents that should be produced during either type of proceeding.

There will always be those on both sides who accept the credit for good investments but not the blame for bad ones. Our book cannot do much to help them. Many arguments, however, find their roots in genuine misunderstandings of the nature of financial instruments, strategies, how the finance business operates, or the motivations of those with whom one is dealing. Others are caused by nothing more than misinterpretations of the meaning of arcane financial jargon. If we can eliminate or reduce such misunderstandings, perhaps some losses can be avoided, or at least not result in formal, expensive, and time-consuming disputes.

* * *

The authors share a wealth of personal experience with the readers. One has specialized as a financial practitioner, consultant, and expert witness. Another has acted as sales, compliance, and training officer for a major financial firm. The third is a practicing attorney with substantial experience in disputes between customers and brokers. All have an extensive theoretical base and long practical experience to justify their suggestions and advice on methods to avoid trouble, or to deal with it if it cannot be avoided.

It would be impossible to thank everyone who contributed to this book. Special mention is due to Edward B. Horwitz, who was never too busy to provide his thoughtful comments on several subjects discussed herein. John B. Shimizu deserves special mention as an attorney whose legal competence, diligence, and dedication contributed to the content of this book. We are also grateful to our families who tolerated the disruption of their lives while we worked on this book.

Richard J. Teweles
Edward S. Bradley
Cedric Choi

Abbreviations

AMEX	American Stock Exchange
CBOE	Chicago Board Options Exchange
CBOT	Chicago Board of Trade
CFTC	Commodity Futures Trading Commission
CME	Chicago Mercantile Exchange
CPO	Commodity Pool Operator
CTA	Commodity Trading Advisor
NASD	National Association of Securities Dealers
NASDAQ	National Association of Securities Dealers Automated Quotations
NFA	National Futures Association
NMS	National Market System (NASDAQ)
NYSE	New York Stock Exchange
OTC	Over-the-counter
REIT	Real Estate Investment Trust
SEC	Securities and Exchange Commission
SRO	Self-regulatory organization

Contents

THE COMPLETE GUIDE TO PREVENTING AND RESOLVING BROKERAGE DISPUTES

1

Fair Dealing in the Investment Business

Let us begin by making clear what this book is not. It is not a primer for those interested in learning how to sue their brokers successfully. It is not a guide for brokerage employees who seek ways to place their own interests ahead of those of their customers and get away with it. It is not a hornbook for lawyers concerned primarily with their fees, contingency or otherwise, or with profiting from "nuisance" settlements. It is certainly not a law book.

Rather, the book is designed as an aid for keeping the peace. Even this constructive purpose cannot lead to a complete solution of all investment business problems. There will always be some boiler rooms or bucket shops established for the primary purpose of cheating the public. There will always be customers more interested in cheating brokerage companies than in trying to invest successfully. There will always be some lawyers more interested in their personal economic well-being than in the pursuit of justice. If readers become aware of such problems they may act with more caution than they otherwise would have.

There are many professionals in both the financial and legal professions who exhibit honesty, integrity, and concern for the best interests of their clients. Nevertheless, the complaint files of the Securities and Exchange Commission have reached all-time highs. The number of disputes

submitted to once obscure arbitration panels has exhausted their resources, resulting in ever longer waiting periods. Some financial machi-
nations have moved from the financial pages of newspapers to the front
pages and are discussed on television's nightly news. Perhaps if financial
advisors and their customers become better aware of some of the pitfalls,
they will act with more caution and avoid disputes, or at least minimize
the losses and costs.

Even this constructive purpose cannot lead to a satisfactory solution
of all brokerage business problems. Most financial disputes do not begin
with evil intentions. Even well-known financial institutions which are
run by managers with high moral and ethical standards may sometimes
find that they have hired some people who should not have been hired,
are improperly trained and poorly supervised, or who react unfavor-
ably to unexpected changes in personal circumstances. Customers who
opened accounts in good faith but with unrealistic expectations concerning the potential rewards and risks in their choices of financial instruments or trading strategies may react adversely, albeit unreasonably,
when they find that they have made less money or lost more money than
they had anticipated.

If a legal dispute evolves, customers have a right to know their wisest
course of action. An innocent brokerage house and its employees have
the right to protect themselves against unfair allegations. All parties are
entitled to have counsels represent them who understand the structure of
the financial business, its terminology, and the nature of typical disputes.

As a first step, it should be productive to comment on three broad
problems in the brokerage business that underlie many of the narrower
issues that will be discussed in detail in the chapters that follow. These
are conflict of interest, the efficient markets hypothesis, and failures to
communicate effectively.

CONFLICT OF INTEREST

The basic relationship in the brokerage business, regardless of the type
of financial instrument involved, is usually between a salesperson and
a customer. Changing the titles of the parties does not change the relationship. Salespersons may refer to themselves as account executives,
financial consultants, investment executives, brokers, various levels of
vice president, or some other high-sounding title that looks good on a
business card, but they are salespersons nevertheless.

There is, of course, nothing wrong with selling if the salesperson
represents a reliable company and sells respectable products in proper

quantities to those who have a real need or desire for the products. (This might make one wonder why there are so many euphemisms for an occupation which is basically perfectly respectable.) The customer may be called an investor, a speculator, or a client, but is basically a customer of the salesperson. In any such relationship, the parties have fundamental motivations. Sometimes the motivations of the salesperson and the customer may collide.

The financial world provides many examples of conflict of interest problems stemming from agency or dealer relationships. Much has been written about the abuse of insider trading. Managers of companies who should be primarily concerned with increasing the wealth of the company's stockholders are sometimes more concerned with their own incomes, perquisites, or job security.

The problem leading to a collision of motivations in selling financial merchandise may not be readily apparent. After all, most customers want to make more money or conserve what they already have, and honest salespersons want their customers to make more money and keep what they already have. Customers who make money are less likely to transfer their accounts to a different salesperson, or to another firm, or to give up investing altogether. Their accounts become larger. Satisfied customers may refer their families and friends. Well-trained salespeople who have good judgment know better than to live for today alone. They do not want to spend their lives endlessly replacing customers who have taken their accounts elsewhere, or who have lost their capital and have little left to do but tell all who will listen about their bitter experiences. Given the seemingly parallel interests of the parties, one might wonder what causes conflict. High on the list of causes are the manner in which brokerage salespeople are often compensated and the bases upon which fringe benefits are bestowed.

The Basic Conflict of Interest

Simply stated, salespersons make their livings directly or indirectly from commissions or sales spreads involved in buying or selling financial interests. Thus, their own financial interests can conflict with their clients' needs and objectives. Salespeople, as agents or fiduciaries of clients, must always suppress this conflict in favor of serving their clients' best interests and needs. At times, this conflict of interest is subject to tension, but the order of things cannot change; it is always the clients' best interests which must come first.

Brokerage firms may place great pressures upon salespeople to sell certain items or to achieve certain levels of gross income production.

Such pressure can range from granting of perquisites such as private offices, to continued employment. Similar conflicts may exist between real estate salespeople, attorneys, insurance brokers, and other professionals and their clients, and are not exclusive to the financial business. The solution for all such conflict generally is simply to place the client's interests first.

Compensation of Salespersons

The basis for compensation of salespersons in the brokerage business is primarily from the gross revenue realized from their sales efforts. Such revenue might consist of commissions, sales credits, markups, markdowns, or fees for specialized products or services. Regardless of the form of such revenues, most come from purchases and sales of financial instruments. Whether the salesperson receives a designated percentage of the gross revenue designated as net commissions, or compensation is disguised as salary, bonuses, or expense payments, the source is most likely to be transactions.

Most customers are best served by paying as little for trading as possible. The lower the rates and the fewer trades that are made, the better for the customer. Most salespersons, however, start every day with an income of zero. If no customer buys or sells anything, there is no short term benefit to the salesperson. Until the customer rebels or the account is destroyed, the higher the commissions and the more often commissions are generated, the better it is economically for the salesperson.

BONUSES AND OTHER FRINGE BENEFITS

In order to stimulate their revenues, some firms pay their salespeople higher rates when total commissions reach a predetermined level during a year and, in some cases, even month by month. Sometimes the increased payments are even retroactive for the calendar year. The incentive for a conflict of interest which existed in January may therefore reach a considerably higher level by October or November.

Sometimes other incentives to increase commission revenue are utilized, such as sales contests, private offices, impressive titles, clerical aides, expense accounts, or invitations to attend meetings at glamorous vacation spas (usually at times when business tends to be slow). It is interesting to note how many of these fringe benefits are bestowed based entirely upon production levels. If they were based upon the number of accounts opened, maintained, well serviced, or showing favorable economic results, this book would be appreciably shorter.

There is considerable incentive for firms to hire successful salespeople from other firms. After all, they are already trained, have a proven track record, and may be able to bring most of their clientele with them. Such stars may be attracted by such considerations as a more desirable location, cash bonuses, more effective research, more managerial and clerical support, or a better firm reputation. None of these presents any great problem unless someone violates an enforceable employment contract or if the firm losing its personnel counters with some other legal or economic response.

Some salespeople, however, are attracted by bonuses based upon higher rates of payout for some period, such as the first six months or the first year of their employment with a new firm. This, of course, provides an incentive to induce customers to trade actively during such a period because of the bonus, rather than for the benefit of the customers.

Although there is nothing inherently wrong with selling, paying more for effective selling, or paying bonuses, there is great wrong in selling for the benefit of a firm or its employees without proper regard for the benefit of the customers. Customers should be sold products that fit their individual needs and wants in proper quantities. The revenue generated should be enough to compensate financial firms and their employees adequately for their contributions. In short, if selling is fair and honest, all parties to the sale can do well.

On the other hand, if representations are made in good faith and reasonably based, a fair customer can hardly blame salespersons or their employers whose recommendations do not always yield good results after the fact. The customer who expects safety of principal, no adversity, and invariably favorable results expects more than can be delivered. Although full-service firms may maintain expensive research facilities and provide salespeople who are well trained and well intentioned, even the most suitable recommendations are not guaranteed or insured.

THE EFFICIENT MARKETS HYPOTHESIS

Whether markets are efficient, and to what degree, has been argued for many years and the argument seems destined to rage on for many more years to come. This subject may seem academic to some, but it is important and should be carefully noted by all who are interested in financial markets. It is particularly important to realize that there are those who reject the concept, but ignore evidence that does not support their position or simply make up their minds with no evidence at all.

What Is It?

A detailed analysis of the efficient markets hypothesis is left to specialized investment books, but the concept deserves careful consideration here.

Basically, it is assumed that the marketplace is made up of large numbers of well-informed seekers of profits who have the financial means and incentives to act quickly to take advantage of opportunities. There are a limited number of financial vehicles relative to the large numbers of researchers, salespeople, advisors, and customers who wish to take advantage of them. Only a few thousand security issues, futures, and options trade actively, whereas the number of people actively interested in trading is in the millions. There is great incentive to acquire information and act upon it quickly while it still has value.

Given the speed with which information gets disseminated, its influence on prices is quite likely to exert itself quickly and accurately. A market which adapts quickly and accurately to events or anticipated events is said to be efficient. If opportunity is already reflected accurately in price, there is small comfort for those who seek opportunity in financial vehicles regarded as overpriced or underpriced.

Various degrees of efficiency have been described, but the most popular description is that which considers efficiency in three versions: weak, semistrong, and strong.

The weak form indicates that all information that can be yielded by price alone is immediately reflected in price and therefore cannot have forecasting value. This does not set well with those who like to draw trendlines on charts, follow one or more moving averages, or rely upon simplistic, inadequately researched computer programs.

The semistrong version maintains that all publicly available information is immediately reflected in price. This means that reading financial newspapers, magazines, and market letters, or listening to brokerage house gossip, financial reports on the radio, or developments on the television might be interesting and explain why prices have already moved, or what events might cause them to move in the future. These sources, however, would have no value for forecasting prices. Events which have occurred and the anticipation of events which might occur are both already reflected in price. This version of the hypothesis is hardly popular with purveyors or users of such information. It reduces fundamentalists to explainers of the past rather than predictors of the future. Although this may be of intellectual interest to some, it is certainly much less exciting than successful forecasting.

The strong version of the theory is even more discouraging. It maintains that all legitimate information, published or not, regardless of the effort needed to obtain it and no matter how quickly it is acted upon, is already reflected accurately in price. Even illegitimate forces such as trading based upon inside information or the activities of manipulators are reflected quickly in prices and therefore exemplify rather than defeat the concept of efficiency.

Implications of the Theory

The efficient markets hypothesis does not maintain that prices will not change, or that price levels cannot change rapidly and materially, or that large amounts of money cannot be made by some investors. Neither does it maintain that some investors will not make money consistently. Naturally, if the price level of any market, whether American Telephone & Telegraph preferred stock or options on hogs, moves significantly higher, those who are long will make money and those who are short will lose. The point is that if the change in price levels is random, such changes cannot be consistently and accurately predicted by most people and, possibly, not by anyone. It is further likely that those who are long, for whatever reason, will credit their financial acumen and those who are not long or who are short will blame their bad luck or their brokers.

The undisputable fact is that there is no credible body of evidence in the financial literature that indicates that the weak and semistrong forms of the hypothesis are not true. There are some who maintain, probably correctly, that there are apparent exceptions to the strong form, but this makes no difference to most investors who do not have the resources, skill, judgment, and personal discipline to achieve good results in markets which are so close to pure efficiency.

What this means is that those who make unusually high returns in the markets over time are those who have good resources and extraordinary judgment. Consistently high returns cannot be made by those who rely exclusively upon naive charts, simple programs designed for their personal computers, or suggestions made by advisors who in turn rely upon equally simplistic devices. Most people who invest are usually long and most markets, particularly in stocks, usually go up, so it becomes rather easy to give credit where credit is not due.

Actually the best that can usually be done is to be long in a diversified portfolio of financial instruments in a rising market, and short in a falling market. Of course, it would be most attractive to find a device which would outperform such investing, and it is still necessary to forecast the direction of the market, but there is simply nothing in the financial literature to indicate that there is anything better for most investors than the basic strategy of buying and holding a portfolio incorporating a satisfactory level of risk.

For those who live on the sale of information and commissions on trading, the efficient markets hypothesis is, of course, anathema. The investor who rejects the theory should do so based upon acceptable evidence of its deficiency rather than because of a brush of the hand from those who may have considerable personal interest in its rejection. One should be particularly careful not to be misled by those who claim an outstanding record in the market, but who are unwilling to provide specific significant evidence of satisfactory performance.

The implications and dangers of this concept from the point of view of those who have the duty to make reasonable recommendations should be evident. Making recommendations without reasonable (valid) support may well be taken as fraudulent. If brokers wish to take positions in the market in their own accounts based upon a formation on their dogeared charts, the only risk is to their own pocketbooks. When they suggest that their customers trade on such a basis, however, either the trades had better be profitable or the brokers should be prepared to support the predictive ability of their "chart signals." This is not to imply that brokers insure their recommendations or that charts may not help sharpen and focus personal judgments. If brokers, however, assert that chart formations lead to consistently adequate investment returns, the evidence had better support the assertions. The same is true of recommendations based upon shallow fundamental analysis.

COMMUNICATION FAILURES

The third cause of problems is the air of mystery caused by the increasing complexity of the financial world and its terminology. Some investors who are bewildered by financial terminology conclude that those who seem to understand the terms also understand how to succeed in markets. This results in increasingly greater reliance upon their financial consultants, even by those with considerable sophistication in related financial activities.

In years past, there were many who felt defeated by such concepts as short sales, butterfly spreads, participating preferred stock, and special memorandum accounts. In recent years, however, the complexity has increased to the point where even some in the financial business sometimes feel defeated by it all.

To the venerable basic business of stocks and bonds have been added new or greatly expanded types of new instruments, such as listed options, zero coupon bonds, adjustable rate preferred stock, and index trading. Futures trading, which once emphasized basic tangible, storable commodities, such as corn, wheat, and cotton, has added meats, precious metals, and such financial instruments as treasury debt issues, currencies, and futures on stock indexes. Option strategies alone are complex enough to challenge even the most scholarly of salespersons, to say nothing of a typical customer. The salesperson is further burdened with having to deal with entire product lines which formerly were not carried by brokerage firms, such as real estate, insurance, and executive search and placement services.

The financial business has always had a virtual language of its own. Terms like *red herring, short sale against the box, blue sky laws, repurchase agreements,* and *bullish or bearish* are familiar to many who deal in the financial world. Of late, however, the esoteric vocabulary of the business has expanded at an explosive rate. Takeover mania and leveraged buyouts lead to discussions of *shark repellants, poison pills, white knights, golden parachutes, greenmail,* and *bear hugs.*

Option trading has added a glossary of its own, going far beyond the basic puts and calls. Now option investors must be concerned with spreads, straddles, and combinations which can be vertical, horizontal, or diagonal. Some combinations are described with such fearsome aliases as *guts* and *strangles.* There are credit spreads and debit spreads. Options may be covered or uncovered, or act as hedges. There are conversions, reverse conversions, and ratio spreads.

Measures of stock market movements, such as the Dow Jones averages, the Standard and Poor Index, or the Value Line Index are now accompanied by a horde of others, some narrower and some wider in scope. Aside from using them to measure markets, it is possible to trade options on the indexes, futures based on the indexes, or options on the futures.

Preferred stocks and bonds have not escaped the trend toward increasing complexity. Efforts to attract buyers of securities, combined with efforts to turn away those who might be trying to acquire the issuer, have resulted in new types and hybrids of securities that can be downright bewildering to all but the investment bankers who devise them. Stripped bonds, for example, are designated with enough such names as Tigrs, Cats, Cougars, and Lions to populate most of the feline world. What is a high yield bond to some is a junk bond to others.

Because of these trends toward increasingly complex devices and descriptions of them, a dangerous situation has evolved. The investor who has long been urged to investigate before investing finds that thorough investigation could take so much time that it would replace the time needed to earn the funds to be invested. As a result, many investors simply rely increasingly on financial specialists who are themselves sometimes so confused by the proliferation of new products and complex strategies that they must struggle even to use their quote machines properly, or to interpret accurately the statements issued by their firms to its own customers. Most manage, however, to stay far enough ahead of the customers so that their ignorance is not always apparent. Of course, they could turn to their managers or computers for assistance, but this does not help much if the managers and computer programmers are also confused.

The financial business has become so complicated that it taxes all but truly scholarly professionals. The confusion, of course, leads to the offering of all sorts of misinformation. Although it might not be given in bad faith, it leads inevitably to charges of neglect or fraud.

Miscommunication is probably the single greatest cause of a breakdown in any professional–client relation. Given the confusing terminology and complex strategies involved in the world of finance, the opportunity for misunderstanding is especially high. It is also relatively easy for misguided or dishonest professionals to mislead people who are unsophisticated or too trusting.

If disputes cannot be settled between a customer and broker, they might be argued before arbitrators or in court. In such cases, arbitrators, attorneys, judges, and juries struggling to understand financial problems must also absorb another layer of specialized terminology emanating from common, state, and federal laws. The parties will find themselves arguing about concepts such as fiduciary duty, suitability, churning, price manipulation, various levels of fraud and negligence, and misappropriation of customers' funds, all of which may constitute violations of any or several of a long list of laws or reasonable levels of trade practices.

SUMMARY

The three broad problem areas discussed in this chapter do not purport to go to the root causes of everything that can go wrong in financial relationships. This book cannot eliminate all problems in the investment world and will not attempt to describe all the variations of dishonesty by those determined to be dishonest. It will not offer a detailed list of broker's practices which constitute or approach white-collar crime, such as switching trades from one account to another to favor one customer over another, stealing money or securities, insider trading, falsifying prices or documents, or concealing vital information from customers or management. Similarly, it is not intended to emphasize equally heinous practices by customers such as denying trades were made, maintaining that quantities bought or sold should have been larger or smaller, alleging that the wrong vehicle was traded, asserting that a buy should have been a sell, trading without funds, lying about what was said or not said by the parties to a transaction, or claiming to be highly conservative only after a loss results from a wildly risky transaction that was entered into with great enthusiasm.

It may be possible, however, to reduce some problems in a constructive way. The first step is to understand how the financial business works and what causes problems to arise. The second is to suggest the means to eliminate some of them. A third is to suggest what can be done if problems arise despite efforts to prevent them, in order to keep losses of money and good will to the minimum. Finally it will describe and compare the various venues where justice may be sought if all else fails. It should be clear at the outset that all problems cannot be avoided, but this does not eliminate the value of an attempt to achieve a significant reduction in their numbers and costs.

Part One
The Arena

2

The Participants

Individuals may purchase or sell investment instruments through a wide variety of means. Among these instruments are stocks, bonds, partnership units, mutual funds, options, and futures contracts. Probably most investors think first of the large nationally known brokerage firms whose ads appear regularly on television. Indeed, the names of these firms are familiar even to those who have never purchased a single share. There are, however, many other types of organizations through which securities or futures transactions may be handled. The range of products and services offered varies widely, so a brief description of the players is in order before further discussion.

FULL-SERVICE BROKER/DEALERS

These are the best known firms. They range in size from giants such as Merrill Lynch, Pierce, Fenner, and Smith Inc.; and Shearson Lehman Hutton Inc., to smaller regional ones which concentrate on a particular geographic area. Examples of the latter are First Albany Corp. (upstate New York); Advest Corp. (New England and the Northeast); Wheat, First Securities (the southeast), and Raymond, James and Associates (Florida). In several cases regional companies have been acquired by larger financial concerns, but left to operate under their own names so that their market niches would not be lost. Among such firms are Robinson-Humphrey (Southeast, Shearson Lehman Hutton) and Bateman Eichler, Hill Richards (Pacific Coast, Kemper Financial Services).

Although the term *brokerage firm* is customarily used to describe such organizations, these companies are also dealers. The distinction is important. Brokers are agents for the customer. They act as finders for the other side of the trade and charge a service fee called a commission for that task. Virtually all such transactions take place on the floor of a securities or futures exchange. Dealers, on the other hand, are principals and own the product which is sold to or bought from the customer. Their compensation comes from a markup on purchases or a markdown on sales. This business is inherently riskier from the firm's standpoint because the inventory may depreciate in value when unsold, but it is also usually more profitable. Given a choice, most firms would probably choose to act as dealer rather than as broker. Most bonds, over-the-counter stocks, and all packaged products such as mutual funds are sold on a dealer basis.

Full-service firms are the supermarkets of the financial services industry. A customer may choose from almost any exchange-traded security, option, or futures contract, many different corporate, municipal, government, or government agency bonds, thousands of over-the-counter stocks, and many different mutual funds and unit trusts. In addition, it is often possible to acquire investment advisory services, estate and financial planning, life insurance, and even real estate through many of these companies or their closely linked affiliates.

Most of these brokers advertise extensively in the press and the larger ones also use television, radio, and direct mail. They frequently have coast-to-coast branch office networks and private communications systems; hence the term *wire house* is still occasionally used to describe them. They generally publish a substantial quantity of research reports and various other sales promotion materials. The larger firms and many of the smaller ones must also train their salespeople not only to be effective in producing business, but also to provide advice and guidance to customers when necessary. All this is expensive. Their registered representatives (what most persons would call stock brokers) take from between 25 to 50 percent of each commission dollar or sales credit received. Commissions are shown on each transaction confirmation. Sales, or production credits, are the acquisition costs of principal transactions or packaged products. Most bond, mutual fund, and over-the-counter stock transactions are done on a net basis, where the broker's compensation is built into the final price and is not revealed. Recovering these costs requires the full-service broker/dealer to charge higher transaction costs than firms not burdened with the same expenses.

DISCOUNT BROKERAGE FIRMS

Investors may save significant commission charges by dealing with discount brokers. These firms provide order execution service and little else. If investors know precisely what they want to do and require no research or other advice, the commission savings may be substantial. For example, according to the schedule of typical commissions shown in Table 2–1, a customer of a discount firm could save 50 percent or more in execution costs.

TABLE 2–1   Full-Service and Discount Commissions Compared

Transaction (listed shares)	Full-Service Broker	Discount Broker
300 @ 15	$114.68	$ 61.42
800 @ 25	$357.42	$128.81
1000 @ 60	$630.86	$180.17

Discount firms are low overhead operations. Registered representatives must pass the same qualification exams as those required for full-service brokers, but otherwise perform a largely clerical function. Large use is made of the automated execution systems provided by most exchanges and the NASDAQ over-the-counter market. These systems are perfectly adequate for the typical customer order, but lack the flexibility to handle more sophisticated transactions.

Discount firms do not offer the diversity of products and services offered by the full-service operations. Some discount brokers accept almost any size account; others favor only those which promise active trading. Many are affiliated with banks, often as subsidiaries. With few exceptions, employees of such discount brokers are salaried and derive little if any benefit from the activity in a customer's account.

SPECIALTY FIRMS

There are numerous firms that do not fit into either of the categories so far described. The individual investor is most likely to encounter the firm which specializes in over-the-counter (unlisted) stocks. There are many such firms, a few of which have extensive branch office networks. In most cases they feature shares of obscure corporations which are often billed as emerging growth companies. The claim is often exaggerated (at best) and sometimes wildly optimistic. It is common for such shares to trade at very low prices, often in cents per share, hence the pejorative label *penny stocks*.

More sophisticated investors may prefer doing business with a "boutique" firm, or possibly with the specialized individual investor services provided by brokers whose primary orientation is to institutional customers. Morgan Stanley, First Boston, Goldman Sachs, and Salomon Brothers all handle a limited number of accounts for well-heeled investors. The minimum size account these firms accept is usually one million, with higher amounts being more typical. Among the types of services some of them may offer are discretionary trading, arbitrage, options, and special situation research. Not only must these customers be wealthy, but they must also be capable of sustaining the losses which must sooner or later accompany any continuing high risk endeavor.

Still others trade with brokers who handle only futures transactions. As will be demonstrated, futures and securities have many similar features, but are different in kind, not just degree. Full-service brokers also offer futures executions and research to their clientele, but often restrict activity only to those who meet stringent net worth and income criteria. The futures counterparts of the big securities firms are major brokers such as REFCO and Heinold Commodities. There are also commodities discount brokers such as Lind-Waldock. Just as there are securities firms not renowned for their ethical standards, so too are there futures brokers whose reputation for probity is not good. A hallmark of such companies is their willingness to accept orders from new customers without inquiring much into their financial means and investment experience. These brokers are generally satisfied if the customer can make the original margin deposit and do not go far beyond that in customer knowledge.

Until the Tax Reform Act of 1986 there were literally thousands of firms dealing in privately placed tax-sheltered investments. Most of these firms had few principals, often only one, and few employees. They sold participations in ventures usually organized as limited partnerships. Considerable risk is associated with these investments. They have limited liquidity and often possess a dubious economic rationale. In addition, investors faced an increased risk of an IRS audit because of the tax features. The Act effectively ended such investments by prohibiting the use of paper losses generated from these partnerships as offsets to earned income. The number of tax-oriented partnerships has thus declined markedly, as has the number of firms distributing them.

Many, however, remain in business trying to develop new means of using their customers' otherwise worthless tax deductions to generate positive investment results. Indeed, the more substantial of these organizations, Integrated Resources and Angeles Corp., to name two, are offering real estate programs that do not borrow large sums of money and are intended to be viable investments on their own merits, exclusive of tax considerations. It should also be noted that the full-service firms offer these partnerships in large numbers and have altered their business in a similar manner.

Finally, most major insurance companies now offer limited investment services. This is in addition to the outright purchase of brokers such as Bache by Prudential Insurance; Donaldson, Lufkin and Jenrette by Equitable Life; Dillon, Read by the Travelers Insurance Company; Tucker, Anthony, & R. L. Day by John Hancock Life; and the previously mentioned Kemper purchase of Bateman Eichler, Hill Richards (and some other regional brokers). The products offered directly through insurance agents ordinarily include mutual funds, variable annuity contracts, and variable life insurance policies, all of which have some securities related features. In most cases, the customers for these services tend to be conservative, first-time investors without prior experience in equity (stock) investments. Sales personnel usually possess a limited registration which allows them to solicit only these products.

BROKERAGE HOUSE EMPLOYEES

The investor's first contact with a brokerage firm is likely to be with a registered representative. This salesperson may bear a title like *account executive, financial consultant*, or even *vice president* or *assistant vice president*. To most people, however, he or she is "my broker." Registered representatives are registered with various self-regulatory bodies— the National Association of Securities Dealers, the New York Stock Exchange, and The National Futures Association, which are the largest and most influential self-regulatory bodies.

Registration involves submitting a detailed personal and business history questionnaire, being fingerprinted, and being investigated for fidelity bonding. The candidate must next pass an examination to demonstrate basic entry level knowledge of the securities business. At most full-service firms this test is the Series 7 examination, a rigorous six-hour multiple choice exercise. It is given once monthly in major cities and less frequently in selected foreign locations. About 40 percent of all candidates fail this exam each month. To handle futures trades the representative must follow the same preliminaries, but must pass the Series 3 exam. This is a 120-question multiple choice test administered on a computer terminal. The National Futures Association has not as yet released significant pass–fail statistics, but consensus opinion holds it to be less demanding than the Series 7.

There are other, less demanding examinations which qualify the successful candidate for only certain areas. Whereas the Series 7 test allows the successful candidate to solicit virtually any kind of securities business, other forms limit the qualification to specific products. For example, there are individual qualifying exams for mutual funds and variable annuities, municipal bonds, limited partnerships, and corporate securities.

Although exams may test knowledge of laws, rules, and regulations, there is no practical way to predict through such means whether a broker is ethical. This should not be surprising, as the same circumstance applies to all professions. The rigor of the bar examination does not eliminate unethical lawyers, nor do professional qualifying standards keep out unethical physicians, engineers, or even clergy.

Regardless of their titles, registered representatives are in fact salespersons. Excepting most representatives employed by discount brokerage firms, these representatives derive much of their compensation from the products sold, and the activity generated in the accounts they handle. The sales profession itself is not inherently dishonest or compromising. A good case can certainly be made for the positive contribution made to the economy by salespeople. There are dishonest salespersons just as there are dishonest practitioners of virtually every trade. The complicated nature of many securities transactions, however, makes the business unusually susceptible to those with less than admirable ethical standards. Although outright fraud is occasionally perpetrated in the securities business, many complaints are leveled against brokers when the facts are less clear. It is an unpleasant corollary of the large profits most seek that large losses may result instead. Indeed, the former usually seem much less common than the latter.

Brokers may not represent themselves to be investment advisers unless they are specifically registered as such under the Investment Advisers Act of 1940. Such registration is rarely possessed by stock brokers, and it is of little matter. For one thing, stock brokers were specifically exempted from the Act's provisions. For another, registration may be obtained by virtually anyone who files an application. There is no examination, experience, or achievement level required to become a registered investment adviser.

Busy brokers are often aided by sales assistants who may or may not be registered. They are typically delegated the function of keeping the broker's records up-to-date, answering customer queries concerning account status, and, in some instances, entering orders. If a sales assistant accepts customer orders as a regular duty, he or she must be registered. Although some make a career of this job, turnover is generally frequent, and one should not assume comparable levels of competence among sales assistants any more than one should assume it from brokers.

Operations Employees

Customers have relatively little contact with personnel employed in nonsales capacities. In the terminology of the industry, such persons are referred to as working in operations, the back office, or—when restricted to the cashiering employees—the cage. When customers live or work in the vicinity of the brokerage office at which they trade, they may find it convenient to make cash or securities deposits and pick up checks in person. This avoids problems caused by mail delays and could possibly reduce errors caused by inaccurate entries, because the customer receives a receipt for all securities and funds deposits. In such situations the customer may become personally acquainted with operations personnel. In most cases, however, these employees remain unknown to the typical investor.

In larger offices, the operations staff usually consists of an operations manager, a cashier, margin clerks, an order clerk, and general clerical help who provide miscellaneous services such as filing, mail distribution and collection, and reception. In smaller offices, typically with ten or fewer registered representatives, these functions are often consolidated, and it is not unusual to find the cashier or the cashier's assistant making margin entries or opening the mail. These employees are rarely registered and, although knowledgeable about their particular functions, are ordinarily not well informed about other aspects of securities or the markets.

The *operations manager* is often a career employee at that post and usually possesses enough knowledge to handle almost any other operations function in a pinch. A good operations manager is an invaluable asset to an office. Unfortunately, operations managers are typically paid considerably less than even average salespeople, leading some to abandon their expertise in operations to try their hand at sales. Most customer complaints involving mechanical procedures are referred to operations managers for resolution.

The *cashier* is responsible for the receipt and delivery of all securities and funds. Included in these duties are such activities as verifying and guaranteeing signatures on certificates sent in by customers after sale, ensuring that the certificates are delivered in proper form, dealing with transfer agents to obtain certificates registered at the customers' request, and paying out checks for dividends, sales proceeds, and account balances. Although these functions are largely automated, it is the cashier's responsibility to make sure they are done correctly.

Margin clerks record the activity in accounts and compute the deposits required to bring the account into compliance with federal, exchange, and firm rules. Despite the term *margin* (*credit* is today's preferred term), these clerks also handle all accounting for cash accounts, the favored type of account for most investors. Margin clerks are not usually allowed to talk directly to customers except in situations where some esoteric rule or computation cannot be readily explained by the salesperson.

Order clerks are extremely valuable employees. In today's hyper-volatile markets, a slight delay in the proper transmission of an order may result in the loss of hundreds or thousands of dollars. Not only must they be expert teletypists, but also they must be knowledgeable about the various types of orders and which kinds are not permissible on certain exchanges. For example, some orders are acceptable on futures exchanges but not on securities exchanges. One such order is the *market if touched*. On the other hand, some securities orders may not be acceptable on futures exchanges (or have different execution criteria). Such orders include *all or none*, a commonplace large order in the over-the-counter market for bonds, and *fill or kill* which could result in a partial execution in the futures market but not on a stock exchange. Registered representatives, of course, have the primary responsibility for proper order entry, but a skilled order clerk can help prevent a bit of carelessness or ignorance from turning into a large loss.

Supervisory Employees

Branch office supervisors and home office supervisors are the two primary types with whom the customer may come into contact. Ordinarily, the customer will first encounter the branch office manager or an assistant, who may be variously called an assistant manager, sales manager, or administrative manager. If the office has three or fewer registered representatives, a New York Stock Exchange (NYSE) member firm may appoint a registered representative in charge. Such satellite offices report to a larger senior office in the area. A number of brokerage firms, particularly those registered only with the National Association of Securities Dealers (NASD), the primary regulator of the over-the-counter markets, may have one-person offices, sometimes operating out of a home, which report to a larger "office of supervisory jurisdiction."

Branch office managers are usually recruited from the ranks of successful salespersons and are familiar with the most common problems and their resolution. Unfortunately, managers are sometimes chosen with scant regard to their managerial abilities. Rather, success in sales is often the principal criterion for selection. Some continue to handle a substantial amount of sales business, which provides them with the bulk of their income. This might well make them less likely to be concerned with complaints from someone else's customers.

Assistant (or sales) managers are usually undergoing an apprenticeship of sorts and are rarely career employees at that position. All qualified managerial employees of NYSE or NASD member organizations must pass the Series 8 branch office manager examination, a rigorous six-hour test, or alternatively, the NASD's principal examination and also the registered options principal examination. The choice depends on the registration of the brokerage firm. New York Stock Exchange members must have office managers registered by the former exam, whereas NASD member offices usually opt for the latter. Because most nationally known brokers are members of both organizations, it is customary for managers to have been through the Series 8 unless they have been grandfathered by passing an earlier qualifying test.

Customers only encounter home office supervisory personnel in the event of serious complaint. Although it is possible that they may encounter a regional vice president or partner, it is more likely that the contact will be with a compliance officer or an attorney.

Compliance officers may or may not be lawyers. Their job is to design and enforce internal policies to keep the firm in compliance with the various federal, state, and industry rules governing the conduct of the securities business. Few, if any, other segments of U.S. industry are so closely controlled through laws, rules, and regulations. Compliance personnel spend much of their time answering regulatory inquiries from the exchanges, the NASD, the CFTC, the NFA, or the SEC as customers often complain to those bodies before they mention their complaint to the broker involved. Frequently, however, the complaints arise from the regulators themselves when they think they have detected a rule violation using their sophisticated computer trade-monitoring devices. In many, if not the majority, of such cases, these inquiries lead to little more than the generation of huge volumes of computer runs and a lot of irritation to the broker's employees charged with this time-consuming and often futile task. Occasionally, though, one of these inquiries uncovers a serious violation of the law. The insider trading schemes revealed in 1986 were at least partially uncovered by these methods.

All substantial brokerage firms employ at least a few attorneys. Large ones may employ many and have specialists in litigation, arbitration, taxation, and legal policy. Some of these are very knowledgeable about select areas of the securities business, but are not usually good generalists. In major law suits, most brokers will enlist the support of their outside counsel in addition to their own lawyers. One can rest assured that when a complaint reaches the trial stage, one will not only be contending with a Wall Street broker, but also often with a Wall Street law firm. In addition, it is the policy of some firms to utilize the services of local law firms when a dispute calls for a specialized knowledge of local law, or when costs of bringing in counsel from outside the area are prohibitive.

Research Analysts

These employees of brokerage firms are charged with analyzing both investment instruments and markets, and providing recommendations for purchase and sale. There are no specific qualifications one needs to fulfill to be called an analyst. The NYSE requires that all research reports made available for public distribution be approved by a Supervisory Analyst, an individual who has passed an examination for this designation. The two-part exam consists of a section dealing with industry and federal rules governing the dissemination of sales literature, and another covering financial and accounting knowledge. A person possessing a Chartered Financial Analyst qualification is exempted from the second part.

Recommendations to trade securities or futures may be made either on a *technical* or a *fundamental* basis. *Technical analysis* attempts to forecast price changes through forces which are internal to the market itself. The tools employed are charts of past price behavior, various ratios that attempt to measure investor sentiment, and theories often based on supposed historically recurring patterns of price movements.

Fundamental analysts, on the other hand, look to financial data provided by their own efforts, the companies themselves, and the public news media. In the case of futures, much of this information is provided by the United States government itself through either the Department of Agriculture or the Federal Reserve System. The recommendations of fundamental analysts are based on projections of business, economic, and financial trends. There is considerable debate over the merits of this type of analysis versus those of technical analysis, or indeed over the possibility that neither type has any value. This is not the place to enter into that debate, but it should perhaps be noted that brokers usually reserve technical advice for active short-term trading accounts, whereas long-term investments are generally made on fundamental factors.

Customers

A great many Americans invest directly in securities. The 1985 NYSE survey of shareownership revealed few surprises and generally reinforced what has been well known for some time. For example, median household income of shareholders was $36,800, while the national median was $22,400. About one in four adult Americans own shares, the number of females and males being almost equal—22,509,000 to 22,484,000 respectively.

As might be expected, professional and managerial occupations predominate, but a significant number of investors have relatively modest incomes. More than 21,000,000 individuals had incomes between $25,000 and $50,000, and only about 11,000,000 had higher earnings levels. The median portfolio was about $6,200.

There are certainly far fewer futures traders than securities investors, but so far the futures industry has not conducted a survey comparable in depth to that of the NYSE. One may assume, however, that the two categories of investor are not separate and distinct. Many securities investors also trade futures contracts, and even those who concentrate on futures may have long-term stock investments which are not considered trading vehicles. It is probable that the average futures trader has greater financial resources than the average stock investor. Major brokers, at least, prohibit or restrict futures accounts with small amounts of equity. These same brokers may not encourage individuals who wish to purchase only odd lots of stock or a few hundred dollars worth of mutual fund shares, but they do not often turn down such orders (when unsolicited) because they feel the service may lead to more substantial business in time.

One can hardly be a passive investor in futures, if, indeed, the terms *invest* and *futures* are not mutually exclusive. One can, however, invest in securities and be quite inactive. Many shareholders have little contact with stockbrokers. Some may have inherited their holdings, and others may have acquired theirs through employees' stock purchase plans. The great majority of the rest are probably infrequent traders and make few transactions. Brokerage firms have long known that the typical customer never repays in commission business the cost of opening and handling his or her account. It is likely that fewer than 20 percent of all accounts opened are profitable to the typical brokerage firm on an overall basis.

Levels of investor sophistication vary widely. Few have the time, knowledge, risk capital, or inclination to engage in in-and-out trading. Fewer still should become involved in the even greater demands of the commodities futures markets. Nevertheless, every self-regulatory body receives numerous complaints each year concerning trading losses in accounts of individuals whose money never should have left the bank or the savings and loan association.

Of course, a great many more persons are indirect shareholders. The NYSE estimated about 133,000,000 such investors in 1980, the latest year in which these estimates were made. Indirect ownership is defined as participation through investments in organizations which themselves have large stockholdings. These include pension plans, life insurance companies, and mutual savings banks. Many, if not most such investors probably have little knowledge of or concern about the stock holdings backing their accounts.

Still other investors invest primarily or exclusively in bonds, particularly municipal and U.S. government securities. The nature of the investment in these cases would seem to preclude charges of inappropriate dealings with a broker. In fact, the largely unregulated nature of the government securities markets and the fragmented nature of the municipal market make them quite susceptible to misrepresentation. Investors frequently confuse the reliability of the issuer with the reliability of the broker offering the securities for sale.

At least 90 percent of current trading volume on both securities and futures exchanges derives from institutional investors, not from individuals. Included in this category are pension funds; foundations; corporations; banks; trusts; and governmental entities, both foreign and domestic. The very size of these investors gives them access to many kinds of professional investment and legal advice not readily available to the investors described so far. One might therefore conclude that these investors are unlikely to have the problems that vex individuals. Such a conclusion is only partly justified. Because they often operate under legal constraints when selecting investments, they have fewer complaints regarding improper advice or recommendations than do individuals, but more numerous (and serious) ones involving order execution and prices. Although they also deal with the brokers previously described, they do a substantially greater proportion of their business with firms that specialize in handling the large wholesale orders necessary to accommodate the huge dollar amounts to be invested. Among such brokers are First Boston; Morgan Stanley; Goldman, Sachs; and Salomon Brothers. These firms have, as noted earlier, minimal contact with individual investors except those of nearly institutional size themselves. The large full-service brokers also handle some institutional trading, but are generally less important in this area than the organizations just cited.

THE MARKETS

The place where the investor transacts business is an important determinant of how the order is handled and priced. There are significant differences in the rules and regulations governing the conduct of business in these different locations. Most of these rules are internally generated by the members and staffs of the various markets. Others are required by federal and state law, and still more by the brokerage firms themselves.

In the United States, unlike other countries, most securities trading does not take place in a central location, but rather through a vast web of telephones and computers referred to as the over-the-counter (OTC) market. Nevertheless, it is still common for most investors to refer to buying shares on the exchange, by which they almost always mean the New York Stock Exchange (NYSE). Indeed, the NYSE maintains a strong grip on common stock trading because it is the home to the blue chip stocks so favored by many investors, especially the institutional ones. On the other hand, the OTC market claims the bulk of trading in all bonds and thousands of smaller, less prominent companies, as well as some larger ones which have not seen the need to list their shares on an exchange. Additionally, all mutual fund and many other investment company shares are traded in the OTC market. Besides the NYSE and OTC markets, stock and option trading also takes place on a number of smaller exchanges. Among these are the American Stock Exchange in New York City, the Midwest Stock Exchange in Chicago, the Pacific Stock Exchange with trading floors in both San Francisco and Los Angeles, the Chicago Board Options Exchange, and the exchanges named for their cities of residence—Philadelphia, Boston, and Cincinnati.

Exchanges are nonprofit organizations owned by their members. They provide the space and facilities for conducting business, and also the staffs that furnish trading support. The rules of business on any exchange are set by the membership, subject to applicable federal and state laws. Like all bureaucracies, however, exchange staffs often develop an independent power of their own and create interpretations of rules with which many members disagree.

Membership allows an individual or that individual's employer to transact business on an exchange floor. These memberships are usually limited in number, so that a membership may only be purchased from a current member. This makes the price highly responsive to supply and demand as prospective members evaluate what future value the membership might convey. For example, in 1969 a NYSE membership, or seat, sold for $515,000. The ensuing bear market and glum projections of future business brought that price to $35,000 in 1977. The rekindled optimism of the 1980s pushed prices to more than $1,000,000 in 1987. Similar price swings have been seen in the value of most other securities exchange memberships. Also, some exchanges offer forms of limited membership, such as options trading permits or electronic access. These permits allow trading in only a specific product or by a specific manner of execution. Some exchanges also allow memberships to be leased.

The OTC market, on the other hand, is much less exclusive. Any individual or firm able and willing to meet the minimum requirements of the regulatory bodies is allowed to trade in these markets. This is at once a strength and a weakness of the OTC securities business. It fosters an innovativeness and a sort of democracy which put a small premium on vested interests. It also allows for the participation of a large number of players in the game and makes policing the unethical few a large problem.

In the commodities futures business there is no OTC market although leverage and cash forward contracts look suspiciously like futures contracts to some. Indeed, federal law prohibits the trading of futures contracts anywhere but on an exchange floor. The futures exchanges have many organizational similarities with the securities exchanges. Chicago is the main focus of domestic futures trading and contains the world's two largest futures markets, the Chicago Board of Trade (CBOT) and its nearby rival, the Chicago Mercantile Exchange, or more simply "the Merc."

These exchanges dominate agricultural and financial futures trading. New York futures trading has historically been most successful in metals, particularly gold, silver, and copper. More recently, petroleum has supplemented this list and has in fact proven the most successful of the nonfinancial commodities contracts. Given oil's place in the world's economy and its pricing in dollars worldwide, one could make a case for its being nearly a financial future. The two largest New York exchanges are the Commodities Exchange Inc. (the Comex) and the New York Mercantile Exchange (the NYME, or "the New York Merc").

Because of the stronger influence of individual membership holders, or locals, futures exchanges have a more unstructured appearance than most securities exchanges. Whereas a stock exchange's policies are likely to be strongly influenced by its largest, most financially potent member firms, futures exchanges tend to reflect the views of the individual trader, a risk taker by definition. Thus, the rules tend to place less emphasis on protecting the customer from his or her own follies, and more on the fair and accurate execution of transactions. The wording of the rules on futures exchanges also tends to be more general than the specific wording often seen in securities rules. For example, futures exchanges require the deposit of funds be made "promptly" without specifying how long promptly might be. Securities exchanges, reflecting more precise federal and industry requirements, demand payment within specific limits, for example, five business days.

One thing all exchanges, securities or futures, have in common that distinguishes them from the OTC markets is the agency nature of the transactions. Exchange trades are *brokerage* transactions where the floor broker is charged with the duty to get the best possible price for the customer in an open outcry market on the floor of an exchange. An execution will be confirmed to the customer as an agency trade, and a commission will be charged. Brokers may not sell their own positions to investors. The OTC markets, on the other hand, are almost entirely principal or dealer markets, where the customer and the dealer bargain for the best price with each other. This type of market is also sometimes referred to as a negotiated market, to contrast it to the auction system typical of exchanges. When an investor buys a security in the OTC market he or she is usually not charged a commission but rather a net price which includes, but does not normally disclose the amount of, the dealer's markup or profit on the transaction. Government, corporate, and municipal bond orders are almost always reported to customers on a net basis, such as: "As principal we sold to you $50,000 face amount State of New York 8%s of 1998 @ 100%, net amount due $50,000." Most OTC stock transactions are similarly confirmed to customers, although some of the larger dealers like Merrill Lynch will display a sales charge or markup separately.

ADVISERS

In many ways it seems logical that the function of the investment adviser should require closer regulation and more qualifications than that of a registered representative, who, after all, frequently acts only as an executor of customer orders and may give little or no advice. In fact, one can become a registered investment adviser by merely filing a form with the SEC and avoiding convictions for felonies involving securities. *The Wall Street Journal* once succeeded in registering a French poodle in this status. This is not to imply that all (or even most) investment advisers are unqualified. It does, however, suggest that the title *registered investment adviser* of itself carries little significance.

Investment advice may be offered without fee by brokers, who are exempted from the provisions of the Investment Advisers Act of 1940. Bank trust officers may also offer such advice without registration. Major investment advisory firms offer services on a fee basis and generally require a minimum portfolio size anywhere from $250,000 to $1,000,000. A typical fee approximates one-half percent of the amount managed. The investor must also pay standard brokerage commissions and fees, because trades must still be executed through a broker. Among major advisory firms are: Martin D. Sass and Company; Stein, Roe and Farnham; Scudder, Stevens and Clark; and Alliance Capital Management. There are dozens of others, including affiliates of major broker/dealers such as Merrill Lynch; Shearson Lehman Hutton; Prudential-Bache; PaineWebber; and Morgan Stanley.

There are many investment advisers who offer subscriptions to newsletters and telephone hot line services. Some of these are well established. More are short-lived magic formula schemes that rarely produce anything worthwhile in the way of sound investment advice, although some may have an occasional short-term winning streak. Some technical analysts actually compare bullish to bearish sentiment as expressed in these letters as an indication of market psychology, generally reaching the conclusion that the advisers as a group are usually wrong. To these analysts, the greater the degree of bullishness displayed in these market letters, the more likely the market is to go down.

In futures, the function analogous to the investment adviser is that of the Commodity Trading Advisor (CTA). Under federal rules, all CTAs must be registered with the Commodities Futures Trading Commission (CFTC), that industry's counterpart of the SEC for securities.

REGULATORS

As noted earlier, the securities and futures businesses are subject to much regulation. This regulation may derive from federal, state, or internal industry requirements. There are several national laws which are the basis for most of this regulation. These laws are enforced by the SEC and the CFTC. Each of these federal authorities has the power to close down a firm operating in contravention of the law. Each also has the authority to fine a violator or to pursue criminal proceedings against miscreants.

Most of the day-to-day operating regulations, however, are enforced by self-regulatory bodies—the exchanges, the NASD, and the National Futures Association. These bodies have the authority to censure, fine, or expel a member (or employee of a member organization) for breach of their rules. They are also empowered to set competence standards for registered employees, and to require written examinations for such persons.

Finally, all states regulate securities and futures transactions within their borders. Using blue sky laws, each state requires registration distinct from any at either the federal or self-regulatory level. Thus, a major full-service brokerage firm operating a branch office in California, for example, must comply with rules and regulations of the SEC, the various securities and futures exchanges and other self-regulatory bodies, the State of California, and others such as the Federal Reserve System, the Treasury Department, and the Internal Revenue Service.

3

The Products

The varieties of financial merchandise available cover a wide spectrum at any given time, and concentration of sales efforts varies with changes in the appetite of the investing public. There are short-term fads in the finance industry much as in many kinds of consumer products.

Some firms specialize in one or a few products. Others prefer to emulate department stores and offer as many items as it is believed may be profitably sold, or which may encourage the sale of related items also available from the same firm.

Although there are dozens of individual instruments and varieties of forms, financial interests are discussed here in four groups. These are securities; futures; funds, unit trusts, and pools; and limited partnerships, tax shelters, and potpourri.

SECURITIES

Although securities will be discussed in some detail here, the reader who is looking for a definition of security which would satisfy a law school professor is doomed to disappointment. Fewer definitions in the English language are more mercurial. It is, of course, possible to define the term with a virtually synonymous term, such as "investment contract." It is also possible to indicate a broad list of necessary conditions, such as funds placed with another in a common enterprise for the purpose of attempting to achieve a profit, and leave it to the courts to debate the nuances of such conditions. For a basic discussion such as is intended here, however, it is adequate to comment upon the most frequent examples which clearly constitute securities and leave the debate about the fringes to others.

Common Stock

The first security issued by a corporation and the last to be retired are common stock. Typically, it represents the major ownership of a corporation and has the greatest management control. It has a residual claim on earnings; that is, all creditors' claims as well as claims by other equity securities (such as preferred stocks) must be satisfied first. In the event a corporation is liquidated, the common stock also has a residual claim on assets. After the claims of creditors and preferred stockholders are satisfied, the common stockholders receive everything that remains. In many liquidations, however, the assets are gone before the common stockholders reach the front of the line. In such cases, the common stockholders may receive only shares in a successor corporation, or nothing at all.

In successful companies, the holders of residual claims may do quite well. After all prior claims are met, the amount of earnings, dividends, and assets per common share may grow substantially and quickly. This could cause impressive increases in the value of common shares in the marketplace, unless the company's success was already anticipated and therefore discounted in the stock's price. If a company operates with large amounts of borrowed funds or substantial fixed assets, or both, as is quite frequent, changes in earnings may be magnified by the combined effect of such operating or financial leverage. The implications of substantial changes in earnings for a company's future ability to pay dividends or expand its operations are obvious.

Common stock prices respond not only to political, industrial, and corporate events, but to the anticipation of events and to the movement of the market as a whole. As a result, common stock prices tend to vary widely, and prediction of the direction and extent of such variations is difficult at best, and may be impossible. All of this can lead to a problem. Common stocks are basically speculative instruments with a substantial degree of risk. This is hardly surprising in that the price variability which attracts the buyer is the very definition of the word *risk*. To induce buyers to purchase stocks at all, the salesperson is quite tempted to indicate that he and his firm have an impressive record of selecting well-timed purchases of common stocks. Such records are frequently not in accordance with the facts, and even when they are, the track record may be so statistically flawed as to be useless in attempting to realize adequate future returns, although they may technically represent the past accurately.

Common stocks are speculative by their very nature. Although it is not unusual to refer to their purchase as "investing," this is using the word in its generic sense. It should not imply that the common stock is an investment in the sense that its hoped-for indicated return has a high degree of probability or that risk is low. The best that can be said for common stocks is that some are more speculative than others. Obviously, it should not be implied that substantial returns are not possible in common stocks. What is implied is that the price of obtaining such substantial returns is the assumption of risk. It is representations to the contrary that have largely necessitated the writing of this book.

Preferred Stock

Like common stock, preferred stock is an equity security and therefore normally ranks behind all debt in its claims on a company's earnings, dividends, and assets. Buyers of such stocks should not be overly lulled by a description of their holdings as quasi debt. Although the word *preferred* may give some comfort to the buyers, they should note that the preference places them only in front of the common stockholders. If there are no dividends or assets available for the common stockholders, there may be none for the preferred stockholders either.

As is usual in the financial world, any benefit of preference is gained only at a price. The dividend on preferred stocks may preempt any prior payments to common stockholders, but its amount is frequently fixed. As a result, preferred stocks, like debt securities, tend to move more with interest rates than with the fortunes of the company which issued the shares.

It might reasonably appear, of course, that the speculative nature of preferred stocks relative to debt securities would at least offer the buyer a higher return to compensate for the higher risk. Alas, even this is not usually true. Corporate buyers of stock are able to deduct a high percentage of their dividend returns from their income taxes, which they cannot do in the case of interest received from debt instruments. This tax benefit is usually reflected in the price, hence, return on the stocks, with the result that individual buyers may well find their returns lower on investments in preferred stock than on less risky debt instruments.

Aside from ignorance or being misled, why do individuals buy preferred stocks? Often it is because of perceived special opportunities.

The preferred stock of a company that is improving after a period of poor results may one day pay an accumulation of dividends that the company was formerly unable to pay. This, of course, would be true only if the stock had a cumulative provision requiring that such arrearage be paid before the common stock received any dividends. It is also possible that the preferred stock is convertible into the common, and that the combination of price, return, and risk at some point made it appear more desirable than the common stock. This, of course, may be quite true, but it is also possible that the buyers or their advisors have miscalculated or failed to note an impending change in the holders' rights to convert at a particular price or at all. The reluctance of many brokers to handle small bond orders or to handle them only at a substantial cost to the small trader may also result in comparatively high returns on preferred stock to such traders.

Preferred stocks may have any or a combination of a long list of provisions, some of which may be quite complex. Lack of understanding about some of these—in addition to the fact that such stock may be by its very nature (especially if convertible) considerably more speculative than many people believe—is the source of many problems between brokers and their customers.

Debt Instruments

Stocks represent shares of a company's equity. The buyer usually hopes to gain through receipt of dividends and price appreciation. Debt represents loans made to a borrower. The lender's gains come from receipt of interest modified by capital gains.[1] It is widely assumed that debt instruments are safer investments than stock. This is not necessarily true. The equities issued by one issuer may involve less risk than the debt issued by another. What is true is that the debt instruments are safer than equity instruments of the same issuer. Some debt instruments involve a high degree of risk whereas some others involve no risk at all.

Debt may be roughly divided into two broad categories; that which is repayable within one year and that which is repayable after more than one year. Many debt instruments of the first category are classified as money market instruments; whereas those in the second, along with equity securities, are considered to be part of the capital market.

---

[1] The term *capital gains* as used here refers to any profit or loss realized on the investment and does not pertain to the term in its income tax sense. It should be noted that a capital gain may be either positive or negative.

Money Market. Short-term debt instruments may be issued by government or quasi-government bodies or by private companies. Most are of high quality, which combined with their short lives causes many of them to be regarded as risk-free, or close to it. As a matter of fact, debt issues of the United States government maturing within one year are usually used as the standard for risk-free investment. Default is so unlikely and the influence of inflation during a brief period is so small that both may be reasonably ignored.

Private corporations also issue short-term debt, such as commercial paper and repurchase agreements, which qualifies for inclusion in the money market. In addition, long-term debt, regardless of the issuer, which matures within a year is part of the money market although it was originally part of the capital market.

Although money market paper is inherently risk free or low risk, this does not mean that investments involving such paper are necessarily without risk, or that the risk may not be substantial. For example, if purchases are made on credit, the leverage can create financial risk. If positions are utilized primarily for tax advantage, the investor may find that an audit, disallowance, penalties, or a combination of all of them may cause tax risks that were not anticipated.

Long-Term Debt. There are many types of long-term debt, such as notes and certificates of deposit, but individual investors are most interested in bonds. These securities are issued for periods of years and in a few cases, have no maturity dates at all.

Bonds issued by the federal government are usually called either *government bonds* or *T-bonds*. Quasi-government bodies, such as the Government National Mortgage Association (GNMA) and Federal National Mortgage Association (FNMA), issue large numbers of securities usually called *agency securities*. Those issued by smaller government bodies, such as states, counties, or cities, or by semi-government bodies, such as school districts, are usually designated as municipal bonds. The latter are usually free of federal income tax as well as state income tax, if the holder resides in the state in which the bonds were issued.

Customer disputes revolving around bonds sometimes involve markups or markdowns discovered to be higher than expected, particularly in cases where sales credits may be especially difficult for customers to compute, such as zero-coupon bonds. More often, problems arise from risks which prove to be greater than expected. Municipal bond buyers may belatedly discover that some such bonds depend upon specific designated revenue for the payment of interest and principal and that lacking such revenue, default is quite possible. In more unusual cases, even some taxing bodies have been unable to generate enough money to pay off obligations designated as general obligation.

High-yield (junk) bonds may provide substantial risks even when carried in carefully designed portfolios, and much more when bought individually by small investors. Sometimes those who market such bonds tend to overemphasize the yield, understate the risk, and are sometimes motivated more by the sales credit to be gained than by the welfare of their clients.

Options

Many securities give their holders, for a price, a given period to make a purchase or sale of a financial interest at a designated price. Stockholders may receive rights, usually with a life of only a few weeks, to buy newly issued stock at a fixed price. Warrants, usually with a life of some specified period of years, may be issued separately or in conjunction with some other security. Not many disputes revolve around these types of options.

Puts and calls are another matter. Since the listed versions of these options began trading actively in 1974, they have become increasingly popular. The buyer of a put or call may lose his entire investment with surprising speed. Although the amount lost may be small when measured in terms of cost per unit, it still represents 100 percent of the buyer's investment, which may not be small in total or when measured against the buyer's discretionary capital. The sale of puts or calls may represent little or great risk depending in part upon whether they are acquired against an underlying stock position (covered) or without one (uncovered or naked). The risk of an uncovered call position is technically infinite.

There are many customer disputes involving options. Some involve alleged churning. Others are caused by misunderstandings concerning risk, particularly when a customer loses the entire intended investment, or even more, because the risk was not understood or because of the hazards which sometimes accompany the use of such complicated strategies as spreads, straddles, and combinations.

FUTURES

Most investors are well aware of the reputation borne by the futures markets for high risk. The reputation may be justified, but the reason is not always so clear.

Risk is a function of an investor's actual return relative to her expected return. That is, if she is certain to receive what she expected, or close to it, her investment was no risk or low risk. If she might receive far more or less than what was hoped for, the investment is high risk. Prices of most futures, however, do not move significantly most of the time. The volatility of one's investment, hence, risk, is caused rather by leverage. Margins are so low for most futures that small moves are greatly magnified by the small capital needed to support a position. Hence, the risk relative to the capital deposited can be greatly reduced simply by depositing a greater percentage of the value of the future. If an investor deposited an amount equalling the entire value of the future position, she might find risk to be miniscule. As is usually the sad case, however, the return possible on the now low-risk position would be equally miniscule.

Because many people want to utilize their capital as completely as possible, most futures positions are highly leveraged and there is little room for error. As a result, most investors in futures lose their money, which is acquired by the relatively small number of winners. Here, as elsewhere in the financial world, it is not unusual for winners to credit their financial acumen, whereas losers blame the marketplace, its personnel, or bad luck. This creates a dangerous situation for brokers and advisers who are not sufficiently cautious about their representations or their choices of customers.

Futures Options

Just as puts and calls may be traded in the securities markets, it is possible to trade puts and calls representing futures positions. These may be covered or uncovered. The latter may involve risk equal to or exceeding the investment in the option. Covered options are much less risky and may well reduce the total risk borne by an investor, but at the usual cost; that is, possible return is reduced at least as much as the risk.

Customers who choose to trade futures options should have some understanding of the underlying futures markets, the nature of options, and the strategies employed in trading them. They should also note that some firms charge fees far in excess of those charged by others for identical positions. Sometimes such large fees are deemphasized, passed over too quickly and lightly to be noticed, or justified by dubious "benefits."

FUNDS, UNIT TRUSTS, AND POOLS

Investors sometimes prefer to place their funds partially or entirely in the hands of others. Sometimes they choose investment advisors, bank trust officers, or a trusted third party to whom they give a power-of-attorney. Others choose to utilize funds administered by one or more managers. There are many reasons for investing in this way, but the two most common motivations are the desire to achieve diversification and obtain professional management.

Investment Companies

Securities may be bought through investment companies which pool funds and, in turn, invest them in other securities. Some of these investment companies issue a limited number of shares which then trade on exchanges or over-the-counter like many other securities. Others sell as many shares as investors may want and stand ready to redeem them from those who wish to convert to cash. The latter are known as open-end investment companies or mutual funds.

Some funds buy all types of securities whereas others specialize. They may buy securities of only one type, such as bonds, or they may restrict themselves to investments in certain industries, such as electronics or energy, or may limit themselves to stocks issued only in selected geographical regions or even individual countries.

The purchase of a closed-end fund may involve a commission if it is listed. If unlisted, the cost of trading may involve either a commission, a markup, or a markdown. Mutual funds are typically sold at their current net asset value, sometimes with a markup called a *load* which may be as much as eight and one-half percent. In addition to the sales cost, there may also be redemption costs and management fees deducted from the income received by the holders.

A detailed discussion of the types of funds is best left to investment texts and prospectuses describing such funds. The emphasis here is best placed on problems and how to avoid them.

Most problems involving funds have to do with misrepresentations designed to induce the investment, or, at least, to justify the cost. Salespersons should, as always, be especially careful when utilizing track records to make certain that the facts are accurate and to avoid implying that track records are predictive of future performance. This subject is discussed in detail in the chapter which follows.

A salesperson usually benefits more from selling a fund with a high load than one with a low load or no load at all. Few brokers are willing to accommodate customers interested in no-load funds, with the exception of money market funds. Lacking evidence, the salesperson should be careful not to imply that the sales load somehow tends to improve the potential performance of the fund. Usually the size of a sales load varies with the size of the purchase. Abuses sometimes occur when a salesperson sells a client several funds in amounts just below the level where the cost per unit becomes cheaper (breakpoint). Similarly, some salespersons recommend unjustified changes from one fund to another. Such changes may or may not involve additional sales costs, but if they do, the salesperson is well advised to be able to justify a recommendation to switch.

The buyer of a fund should be provided with a prospectus as quickly as possible, and the salesperson should be careful to make no material statements which contradict the prospectus. A client primarily interested in diversification should not be led to believe that there are no ways of accomplishing it other than purchasing a high-load fund, or that a high load in itself somehow leads to improved performance.

If a firm and its personnel are trying to avoid problems connected with the sale of funds, the best advice is basically quite simple. A recommendation to a client to buy securities should be based primarily on the welfare of the client rather than that of the firm and its personnel, and costs of buying, selling, and management must be fully disclosed.

Unit Trusts

Unit trusts have become extremely popular since the 1960s and so deserve mention here. They have not been the center of many disputes, however, aside from the problem of possible misrepresentation which applies to all investments. Basically, a unit trust is used to package a specialized group of securities such as corporate bonds, government or agency securities, certificates of deposit, and occasionally, common stocks. A portfolio is assembled by a dealer who then sells units of participation in the trust.

Like the mutual fund, a unit trust offers a small investor diversification and skilled securities selection in areas where an investor, especially one with limited means, would have difficulty choosing financial instruments wisely or would not be able to find instruments in small enough denominations to afford buying at all. The usual selling points offered to induce clients to buy such securities (other than diversification), are generous returns, liquidity, the ability to buy in small units (typically $1,000), and, payment (usually monthly), of interest or dividends and possibly principal.

Units typically are sold at markups of about four percent and are redeemed at no charge either by the dealer or a trustee. Trusts, like bonds, usually have stated maturities after which par value is returned to the investors, unless there have been defaults of any underlying securities.

Maturities may range from a few months to many years. If the trust consists of stocks, it may not be possible to indicate a stated maturity. Because the underlying securities are held to maturity and not managed, there is no management fee.

Pools

As the name implies, a pool involves the commingling of the funds of numerous investors into a single account in which profits and losses are divided in proportion to the funds invested by the participants. Pools are utilized both in securities and futures, but individual investors are more likely to be solicited to participate in pools dealing in futures. Pool operators may be subject to registration under federal or state regulations. Pool operators who trade in futures must register as commodity pool operators (CPOs) with the Commodity Futures Trading Commission (CFTC). In some cases the formation of pools is accompanied by prospectuses or offering sheets, but not always.

Although the number of such pools is relatively small, the number of disputes involving them is disproportionately large. Problems sometimes occur because the pool operator or his sponsor is disreputable or self-serving. For example, so-called "blind pools" have been utilized by their sponsors as a convenient device to churn accounts either by engaging in an unreasonable number of transactions or by charging unreasonably high fees, commissions, markups, or markdowns. They may also be used as a convenient place to eliminate from inventory stocks that cannot be placed anywhere else except at a loss, if at all.

A much more frequent cause of disputes is the propensity of those who speculate, especially in futures, to lose money. Those who lose money, of course, are much more likely to demand redress than those who do not.

Accordingly, pool operators who are not properly registered; fail to provide proper, complete, and timely documentation; misrepresent their product or performance; make material omissions; or conceal essential facts; are unusually vulnerable to legal action or become the subject of complaints to regulatory bodies.

Those who wish to become or to sponsor pool operators would be wise to seek competent legal advice concerning possible registration, accounting, reporting, and other requirements before entering the field, unless they are unusually experienced. Those who invest in pools should ask many searching questions about performance and approaches to market strategies before making their investments. For example, if a track record is offered as an inducement to invest in the pool, the customer, as usual, should attempt to make certain that the record is valid. If the customer shares in profits, the definition of *profit* and *share* should be completely clear. Profits may be defined as net by one pool operator, whereas another might intend to share in all profits, but not in losses. Some pool operators might consider only closed profits in calculating the investors' shares, whereas others might consider both closed and open profits.

Having these answers in writing and keeping good records may one day prove comforting if a dispute should arise. Brokers dealing with pool operators who prove to be disreputable may find that failure to know their customers (the pool operators) may cause them to become a party to a dispute when they had considered themselves nothing more than order takers.

LIMITED PARTNERSHIPS, TAX SHELTERS, AND POTPOURRI

Limited Partnerships

Although the subjects of pools, limited partnerships, and tax shelters are separated here for purpose of discussion, it should be realized that there is considerable overlap among these subjects. Pools might be organized as limited partnerships and some of the latter are formed primarily with tax considerations in mind.[2]

Limited partnerships are utilized primarily to facilitate direct investments in financial areas where financial intermediaries perceive public interest. Two of the most enduring such areas are real estate and oil and gas. Real estate partnerships are usually managed by a general partner who is a professional in that business. The general partner is motivated by management fees, the ability to assess expenses, and, perhaps, by some personal ownership of a share of the fund. Proceeds received from investors may be used to purchase, develop, or manage property which may be residential or commercial. Income may be received from rental income or profitable sales and is divided among the partners according to a formula stated in the partnership agreement. Investors, as in most limited partnerships, are offered a chance to receive income or build equity in a field which might require too much capital to enter on an individual basis. In addition, it is possible to diversify among various types of property of different natures, various locations, or both. The limited partnership should be distinguished

---

[2] A further discussion of these subjects is offered in Chapter 6.

from a joint venture and from a real estate investment trust (REIT). In a joint venture, the investors share in active management and, therefore, incur a greater individual liability. A REIT must comply with various complex federal regulations which allow it to invest in real estate property, mortgages, or both, and pass income directly through to its investors without itself paying tax on the income, even if it is organized as a corporation.

Most oil and gas partnerships have as their goal the accumulation of energy reserves. They hope to profit either by selling the products or, less often, the leases which have been accumulated. The perceived advantages to the limited partners are similar to those in real estate. It is possible to participate in expensive drilling programs or the purchase of leases which would involve too much capital for an individual investor. As in most joint programs, professional management and diversification are offered as advantages.

Aside from these two most popular areas, some limited partnerships invest in minerals, livestock, movie production, windmills, railroad freight cars, and almost anything else that the public will buy and the government will allow.

The broker's motivation in selling shares in partnerships is, of course, income. The broker's risks center around failure to provide proper documentation; such as prospectuses, offering circulars, or suitability questionnaires; selling shares in unregistered partnerships which prove not to be exempt; and, above all, making misrepresentations or omissions concerning the potential risk and reward of such investments.

Compliance personnel of brokerage houses, of course, are generally aware of federal regulations which require the registration or offer exemption from registration of limited partnerships. They should also keep in mind that a partnership might have to comply with blue sky laws in the states in which partnership units are offered. Failure to obtain such approval may result in serious repercussions for those who sell unregistered shares. Firms that register shares in some states, but fail to control salespersons who make interstate sales in states where the partnership units are not registered also face liability.

Tax Shelters

Changes in the federal tax laws which lower top brackets, strengthen alternative minimum tax requirements, and largely eliminate the creation of deductions from tax shelters have reduced and narrowed the interest in vehicles designed primarily to shelter taxes. Many shelters created when tax laws were more favorable still exist however, and some of the disputes that will result because of them will still exist too. Furthermore, new types of shelters may be devised and tax laws may once again change to allow some variation of shelters to be created by imaginative managers and their tax attorneys. Therefore, even though it may prove to be largely of historical interest, a brief discussion of limited partnerships designed primarily as tax shelters may be useful to some readers.

As used in the financial industry, tax shelter investments are designed to provide a tax benefit as well as an economic profit. The tax benefit may take one of several forms or a combination of them.

A deferral offers the investor the opportunity to deduct material tax dollars in the early years of her investment and pay the taxes on those dollars some years later. The benefit may be an opportunity to invest profitably the money that would otherwise have been paid in taxes, or to pay lower taxes later if the taxpayer is in a lower bracket or if tax rates have been reduced. Investments designed primarily for deferral are exemplified by animal feeding programs, equipment leasing, and movie production.

Other programs emphasize write-offs in the near term which accompany the creation of capital assets. The assets may be sold later, may create a flow of income to overcome the earlier expenditures. Most real estate and oil and gas programs have the objective of providing early deductions, allowing the creation of assets such as shopping centers or oil fields which will provide income later.

Investors in high tax brackets may even benefit from programs designed to produce unusually high deductible losses, but which have no reasonable expectation of providing income or assets sufficient to overcome the losses. Naturally, losses generated must conform with legal constraints concerning what may be properly deducted. For example, under the Tax Reform Act of 1986, the distinction between active and passive income did much to eliminate the creation of new tax shelters following the somewhat standard forms that were popular for many years.

Strictly speaking, a tax shelter implies the creation of deductible expenses justified by an accompanying benefit, but there are those who would also include investments that provide tax-sheltered income. Examples include most municipal bonds and the purchase of existing real estate with established income flows. The income from the former is legally deductible from federal income tax as well as state income tax in the state in which the bonds are issued. The income from real estate may be sheltered by depreciation, but does not provide current deductions for construction cost.

Most tax shelters are merely specialized types of limited partnerships. They may be public or private, registered or unregistered, and are designed to provide a tax benefit as well as an economic benefit to those who subscribe to units or shares of such programs. Limited partnerships that are designed to produce passive income to enable the write-off of previously generated tax losses, although designed primarily with tax benefits in mind, would not usually be described as tax shelters. They may, however, help shelter those who designed earlier tax programs from the wrath of investors who took losses which were later found not to be deductible.

Details of the form of such programs as are discussed here are best left to specialized investment treatises. This discussion emphasizes compliance. Although the investments themselves may be quite complex, the compliance aspects are not. Most problems center around lack of suitability and representations.

Some tax shelter programs are sold to investors who do not have the need to shelter income. In some cases, the sale of such programs appears based rather upon the need of the salesperson for immediate non-sheltered income.

The problem of representations usually centers upon understatement of the risk or overstatement of the return. Sometimes there is no problem creating the short-term losses, but the income to be realized later never appears. Sometimes a general partner lacks the ability to manage the program successfully. Sometimes the buyer finds he has become subject to tax risk which was not discussed when the product was being considered. Tax risk includes the possibility of disallowance of deductions by the IRS, sometimes with the addition of unexpected interest and penalty charges. Even the increased likelihood of a tax audit in itself is a risk that some taxpayers would rather avoid.

Although tax shelters provide an attractive source of revenue for brokerage firms, their personnel should realize that clients rely upon their advice when they buy such products. The client does not know the general partner of the shelter, but she does know her broker. The latter should be certain that due diligence relative to specialized programs is carried out carefully, and that clients who are solicited are suitable to make such investments. (See Chapter 6.) Tax advice should be offered only in good faith and offered only by those qualified to offer it.

Potpourri

In recent years there has been a tendency for investment firms to offer a longer list and wider range of financial products. The line of demarcation between banks and brokerage firms has become blurred. Small firms finding it ever more difficult to compete have chosen either to specialize in one or a few products or have become absorbed into larger firms.

Large firms have become virtual financial department stores, entering or expanding their presence in fields such as real estate, insurance, estate planning, executive relocation, the sale of cash commodities, and many others. Despite this expansion of product lines, the general implications for the compliance area emphasized here have changed little.

If the sale of products is governed by federal or state laws, or by custom and trade practice, sales should be made in accordance with any such rules or precedent. Representations should be accurate with no material omissions or concealments. Merchandise offered should be suitable for the clients to whom it is offered. Revenue from sales should be held to a reasonable and fair level. Supervision should be thorough and efficient.

All in all, it really does not matter much whether a firm's product lines are wide or narrow or how esoteric some of the items offered for sale are. If a firm has sound policies, selects, trains, and supervises its personnel efficiently, and makes a conscientious effort to follow the rules, it has gone a long way to solve most problems and should not suffer unduly from those which it has somehow failed to avoid.

Part Two
Breach of Trust and Its Causes

4

Solicitation of Accounts

TYPES OF ACCOUNTS

Customers may carry several different accounts with the same broker, just as they may have several different accounts with the same bank. Some of these accounts may be matters of convenience, set up to separate certain types of activity—long-term growth, speculation, and the like. More likely, however, the accounts are separated because they have different ownership and tax considerations. For example, a married couple with substantial assets might easily have six or seven entirely different accounts with the same broker, and several accounts with other firms. The couple might have a joint account for their regular investment portfolio, individual accounts for each spouse's personal property, two separate Individual Retirement Accounts (IRAs), and three custodial accounts for children under the Uniform Gift or Transfer to Minors Act.

There are two basic types of securities account, cash and margin. In addition, there is the futures account which is a margin account by definition. Certain types of transactions can only be executed in one or another of these accounts. The cash account is limited to the purchase and sale of securities on a fully paid basis. No credit may be extended in this account, nor may short sales or futures transactions be effected. Margin accounts allow for almost any type of securities or securities option trade, including any requiring partial financing or short sales, but no futures. Futures accounts cannot be used to trade anything other than futures contracts or options on such contracts. There is considerable confusion among both experienced and novice investors about the differences between some futures options and options on the actual indexes or securities. A contract calling for the delivery of 40,000 pounds of pork bellies is clearly a futures contract. A U.S. Treasury bond is clearly a security. What of, however, an option on the Standard & Poor's 500 stock index? There is an option on the actual index traded on the Chicago Board Options Exchange. There is also an option on the Standard & Poor's 500 Stock Index *futures* contract traded on the Chicago Mercantile Exchange. The former must be traded in a securities account, whereas the latter requires a futures account. It might, therefore, be useful to describe the basic types of account before discussing the manner in which these accounts are opened and used.

Cash accounts for securities are the easiest accounts to open. At many brokerage firms, no special documentation is required. They may even be opened with information provided over the telephone by the customer. Some firms may require the customer to provide a specimen signature, but this is not a widespread practice. An agreement to submit disputes to binding arbitration may also be required by some brokers. Any purchase of securities that may be paid in full may be executed in a cash account. Likewise, any fully paid security may be sold in this type of account. Payment (or delivery) is regulated by both Regulation T of the Federal Reserve System and NASD/NYSE rules. In fact, there is a slight but sometimes important discrepancy between the two which will be explored in more detail in Chapter 8. The basic rule is clear—full payment or delivery shall be made promptly. This is interpreted by members of the self-regulatory bodies to mean no later than five business days following the date of the trade; for example, a purchase of stock on Tuesday must be paid for no later than the Tuesday of the following week.

Most individual investors do not need any other type of account. The only types of trade that cannot be executed in a cash account are those whose speculative nature should restrict their use to high-risk trading. Although individual investors often try to beat professional traders at their own game, they are seldom able to do so, and most are ill advised to make the attempt.

Margin accounts permit the investor to trade with the use of borrowed funds. Under current Federal Reserve requirements, the buyer must deposit 50 percent of the purchase price in cash (or 100 percent in fully-paid marginable stock) to buy shares in a margin account. The remaining 50 percent is borrowed through various forms of loan, the most common called a *call* or *broker* loan. The advantages are apparent if prices rise because the investor can buy twice as many shares as can be bought on a cash-only basis. This magnifies the profit when the forecast is accurate, and obviously magnifies the loss when it is less prescient.

Brokers encourage customers to open margin accounts because they are generally more profitable for the firm than are cash accounts. The customer can afford to take larger positions, meaning that commission revenues are likely to be greater than those of a similar account where the shares are fully-paid. In addition, the margin investor is likely to be a more active trader than the typical cash account customer. The margin account permits a broader selection of investment and trading tactics than does the cash account. Although not suitable for most investors, short sales and several options positions, including spreads and short straddles, must be done in margin accounts under industry rules.

Few institutional investors are permitted to use margin because of their own policies or legal restrictions. Most margin customers, therefore, are individuals. Although they are often thought to represent the "smart money," there is little evidence to support this contention. They are indeed usually more active and informed than typical customers, but this may in fact be a contrary indicator. The weight of academic studies to date suggests that buying and holding stocks for the long term is a sound practice and produces attractive rates of return. Cash accounts are perfectly suitable for this kind of investing. Active trading, on the other hand, has not been demonstrated to produce results superior to simply buying and holding. Practical experience leads to the inescapable conclusion that there is probably an inverse relationship between successful investing and active trading. That is, the more active the trading, the less successful the investment result.

Futures accounts are often carried by securities firms as well as by those specializing in commodities. They have some characteristics which make them appear similar to securities accounts but are in fact quite different. For one thing, all futures accounts are margin accounts by definition, although the type of margin is different from securities margin. In futures accounts there is no creditor-debtor relationship because no credit is extended, no money borrowed, and no interest charged. The futures trader deposits about five to eight percent of the contract value as a good faith deposit or earnest money. The contract is a pledge to make or take delivery of the entire contract amount in the delivery month, if the contract is not offset. The long, for example, agrees to accept delivery of 5,000 bushels of soybeans and pay the prevailing cash price, possibly $5.50 per bushel or $27,500 for the contract. A margin deposit represents a show of good faith that the purchaser will honor the contract terms. Few futures traders (other than commercial firms) intend to let a delivery occur because they plan to offset their positions prior to the possibility of a delivery.

When adverse price changes cause an open loss in a futures account, the amount of the loss is actually removed from the account on a daily basis and credited to an account which has a favorable mirror-image profit. Accounts must always be above prescribed maintenance levels or a margin call for new funds will be issued. Because of the low initial margin requirements, a small price change is often enough to trigger a margin maintenance call. Customers must be prepared to take quick action to cut off losses before they become hemorrhages.

There are few patient long-term investors in futures contracts, although it is possible to maintain a position in some contracts for a year or even longer. A contract is exactly that: it pays no dividends and conveys no rights of ownership similar to those of securities. A holder might have to answer several margin calls throughout the life of a position, even one that ultimately proves profitable.

Futures accounts are usually divided into two broad categories, speculative and hedging. Almost all individual accounts fall into the former category. Speculators have very short-term horizons, and even when following long-term trends, many use short-term tactics such as stop orders. Hedge accounts, on the other hand, are used by commercial interests which either produce the underlying commodity or use it in the course of their businesses. Typical of hedgers in the futures markets are food processors, petroleum refiners, metals fabricators, and financial institutions. Most hedgers use the futures markets to shift risk.

Other Accounts

Besides the basic accounts, there are numerous variations. One of the most common is the advisory account, which may be used with either securities or futures. In such accounts the customer, or principal, assigns decision-making authority to another. This other party may be anyone of legal age to transact business, but is usually an investment or commodity trading advisor, another family member, or a friend. The authorization to act in this capacity must always be in writing regardless of the relationship between advisor and principal, even if the advisor is the spouse of the principal. Should this written authorization be made in favor of a registered representative the account is termed a *discretionary account* and comes under especially strict rules governing account conduct.

Organizations may also open accounts although such accounts are only variations of the accounts already described. For example, corporations other than investment companies usually do not attempt to trade securities actively on a speculative basis. They are more likely to invest in short-term cash equivalents in order to manage their cash flow effectively. Typical of such short-term investments are Treasury bills, commercial paper, or certificates of deposits, any of which provides a better return for temporarily excess cash reserves than allowing them to lie fallow in checking accounts. Insurance companies are major buyers of preferred shares because of the preferential tax treatment received from the dividends paid on these investments. Corporations sometimes are restricted from margin trading by internal prohibitions, so corporate cash accounts are the more common type.

The last decade has seen a rapid growth in corporate futures trading. When commodities trading was dominated by agricultural and industrial products such as grains and metals, the corporate users of futures were the likes of Continental Grain, General Mills, General Foods, Hershey Foods, and Phelps Dodge (copper). The advent of financial futures and growing sophistication in corporate treasurers' offices have led to the opening of futures hedging accounts not only for major industrial corporations, but also for financial ones as well. Banks, insurance companies, savings and loan associations, and mortgage bankers have all discovered the potential advantages of hedging their business activities through the use of the previously arcane futures markets. The very nature of the futures markets makes it more difficult to open corporate futures accounts than their securities counterparts, and considerably more detailed documentation is required for the former.

Brokers may also handle certain forms of trust accounts but more often serve only as the executor of orders. Large trust funds are usually placed in the hands of banks or trust companies whose officers make the investment decisions and use brokers as sources of investment information and order execution. Broker activities in the trust area other than those described are usually concentrated in acting as trustee or custodian for Individual Retirement Accounts or self-employed retirement accounts (SEP or Keogh plans). They also handle accounts for the benefit of minors under the Uniform Gift or Transfer to Minors Act. These accounts have an adult designated as custodian for a minor. The custodian is charged with making investment decisions for the benefit of the minor. The broker is responsible for forbidding certain types of prohibited transactions such as margin trades and some types of options activity, but is otherwise not legally charged with responsibility. There have been, however, cases where the broker has been charged with negligence in allowing the custodian to continue activities that were deemed too speculative to have been in the best interests of the minor.

Another type of account is the guaranteed account. In itself, the account is not different from others already described, i.e., it could be cash or margin, securities or futures. The "guaranteed" feature means that the equity in one account is used to guarantee the broker against losses suffered in another. For instance, a customer with substantial equity in one account might guarantee another account opened by a son or daughter with less equity than the firm might otherwise require for that type of account, often a speculative one involving options or futures. Should the guaranteed account incur losses in excess of its equity, the broker is entitled through the guarantee agreement to tap the other account for any deficiency.

Methods of Solicitation

Securities and futures accounts may be opened without solicitation. Customers may simply walk into a brokerage office, complete whatever documents that may be required, make any deposit the broker calls for, and transact business that very day. The process is not much different from opening a bank account except that in some cases more paper work may be involved. Some brokers discourage walk-in business because they have no control over who might appear, particularly when minimum size accounts only are accepted. Most financial firms, however, welcome walk-in business and often assign a "person of the day" to handle this type of inquiry. Typically, the person so assigned is a relatively new representative, and the duty rotates on a daily or weekly basis. Most persons who walk into a brokerage office are seeking information and are usually not interested in doing business immediately. The potential is such that brokers will normally not turn away anyone who appears to be a prospect for future business. Almost every branch office has some story of an indigent appearing individual who walked in unannounced, asked for a few quotes, and walked out, only to reappear a few days later to place sizeable and legitimate orders with the person who was considerate enough to listen to his earlier requests.

In much the same manner investors may phone in unsolicited requests to open accounts. The process is not much different from walking in, although brokers tend to be more wary of fraudulent orders when the customer is not known to the firm or to the representative handling the call.

Unless, however, the registered representative is well connected or phenomenally lucky, some method other than the chance walk-in or phone-in must be used to develop sufficient business to justify her position and expenses. Many techniques for this purpose have been developed over the years, and such techniques for the most part are not unique to the finance industry. Representatives are continually reminded by their managers that they are first and foremost salespersons. The business is often represented as a numbers game. That is, see or be seen, and talk to enough people about investments and success will follow. Success does not depend on the ability to forecast the market correctly or to give profound advice. Rather, success comes from writing order tickets, the more and the larger the better. One can only accomplish this by having a large enough account base to take advantage of the variety of possible investment choices now available. Not everyone wants to buy a mutual fund, a municipal bond, or an option on a Swiss franc futures contract, but in a large enough account book the representative will often find individuals who will do one or two of those things. Some representatives ultimately refine their business to handle only the type of business they like best—option writing or municipal bonds, for example. Few, however, start out that way. Of course, if the customer deals with a representative employed by a futures-only firm or one that deals only in OTC stocks or mutual funds, he is unlikely to receive advice about making other kinds of investments.

The new representative is likely to try several different methods of developing business before settling on one that best fits his or her style and achieves the desired results. Representatives of large national full-service firms can rely on a steady stream of coupons returned by persons who have clipped them from ads in local or national magazines and newspapers. Many are returned by the idly curious, others by school children seeking material for reports, and still others by investors with the real possibility of doing significant business. The serious representative will follow most of these requests with a phone call. Allocation of these leads varies from firm to firm, and occasionally some are given to representatives who are already established. These salespersons are unlikely to do much more than mail the requested information, and sometimes not even do that. Given the sophisticated marketing techniques employed by large firms today, certain prejudgments on a potential customer's financial abilities may be made from such things as zip code or telephone area codes. Thus a coupon returned from an affluent suburb is more likely to be followed by a phone call than one returned from an address on skid row.

Direct mail has been used successfully by many representatives in developing new business. Here too, mailings have been refined to the point where they are made only to those who are likely to be interested. It should come as no surprise that lists of subscribers to expensive and influential periodicals are readily available for purchase. Indeed, obtaining even the most confidential of lists seems to be a skill in which financial firms are particularly expert. Some of these lists are easily obtained by the person willing to put in the effort. One could, for instance, simply go to the local town hall and examine the list of recent property transfers, usually a matter of public record. Various other lists can be obtained through methods which range from the unethical to the illegal. At one time or another it has been possible to acquire lists of recent purchasers of luxury automobiles, owners of private airplanes, nonbusiness travelers who habitually fly first class overseas, tourists who frequent luxury hotels, etc.

Other brokers find direct mail too slow for their purposes and may try using these lists for cold calls. In the cold call, the broker simply phones the person on the list, introduces himself and his firm, and attempts to hold the target's attention long enough to see if another call is merited and if so, when would it be accepted—two days, next month, six months, or just "when you come up with a good idea" (this latter suggestion is usually read by the broker as "tomorrow"). Naturally, many are annoyed at receiving such calls, and others are downright hostile, but the persistent representative who can shrug off rejection after rejection will ultimately contact enough persons who are receptive to his message. In some areas, particularly large metropolitan ones, the cold call is usually regarded as one of the most efficient techniques. For one thing, the phone book itself provides a virtually inexhaustible supply of names— physicians, lawyers, architects, and other professionals. For another, simply sitting at a desk a representative may discover which potential customers are more likely to merit a personal visit and which can be quickly discarded as unpromising. In other areas, however, such solicitation is not viewed any more favorably than similar calls soliciting magazine subscriptions, new storm windows, or aluminum siding. This is especially so in rural areas or small towns where few do business with someone who is neither a friend nor an acquaintance.

Another favorite device for developing a clientele is the investment lecture or seminar. These are especially well received in areas where there are large percentages of retired persons who often regard these presentations as an evening's diversion. Because these investors often have both a goodly amount of discretionary income and plenty of time to attend these talks, they are looked upon as prime new account candidates. Seminars on specific (and often esoteric) topics are likely to draw a different type of audience and may well be popular regardless of the geographical location. Tax and estate planning, options trading, and futures are topics that are often favored in these seminars. Industry rules require that a talk before a general social or fraternal group be on investing in a general sense only. No specific securities may be recommended, and any literature to be distributed must be on a pick up basis only. The essence of the rule is that it is impossible for the registered representative to ascertain in advance the investment objective of each audience member, and even if it were possible, there is no way to determine the suitability of any single recommendation for any individual member of that group. From the broker's standpoint, this method allows one to be seen by a large number of prospective investors in a brief period. If the broker has a good stage presence, he or she may make a number of favorable impressions more quickly than would be the case with other methods of account development.

Although they are not solicitations, referrals are a representative's favorite way of obtaining new business. Referrals can be requested, and successful representatives make it a point to ask satisfied customers for the names of family members, friends, and others who might do business with her. Although there is a built-in receptivity to a call from someone recommended by a friend, persons being contacted by someone they don't know aren't often willing to drop currently satisfactory relationships. Once the initial contact has been made, the prospective customer must be developed in much the same manner as an equally receptive lead from a cold call. Sometimes, referrals simply walk or phone in, citing the name of the customer who referred them. This is often welcomed by the representative because no effort was expended in making the contact. It can be assumed the investor would not have made the contact unless she were ready to invest. The representative therefore has already overcome two major obstacles to a sale without doing anything. There is, however, a potential danger. Many times referrals will call wanting to buy the same security purchased by their friends although this particular investment may be unsuitable for them. If the new customer is unknown other than as a friend of another customer, the ethical representative should go through the same fact-finding process necessary to qualify any new account. Customers should be wary of representatives who simply accept orders without more questioning than the basic minimum required to complete a new account document.

REASONS FOR SELECTING BROKERS

From the foregoing it may be apparent that many investors have the choice of their broker thrust upon them by the charm, persistence, or personality of the registered representative. There is nothing necessarily perverse in this because everyone obviously reserves the right to say no. Furthermore, everyone likes to deal with someone who is pleasant to deal with, and it can be assumed that most persons will not open accounts with those whom they find unpleasant. On the other hand, if the salesperson's charm, persistence, or personality is supplemented with exaggerated claims of the abilities of either the salesperson or the employer, the customer may well be induced to open the account on false premises.

Full-service firms offer a staggering array of services but no investor can use them all. Few, indeed, will have the need for more than a couple. Some will require accurate order execution and little else. Others will need investment ideas developed by research departments. Still others will need (or at least desire) a broker who will hold their hand through difficult periods and patiently explain even the most simple investment concepts. There is a place for all these desires and needs, and there are brokers who will satisfy them. It is unlikely that any broker can satisfy them all if he or she intends to become productive to the employer.

A common complaint among investors is that they are courted solicitously until the account is opened and then quickly forgotten. The reason for this is readily apparent to those familiar with salespersons in any industry. If the investor has, for example, $25,000 to invest in an instrument such as a mutual fund or a municipal bond that is not going to be actively traded, the representative has a strong incentive to press for the sale because it will generate a substantial sales fee or credit. The customer is typically barraged with letters and phone calls offering all sorts of assistance in coming to the investment decision. Once that decision is made, however, and the potential for further activity eliminated or reduced, the salesman's ardor cools quickly. Anyone who has purchased a new automobile can relate to the phenomenon.

Potential customers should thus be wary of unrealistic promises of continuing service and portfolio monitoring. Unless the investor has an unusually large and active portfolio, not only should he not expect this service, he shouldn't even desire it. A broker who calls daily with a new investment idea for the investor with an average portfolio is probably trying to churn the customer's account.

Some of this can be ascribed to the normal process whereby new representatives enter into the securities business. The major firms all have training programs that run for about four months. The period is determined by the time necessary to complete the industry's basic requirements and to prepare for the registration examination. Fledgling brokers usually do not have enough accounts awaiting them to ensure a productive business and must thus attempt to develop new ones by the processes described. When a broker has few accounts it is possible to lavish extra service on smaller accounts, but as more business develops attention is diverted to the larger, more active accounts. As the broker's account book builds, the odd-lot buyer, once a prized account, is now relegated to a lower place and rarely receives phone calls or mailings. These investors in fact become used to a periodic letter from a new representative with whom they have never spoken. The contents of the letter usually inform the investor that the previous broker has either left the employment of this firm, or that the new representative will be able to provide more personal service, which generally means that he or she is new and doesn't have any accounts.

Besides exaggerated claims of personal service, the prospective customer should be wary of claims for superior executions. All such claims are not necessarily false, but one should carefully consider the need for exacting executions, as well as the substance of the claim in the first place. If one is trading in futures this element can be crucial. A faulty execution or the failure to execute as instructed can lead to substantial losses in such volatile markets. Some firms maintain their own floor brokers and staff; others rely on the services of independent brokers. It has not as yet been demonstrated that one or the other provides better execution prices. The argument usually given for the use of independents is that they try harder as their own living is on the line. That is, they have a lot of money invested in their membership and can ill afford to antagonize the members who use their services. The argument for the firm-employed broker is that he is more directly responsive to the sales force and customers of the firm because he has no other allegiances. There may be some merit in each opinion but hardly enough to cause a person to open an account with a representative based primarily on it. Unfortunately, the only way one is likely to be able to judge execution service is to experience it first.

Unless the investor is dealing with large securities purchases, the nuances of order execution are not so important. This is not to condone sloppy order execution, but rather to point out that long-term investment decisions are usually best executed at the market. For this type of order, the automated execution systems offered by the major exchanges and the NASDAQ system are perfectly adequate. They have the virtue of making the execution price almost immediately available. The trading customer may feel them inadequate because they can handle only market and limit orders, robbing him of the more sophisticated trading techniques like stop and stop-limit orders.

In the over-the-counter market one sometimes finds dealers who are in effect the market for certain stocks. The investor should be extremely suspicious of securities which are claimed as available exclusively through one dealer. Should a salesperson inform the customer that this security can only be bought from that particular dealer, it indicates no fair and competitive market exists. In other words, the price is what the dealer says it is. This type of purchase is to be avoided at all costs. Much the same can be said for most commodity leverage contracts.

A reason often cited by salespersons as important to investors is the quality of the research provided by that firm. If one is dealing with a discount broker it is customary to offer no research at all, although generic reports like the familiar Standard & Poor's tear sheets (so called because they are easily torn out of the large binders where they are kept) are occasionally offered.

If, however, the firm is a full-service one, its representatives are likely to extol the superior ideas produced by their research departments. One frequently mentioned criterion is the *Institutional Investor Magazine's* annual "All American" team. If a brokerage firm has placed a number of analysts on this team, it supposedly indicates better research ideas than can be provided by a firm with smaller (or no) representation. Institutional brokers pay a lot of attention to this ranking, but it is in fact not much more than a beauty contest. For one thing, it is the result of a poll of those who bothered to respond. For another, the assumption is implicit that these analysts provide the best advice in their specific industries. It is probably true that their opinions are more knowledgeable and better informed than those of a random group of typical retail investors. There is, however, little evidence that their recommendations will be consistently superior to those of other analysts. Indeed, because these analysts usually cover the large capitalization blue chip issues favored by their institutional clientele, they rarely give much attention to the smaller growth issues that often hold out the most promise of return to the individual investor. There is another reason why the investor should not be swayed by the number of "star" analysts a brokerage firm boasts. Much like star athletes, these analysts are subjected to constant offers to switch employment. Their salaries are usually in excess (sometimes *greatly* in excess) of $250,000 annually, and many of them do jump when a better offer is made. Thus, one year's lineup is not very likely to be the same as the next year's.

A greater danger arises when too much emphasis is placed on technical analysis. This is true to some degree with securities, but is a much more serious problem with futures. A brief scan of commodities periodicals will reveal ads for trading systems, all of which have "outperformed" the market for any length of time. There is talk of mysterious devices such as "oscillators" or "stochastics" which are virtually certain to pinpoint the proper time to buy or sell. A moment's reflection should indicate to the serious investor that were anyone actually to possess such a system he would hardly reveal it to the great unwashed for a token subscription of a few hundred dollars. Nevertheless, it does not appear to discourage those who quest for magic formulas to riches. Any representative who claims to possess such a system is making an inherently fraudulent contention.

All investment is to some degree risky. The risks are greater or lesser depending on the investment vehicles chosen and on the tactics employed by the investor. For example, a U.S. Treasury bond is essentially free from credit risk because the holder has the unequivocal promise of the government to pay interest in a timely manner and to repay the principal amount at maturity. Should the investor, however, attempt to *trade* the bond, or even worse, an option or a futures contract on that bond, in anticipation of interest rate changes, the possibility of loss may be substantial. Representatives sometimes minimize the potential risks to prospective customers in hopes of obtaining business which might otherwise be channeled into other forms of investment. Claims are sometimes advanced that losses can be minimized through the judicious use of stop orders or spread positions. Others contend that their firm will always make a market in a particular OTC security, thus assuring the investor of a way to recover the money if the investment does not work out. Neither of these claims is true, and the claim about market-making constitutes fraud if the representative is promising the guaranteed return of the customer's original investment. Indeed, the CFTC requires all new futures customers to be given a risk disclosure document which specifically addresses the promise of risk limitation through the use of stop orders and spreads. Securities options customers must receive the Options Clearing Corporation risk disclosure document which is even more comprehensive in its explanations of risks involved in options trading.

On occasion, some representatives are so misguided as to promise to make up any loss out of his or her own pocket should the investment fail. Such a person must be desperate for new business because this promise violates the rules of all self-regulatory bodies governing the securities and futures business. In short, the process of investment involves risk by definition. Those who can bear no risk to their principal should stay within the safe confines of FDIC or FSLIC-insured bank accounts. Those who desire greater rewards must be aware that these rewards necessitate greater risk.

5

Opening Accounts

The process of opening a securities or futures account is fairly standard. The various exchanges and regulatory bodies have established procedures which, although differing in degree of rigor, are essentially similar. Many full-service brokers will not open a new customer account without a bona fide order, i.e., one with a reasonable chance of execution. There are good reasons for this. The processing of new account forms alone, as well as the time consumed in acquiring and approving the necessary documentation, is expensive. Would-be investors who are not really serious should not be permitted to waste the time and energies of brokerage firms. Discount brokers, on the other hand, frequently solicit new accounts by direct mail and usually do not require an order. In this case, there are fewer costs involved because little if any "professional" time has been spent on developing the account. The documents required for account opening are discussed in Chapter 11.

The account may be opened either over the telephone or by the customer appearing at the broker's office. Sometimes a representative may obtain the customer's initial order on a home or office visit. In such cases, however, the actual account opening must await the approval of the supervisor later that day or even on the business day following the visit. Unless the customer is opening either a futures account or a securities account with a large or speculative transaction, the broker customarily does not require a deposit. For example, if the customer's order is to buy 100 shares of American Telephone and Telegraph at the current market price, the broker typically enters the order after completing the new account procedure. If the order is for the purchase of a volatile security or an option, or for a short sale, the broker is almost certain to demand a good faith deposit to cover itself should the market move against the customer and the customer later refuse to pay. Settlement date for the usual securities trade is five business days from the trade date. For options, it is the business day following the trade date. Should an adverse price move occur between the trade and the settlement date, the customer might refuse to honor her commitment to the broker. In such a case the broker would be forced to use its own funds to complete the transaction and then have to pursue the customer for satisfaction of the claim.

It is customary in the futures business to require a substantial deposit before allowing any transactions. First, the possible loss is usually much greater than with the typical securities transaction. Second, the futures margin must normally be deposited before the opening of the market on the day following the trade. Indeed, the loss on the opening transaction could either wipe out the customer's equity or reduce it to the maintenance level, something that rarely happens with securities. Reputable firms normally set account-opening equity requirements at levels considerably in excess of any possible loss the customer might suffer. The serious prospective customer should not object to this. Brokers must be cautious not to encourage trading in futures and options by those unable or unwilling to undertake the considerable risks involved. It is rather too late to find that the customer has insufficient funds to answer a margin call on the first or second day following his first trade.

DOCUMENTS

In order to open an account the representative must first complete a new account document. Some brokers prefer that the customer fill out this form in his own hand, particularly when options or futures are involved. Stricter suitability requirements are customary for traders in these markets, and they are usually asked to demonstrate net worth and income levels higher than are required for other investors. Experience has shown that representatives eager to open these potentially active and lucrative accounts sometimes inflate numbers to make a supervisor's approval easier to obtain. Thus, a $50,000 income becomes perhaps a $75,000 income; a $60,000 net worth becomes one of

$125,000; and illiquid becomes liquid. Should a loss occur and a lawsuit follow, the brokerage firm would be hard pressed to defend the actions of its representative in completing the new account form. It would be on sounder ground had the customer himself inflated the figures. It should be understood that neither situation is a good one, and the broker is not necessarily freed from its "know your customer" obligations because the customer provided false information.

Normally, the representative fills out the new account document and most often does it with information provided over the phone by the customer. The representative should ask for specific information and not enter estimates or guesses based on the customer's occupation or address. Many people live beyond their means. Not every physician is wealthy, and not every corporate vice president is capable of risking thousands of dollars on a single trade. New brokers are especially reluctant to ask straightforward questions about income or net worth for fear of alienating a potential customer who has been cultivated carefully for some time. Really worthwhile prospective customers do not object to answering questions and indeed are often proud to state sums which they know are impressive. A guess or an unsubstantiated estimate of important facts is worse than no information at all.

A typical new account form at a securities firm has entries for the following information:

Name

Address (home and business)

Citizenship

Social security or taxpayer identification number

Employment

Annual income

Age

Dependents

Bank and personal references

In addition, options accounts also require disclosure of the customer's net worth (exclusive of equity in the principal residence), liquid net worth (cash and securities), and investment experience.

Some investment firms require the representative opening the account to verify the bank reference for all accounts. Others demand this check only if the customer is proposing an unusually large or speculative transaction. Banks do not ordinarily disclose much information about a customer's checking account, especially in response to a broker's phone inquiry. Although they generally provide more data in response to a letter, the process is too time-consuming for the typical account opening situation where a transaction is pending. At best, the bank reference may indicate that the investor has been a good banking customer for some time. This gives some insight into the customer's business reputation. It is, however, not likely that customers will give as a reference a bank with which they have had an unsatisfactory relationship. From the broker's viewpoint, the most telling information that may be derived from this reference is the naming of a bank where an account has only recently been opened. Of course, people are as free to change bank accounts as brokerage accounts. Unless the customer has recently moved into the area and is reestablishing financial relationships, the nearly simultaneous opening of two financial accounts should indicate to the broker that some caution is in order.

Futures Accounts

If the account is for trading futures the information already noted is required, and company policy may well demand more. If the customer proposes substantial transactions or activity, the broker might require some form of credit analysis such as those provided by Dun and Bradstreet, TRW, Hooper Holmes, or CDC.

Federal regulation requires that the customer be provided with a risk disclosure document which contains clear warnings that futures trading is inherently risky. In addition, there are separate disclosure documents for futures options, accounts controlled by commodity trading advisors, and investments in a commodity pool, a mutual fund-like vehicle for futures trading. Although these papers give clear warning that certain risk limiting devices like stop orders and spreads are not guarantees against loss, they do not (and cannot) enumerate all potential risks in such volatile markets. Representatives should be careful not to imply that these documents are only formalities. The CFTC rules require the customer to sign them, giving evidence of familiarity with the risks described. Should the representative urge the customer into a hasty signature before a complete perusal of the documents, the broker would have difficulty defending against later charges of unsuitability. Too many representatives have assured customers that their judicious use of stop orders as well as personal attention to the market preclude the large losses incurred by others not blessed with a similar trading system.

The completed documents must next be presented to a supervisor for approval. If the brokerage firm is a member of either the NYSE or the NASD, the branch office manager is the usual source of this approval. This person is often an officer or partner of the firm. In order to qualify as an office manager an individual must be so registered with the regulatory bodies and have passed one or more examinations pertaining to that function. Because futures and securities regulators do not have common standards, many office managers must satisfy both authorities separately.

Options Accounts

If the customer intends to trade listed securities options the account must be approved by a registered options principal. Most branch office managers are so qualified, but if the office is served by only one or two representatives, the account must be approved by a regional or home office options principal. All customers must receive a copy of the options disclosure document no later than at the approval of the account. This booklet describes the risks of options trading, but has a considerably different tone from that of the futures disclosure document. The latter concentrates on warning the prospective trader that risks are not limited to the margin deposits she makes, and that use of certain trading tactics do not necessarily prevent loss. The securities option disclosure document, on the other hand, describes in more detail the nature of the most commonly employed strategies and indicates the potential dangers in each.

In addition to the disclosure document, the new options customer must receive an options agreement and a copy of the information used to approve the account. These items are often consolidated on a single sheet by printing the agreement on the reverse side of the new account form. The investor is asked to review the information on the new account form for accuracy and completeness, and to make any changes necessary. The customer is thus alerted to the possibility of inflated figures entered by the representative.

The options agreement requires the customer to abide by the rules and regulations of the exchanges that trade listed options, and also of the Options Clearing Corporation, the central body through which all listed options transactions are cleared. If the customer does not return the signed agreement within 15 calendar days of the date of the approval of the account by a registered options principal, the account is blocked. Such an account is restricted to closing transactions only, i.e., the customer may liquidate existing positions but cannot create new ones. The block is lifted upon the receipt of the signed agreement. Some brokerage firms require the customer to sign the agreement and any other necessary papers *prior* to the approval of the account. This sound policy avoids not only blocked accounts, but also other trades which are not permitted. For example, spreads and naked call writing may only be executed in a margin account. If the representative does not obtain the margin documents before the trades, they are not allowed. This measure eliminates the need to break trades already made, a frequent source of loss both to customer and broker.

Joint Accounts

Additional documents may be needed if the account is to include the names of more than one person. The most common of these accounts is the *joint account,* in most states titled "joint tenants with rights of survivorship." It is often employed by married couples but is not restricted to such use. A typical account title is "John Smith and Mary Smith, joint tenants with rights of survivorship," or simply "JTWROS." The major value of the account is that probate is bypassed, and in many cases estate taxes are avoided. The parties in the account are co-owners of the property, and the death of one of the tenants makes the survivor sole owner. Because the transfer of property between spouses is unlimited there are usually no estate tax consequences. If, however, the parties were not married, estate taxes can be levied in some circumstances.

Either party is entitled to transact business in the account, and either party may make deposits. Property may not be withdrawn without the written consent of both parties. Checks paid on the account must be in the name of both parties. Both parties must sign a joint account agreement in order to conduct business.

Less familiar is the *tenants in common* account. In this account the parties have a specified fractional interest. The death of one of the tenants dissolves the tenancy with proportional shares going to the surviving tenants and the heirs of the decedent. The growing number of two-income families linked with still ominous divorce statistics have made this account increasingly popular with married pairs, but it is also used by relatives, friends, and others who prefer the economies achieved by consolidating transactions into a single account. Some brokers have a separate form for each type of joint account, whereas others have a single form with separate paragraphs designating the type of account, where the irrelevant paragraph is struck out. In any event, all persons participating in the account must sign the agreement.

Custodial Accounts

Accounts for minors are common, but care must be exercised not to let the minor transact business directly. The reason is that minors cannot be held to honor legally binding commitments. A minor's refusal to pay for a losing trade would therefore leave the broker with little recourse except to swallow the loss and consider it an educational experience. The most common type of account for investment on behalf of minors is the custodial account, which names an adult as custodian for a minor under the Uniform Gift or Transfer to Minors Act. Property in the account represents an irrevocable gift to a minor from an adult, who need not also be the custodian. No special documentation is required, and the account may be opened using the standard new account procedure. The custodian is allowed to make any reasonably prudent investment on the minor's behalf. Margin accounts are not permitted, thus precluding certain types of activity like short sales and naked call writing. Extending the expression *reasonably prudent* to include such speculations begs the question. Because the property belongs to the minor, profits or earnings gained from the account are taxable to the minor. For this reason, the minor's social security number must be on the account document.

Fiduciary Accounts

Other types of fiduciary accounts require more extensive documentation and should not be opened by the representative until the firm's legal or compliance department has granted approval. These include trust accounts, pension fund accounts, and similar retirement accounts which are regulated under the Employees Retirement Income Security Act (ERISA) by the Labor Department. These accounts often have specific limitations on permissible investments, especially options, futures, and other leveraged transactions. If the representative executes an order that later turns out to have been prohibited for this account, the brokerage firm could have substantial liabilities. It is also important to know who may legally enter orders for these accounts. There have been a number of cases where orders were entered by unauthorized employees even though the actual transactions were of the kind usually entered by that account. Worse, there have been others where an unauthorized employee placed orders that the account was not authorized to enter. Copies of resolutions, powers of attorney, or other empowering documents should always be obtained before accepting any orders. Unfortunately, as salesmen, representatives are anxious to get in that first trade in a new account and sometimes overlook necessary documentation as mere paperwork that can always be obtained later.

Corporate and Partnership Accounts

Accounts opened for corporations, particularly financial ones, customarily have numerous limitations imposed by the corporate charter. If the officials opening the account contemplate only the purchase and sale of fully-paid securities, brokers require, in addition to the regular new account documents, a resolution from the board of directors naming those legally entitled to act on behalf of the corporation. If either margin or futures are possible investments, it is necessary to obtain a copy of the corporate charter (or an excerpt therefrom) which authorizes such transactions. An absence of a specific prohibition against such trades is not considered grounds for proceeding. Rather, they should be expressly permitted in the charter.

If a partnership opens an account, a copy of the partnership agreement is necessary. Unless otherwise specified, brokers can usually accept orders from any general partner, but never from a limited one. Some partnerships such as law or accounting firms regularly admit new partners or retire older ones to the status of limited partner. Representatives handling these accounts should be careful to request updates in partnership agreements to assure themselves that those entering orders are indeed general partners or other specifically authorized personnel.

Power of Attorney Accounts

Another type of account makes use of a power of attorney. These accounts are not different from the ones already described except in one critical area: the delegation of investment decisions to someone other than the owner, or principal, of the account. The document conveying this right is called a *limited power-of-attorney* or a *trading authorization.* The owner of the account authorizes the person named in the document to make trades without the owner's specific approval. It is the standard arrangement for the investment advisory accounts used by substantial investors who lack the time, desire, or knowledge to manage their own investments. It is also occasionally made out in favor of a relative, friend, or lawyer who is presumed more familiar with investments than the principal. This written authorization is also required (although frequently neglected) when a spouse's account is concerned. It is not uncommon for a spouse to make transactions in the other spouse's account. For example, when each spouse has an individual account with a broker, the representative may receive a call from one with the instructions: "Buy 100 shares for me and another 100 in my wife's (husband's) account also." Unless prior written consent of the other spouse had been obtained this is an unauthorized order. In many cases no immediate problems arise, but later a divorce proceeding may bring to light numerous, usually money-losing, trades that turn out to have been unauthorized. Unless deemed ratified, these transactions are often settled through a recision of the trades and a restoration of the lost equity.

Discretionary Accounts

When a trading authorization is made out in favor of a registered representative the account is termed *discretionary*. These accounts are not acceptable at some brokerage firms because of the potential conflict of interest involving the representative managing the investments. A discretionary account requires written approval by a senior official of the firm. All of the orders must be approved in writing on the day of entry by a supervisor, ordinarily the branch office manager. Order tickets must be marked discretionary or coded so that they may be easily selected from other executed orders and initialed daily by the supervisor.

A limiting form of discretion may be used with only verbal delegation of authority from the customer. If limited to price and time of execution this type of discretion may be exercised by the representative with nothing more than a phone call from the customer as authorization. Brokers are probably ill-advised to permit this type of control as it can easily lead to misunderstanding and second-guessing on the customer's part.

Margin Accounts

Almost any account, except those under legal restriction, may be opened as a margin account. As noted earlier, margin is not permitted in some accounts. Others may use margin credit for securities dealings, although the typical investor should probably give margin considerable distance. Additional documents are necessary for any margin account. The standard securities margin agreement is really a loan document wherein the customer pledges any margined securities as collateral for loans the broker may arrange or extend. The broker is allowed to hold margined securities and liquidate them if necessary to protect itself against customer failure to maintain the equity prescribed by industry or house rules. The customer is also expected to sign a securities loan consent form which allows the broker to lend margin securities at its discretion. The loan consent is a brief statement, often a single sentence, that reads: "Until you receive notice from the undersigned, you are hereby authorized to lend, to yourselves or to others, any securities held by you on margin for the account of, or under the control of, the undersigned." The loan consent is often on the same form as the longer margin agreement, but is a separate agreement and requires a separate signature. Sometimes a customer may balk at signing the loan consent as it appears to convey nothing of value to him. Although it is not technically necessary to the existence of a margin account, the loan consent provides brokers with valuable opportunities in securities lending, a lucrative part of the brokerage business. The customer's refusal to sign usually makes the account unacceptable as a matter of policy, although accommodations are sometimes made for particularly desirable accounts.

All futures accounts are margin accounts by definition. Futures margin, however, is different from securities margin because the customer is not borrowing anything. The customer agrees to deposit and maintain minimum amounts that the broker calls for as good faith deposits. The futures margin agreement allows the broker to liquidate any position when the customer fails to answer margin calls, and makes the customer liable for losses suffered beyond the account's remaining equity. Because of federal regulation, funds may not be transferred from a domestic futures account to another account, such as a securities account, without written authorization. Customers are therefore asked to sign a transfer of funds agreement if they maintain other types of account with the same broker.

Accounts Requiring Employer Permission

There are a few kinds of account which necessitate the written consent of the employer before they may be opened. These include margin accounts for non-officer employees of banks and insurance companies, as well as any account for the employees (officers and partners included) of other broker/dealers. In the latter case, duplicate confirmations of all trades and duplicate account statements must be promptly sent to the employer. This policy serves as a check on employees who might be tempted to circumvent employer restrictions on certain transactions by executing them through other brokers.

SOME CONCLUDING OBSERVATIONS

Not all accounts are acceptable to brokers, and nothing compels them to open an account for anyone. Brokers are not, after all, public utilities, required to provide service for any and all. The prospective customer may give indication of mental problems or instability. Such an apparent lack of capacity should disqualify a customer from doing business with a broker who could well be held liable for continuing to do business with a legally incompetent individual. In other cases, the customer may be all too competent in his ability to launch lawsuits against brokers for reasons that may range from the frivolous to the blatantly unethical. No broker should be so hungry for business that it would permit the opening of a new account for someone who already has several outstanding lawsuits against those previously so undiscriminating as to allow him to open accounts with them.

Nor should brokers have to entertain unrealistic demands and objectives from prospective customers. The investor who wishes to double her account value annually with no risk to her principal is asking the impossible. A representative who accepts such a customer is asking for problems. Similarly, there is no need to accept a customer who makes unreasonable demands on the representative's time. Some investors feel that the representative exists to service their accounts only. They often want that person to be available at any time to discuss the market even when no order is pending. Although this type of coverage may be fitting for a few large institutional accounts, it is a rare individual who merits such service. Indeed, for a representative to concentrate his activities on a single account, no matter how large or active, is a dangerous practice which is discouraged by most firms. If the customer and the representative have a falling out, the latter loses his entire brokerage income whereas the former simply moves on to a new firm.

Representatives can avoid many problems by setting the ground rules before opening the account. The customer, especially the new investor, should be clearly instructed on settlement procedures. The customer should know when payment or delivery are due and should be made familiar with the broker's policy on extensions. The representative should be firm and specific about which expectations are reasonable and which are not. This applies both to anticipated investment performance and to demands on the representative's time. A stockbroker who takes the time to stress these points will have fewer misunderstandings and problems in these areas than one who does not. Representatives whose primary goal is to get that first order in as quickly as possible deserve much of the trouble they will ultimately get.

6

Suitability

If this chapter could but offer the one best definition of investment suitability, a great service would be rendered to the financial and legal arenas. There is, however, so much disagreement among knowledgeable people about this concept that it is not possible to satisfy everyone here, and it will probably never be possible elsewhere either.

It is possible, however, to illustrate various schools of thought and indicate which approaches seem to have the widest general acceptance. The reader should be aware that there are conflicting versions, although some are held by those with understandably biased views and should be weighed accordingly.

DEFINITION

Suitability in its broadest sense refers to the appropriateness of dealing with a potential client at all. In a narrower sense, it may refer to the basis for specific suggestions that specific investments be acquired or liquidated, or that specific strategies be followed once it has been determined that the broad establishment of a relationship is acceptable. In the brokerage business, the first of these is illustrated by the mere acceptance of an account. The second is illustrated by the transactions made in the account once it is opened. In short, satisfying suitability

73

requirements means that financial fiduciaries should correlate the situation of their customer with recommended positions or strategies after both have been investigated. Essential facts about the customer must be determined and suggestions must be reasonably based. Recommendations that positions be taken in commodity futures or naked stock options for an aggressive young business person might be quite proper, whereas the same recommendations for a retired person interested in capital preservation would be highly improper.

Generally, there are two elements deemed to be integral to the concept of suitability. The first of these has to do with the financial capacity of clients. The second has to do with their financial objectives based upon their needs and desires. These two elements are obviously intertwined in a sense, but can, nevertheless, be productively discussed separately.

Financial Capacity

Investments, by definition, require funds although the amounts and sources may vary. Whether a financial intermediary solicits business or merely accepts orders, it would certainly seem that the intermediary should determine whether the investor can afford the obligations to be incurred. Protection of the firm from people unable or unwilling to meet their obligations is a base line consideration. Accordingly it is usual to inquire as to a customer's income, net worth, and liquid net worth. If the customer is investing with borrowed money, the salesperson should consider the increased risk created by the use of such leverage. Even more caution is necessary if the salesperson suggests borrowing the funds.

Some might argue whether inquiry into a customer's financial position is a fiduciary duty if the financial firm is to act only as an order taker, but, at a minimum, it is certainly a good business practice. Failure to do so might well imply that the intermediary is operating below the standards dictated by usual trade custom and practice.

If a broker inquires of a customer concerning suitability, it might be logically assumed that the broker should inform the customer that suitability will be considered before trading begins. The widespread custom of inquiring into suitability, if only to aid in establishing credit or trading limits, might well create a legal obligation to the broker. Not only might custom create an obligation under common law, but it might also create a contractual duty pursuant to most customers' agreements, which frequently indicate that the parties will conform to the rules, regulations, customs, and usages of the markets in which the customer intends to trade. Few would argue with a conclusion that one recommending trades or acting on behalf of another must consider suitability in all its aspects.

Some maintain that those who sell financial products, whether solicited or not, have a positive duty to determine whether the client has the financial ability to sustain losses. Others believe that a duty to reject orders may sometimes exist but usually does not. Those who take the broader position apparently believe that a broker has a duty to protect customers from themselves, much like a bartender who might be held liable for the actions of a customer who was clearly served one or more drinks too many. Others take the position that a customer who is of legal age and has the mental and physical capacities to act has the right to take risks in an effort to achieve gains so long as there is a reasonable probability that she is able to provide the necessary funds. Most of those who take this view, however, agree that the broker still has the obligation to disclose material facts, and certainly cannot properly conceal or misrepresent them. They would also agree that there are obvious exceptions to a broad assertion that a broker taking unsolicited orders is nothing more than an order taker. It would be a reckless broker indeed who would take an order from a glassy-eyed customer to buy all of the stock in General Motors.

Neither of these views can be definitively determined here to be the correct choice. Logically it would seem that a customer who has acquired all reasonable information from a salesperson has every right to accept or reject risk at his own discretion. Maintaining that only those with substantial assets should be allowed to take great risks, whereas those with modest resources should be allowed to take only conservative positions, despite their knowledge of the possible risks and rewards, leads to some uncomfortable conclusions. Those with substantial assets would be allowed to take great risks and might suffer great losses. Those with quite little would not be allowed to take enough risks to give them a realistic chance to increase their assets substantially.

It may well be argued that those with sufficient means would be better advised to take conservative positions designed to preserve what they have, whereas those with modest assets might well enter into more speculative ventures in an effort to accumulate enough to become conservative. The broker, of course, should make clear that, as always, the opportunity to enjoy large rewards entails the taking of risks at least as large, the effort to gain small rewards still requires taking small risks, and that the mere fact that a risk is taken does not mean that a reward is possible.

Whether salespersons should solicit or accept certain types of accounts, and whether their supervisors should merely go along with the conclusions or make some independent verification of the salespersons' inputs, are discussed elsewhere in this book.

Objectives

The objectives of new clients should be clearly determined and a record made of them. The objectives should be reasonable in concept and degree. It is common for investors, especially those who are unsophisticated, to desire or even to expect complete safety of principal in addition to substantial current income, capital appreciation, and favorable tax consequences. Some investors who lose accept their misfortune unhappily but graciously. Others maintain that they never really understood the risks inherent in their investments. Sometimes this is true and sometimes it is not, but in either case, those who sell financial instruments can eliminate many problems by explaining risks accurately, completely, and clearly. A financial salesperson should make clear that risk accompanies opportunity for reward, that the amount of risk taken tends to equal or exceed the amount of potential reward, and that opportunities to invest in such a way as to increase the chance of reward and, at the same time, reduce the risk of loss are extremely rare if they exist at all. It is wise to make and preserve a record of such disclosure. Salespeople should not gloss over or minimize the importance of such disclosures and clients should beware of such practices. If disclosures were honest and adequate, in writing, not countered by conflicting oral representations, and in possession of both parties, the number of disputes revolving around clients' understanding of the risks would be materially reduced.

Those who sell financial products are also well advised to note that suitability may change with time. Customers can gain sophistication with experience. Their needs may change as they get older, or if there are changes in their health or family circumstances. Their financial capacity may improve or deteriorate in accordance with their investment successes or failures or other financial activities.

Individual Transactions

A firm may conclude that a customer is suitable to open an account, but responsibility does not end with the opening or continued monitoring of a customer's suitability. It is also necessary to consider the suitability of individual investments.

If customers make their own decisions, brokers are generally considered to be basically order takers whose obligations are primarily only to handle orders properly and provide accurate information relative to the account, such as positions held or the financial balance. They are not obligated to volunteer opinions on a customer's choice of investments or trading strategies and, in fact, may even be faulted for delaying orders by taking the time to talk about them. If a customer is talked out of making a trade, one can be quite certain that a profit would have resulted and that the customer will blame the broker for causing the profit to be lost. If a trade is encouraged for which the customer was only marginally enthusiastic, a loss will almost inevitably follow and the customer will maintain that the position would not have been entered without the broker's encouragement. In a word, brokers may always be fiduciaries to some degree, but that does not obligate them to become parties to all positions or strategies selected by their clients. They are also not an insurer of opinions which are reasonably based and offered in good faith. If an order is solicited, most would agree that the degree of fiduciary duty becomes high, and that the position recommended should be suitable to the client based upon facts which should be known to the firm and its sales personnel.

It is widely accepted that a broker represents to all of those with whom he deals that he will do so fairly, honestly, and in accordance with trade custom and practice. This concept has often been referred to as the *shingle theory*, following the use of that term in the case of *Charles Hughes & Co. v. SEC* in 1943.[1] That case held that a broker's duties toward his clients begins when he hangs out his shingle, but it has been cited since to justify a continuing requirement that brokers treat a customer fairly after a relationship with that customer has been established.

Solicited versus Unsolicited

Because it is generally accepted that the need for determination of suitability is higher for a solicited order than for an unsolicited order, it is necessary to distinguish between them, but this is no exact science. Only the extremes are quite clear. If a customer with an open account calls a broker, places an order for something about which there has been no previous communication, asks no questions, indicates no interest in discussing the order, and the salesperson expresses no opinion, it is almost certainly unsolicited. The salesperson should make the record clear that the order is unsolicited by noting that fact on the order form, the mailed confirmation of the trade, or both.

If the broker utilizes a power of attorney and the customer does not learn of a transaction until after the fact, there is clear solicitation. The need for salespersons and their supervisors to be certain of a customer's

[1] 139 F.2d 434 (2d Cir. 1943), *cert. denied,* 321 U.S. 786 (1944).

suitability in such cases is obvious. Especially to be avoided are trades which might indicate a conflict of interest. Salespersons should avoid, for example, placing securities in a client's account from their firm's inventory on a principal basis. If the securities were already in the inventory and were not acquired to accommodate the order; it would be quite embarrassing to the broker if the inventory position appeared to be uncomfortably large, resulted from an underwriting that was not well accepted, or yielded a sales credit to the salesperson that was large compared with a commission on a security purchased as agent. If most trades in a discretionary account were of this nature and the client did not approve them, a conflict of interest is almost a given. Informing the client of such trades by indicating "principal" on the confirmation is probably not sufficient to justify such a practice. Utilizing a trading authorization primarily to generate commissions might be offered as another example of unsuitable trading, but where the quantity of trades rather than the quality is the primary consideration, this is best reserved for the discussion of churning in Chapter 10.

Between the extremes of order taking and discretionary authority there are many possibilities, and the distinction between solicited and unsolicited may become quite blurred. If a salesperson calls a customer, recommends a transaction, and they discuss the suggestion, it is quite clearly solicited. Suppose, however, that the salesperson sends some literature discussing several investment opportunities to a mailing list of her clients. A client then calls and, without discussion, places an order for one or more of the items in the literature. Or suppose that a customer initiates a call and indicates that he is interested in one item on a list of five which he himself has compiled with no input from the broker. The broker indicates her choice from one of the five, which the customer then buys. Are these orders solicited?

Although there are many opinions involving such circumstances, the best conclusion is probably that they are solicited and orders should be marked accordingly. A broker is best advised to assume that, if in doubt, an order is solicited and she would be wise to make an effort to establish the suitability of the order or strategy for the client. This does not mean that a profit will ensue, but merely that the customer is aware of the nature of the transaction or strategy that is recommended.

Sophistication and Suitability

Brokers who are accused of recommending trades or strategies which are not suitable for a client frequently attempt to defend themselves by taking the position that the client is sophisticated. Conversely, clients who lose money often maintain that they were unsophisticated, hence, the suggestions were unsuitable. Sophistication and suitability are related but not synonymous terms. One may be sophisticated and not suitable or suitable and not sophisticated.

Sophistication consists primarily of a broad understanding gained from experience, reading, training, or education. A person who works for a brokerage firm, or is an attorney or accountant, or has a degree from a business school, or has dealt extensively in speculative ventures such as real estate, might well be considered sophisticated. Business executives who regularly deal with taking risks to achieve economic reward certainly are in a position to understand the basic nature of the relation between risks and rewards in financial ventures. Nevertheless, they may be logically considered to be unsophisticated in many circumstances. The successful owner of a hardware supply company who has invested in the real estate market for many years might find it quite difficult to judge accurately the degree of risk in an oil drilling partnership or an uncovered call position in Swiss francs.

Persons who are quite sophisticated but also quite busy, such as physicians, attorneys, or accountants, might well be quite vulnerable because they might place their trust and confidence in a broker to act for them. They might well conclude that the broker is a professional who will act for them with the utmost of good faith and fair dealing, because that is how they themselves are supposed to work with their own clientele. Such people may well pay only scant attention to confirmations and statements, despite admonitions to check them carefully. Their accounts are then subject to abuse by brokers who are aware of the reliance being placed upon them by the customer.

Conversely, a person who is completely unsophisticated in terms of directly comparable or transferable experience may be quite suitable for even the most speculative transactions. Such a person may have only a small amount of experience but may make a conscious decision to risk losing money in the hope of making a substantial profit quickly. If they have not been mislead about the risks and returns relative to their trading, they might well be considered suitable. Clearly, even the most sophisticated traders may well have been unsophisticated when they began trading. If suitability required a client to be sophisticated before trading could begin, most clients could not begin trading in the first place. It is equally clear that under some circumstances, some types of trading may be completely unsuitable for some clients who are highly sophisticated.

DIFFERENCES BY VENUE

In a general sense, suitability in the financial world always implies both financial capability and consistency of salespersons' recommendations with the objectives, wants, and needs of the client. The sources and nature of suitability requirements vary somewhat with the area in which the client chooses to invest. Rules and regulations change with time and are subject to possibly contradictory interpretations by different courts, arbitration panels, regulators, and attorneys. Although some will undoubtedly disagree, it would appear best to conclude that those salespersons who discuss investments with others in any financial area or specific vehicle would be wise to assume that the word *solicit* should be interpreted quite broadly, and that there are suitability requirements and to act accordingly.

Trade Custom and Practice

Although much can be said and written about laws, rules and regulations, it seems safe to assume that suitability, especially where solicitation is concerned, is firmly established by trade custom and practice. A person who solicits business in investments is generally considered to be acting as a fiduciary. The client places trust and confidence in the salesperson and is entitled to the utmost in good faith and fair dealing. Representations about the suggested investments which are incomplete, inaccurate, or which conceal essential information may well be considered fraudulent. Under the common law, a fiduciary may be held liable for constructive fraud even without intent to deceive. Failure to advise clients of unsuitability may thus be actionable under common law principles if the salesperson is aware of the unsuitability. Because brokers customarily inquire into the financial capability and objectives of their clients and set credit limits based upon this information, it would be rather difficult for them successfully to profess ignorance of a client's suitability.[2]

Securities

Suitability in the solicitation of securities business is based not only on long-standing trade custom and practice, but also in rules and regulations

---

[2] Readers interested in reading more about trade custom and practice, and in text and legal references pertaining to this subject will find valuable an article by M. Van Smith in the Denver University Law Review, *The Commodities Futures Trading Commission and Suitability; Now You See It, Now You Don't*, 60 Den. U.L. Rev. 613 (1983).

of state and federal regulatory agencies, such as the Securities and Exchange Commission (SEC), and its industry counterpart, the National Association of Securities Dealers (NASD), and by the rules of virtually every securities exchange and brokerage firm. Although such rules may not themselves provide the basis for a right of private action, they would certainly provide the basis for a clear indication of trade custom and practice. Some courts have enforced these rules as evidence of standards which, when breached, constitute common law negligence. Furthermore, if customers' agreements indicate that rules will be enforced, failure to do so might provide the basis for asserting a breach of contract.

Many rules universally considered to apply to suitability may not specifically mention the word "suitability" but nevertheless so plainly refer to this concept that they are widely called *suitability rules*. One of the most widely utilized and quoted rule is that of the NASD presented in its *Rules of Fair Practice*, Article III, Section 2, as the basic ethical policy of that organization's board of governors. It reads:

> In recommending to a customer the purchase, sale or exchange of any security, a member shall have reasonable grounds for believing that the recommendation is suitable for such customer upon the basis of the facts, if any, disclosed by such customer as to his other security holdings and as to his financial situation and needs.

The suitability concept was strengthened when the SEC established a suitability rule of its own in 1967. This rule established a *know your customer* standard which provided a basis for relief against broker-dealers who made trades not reasonably suited to customers' financial objectives. The rule read:

> Every nonmember broker or dealer and every associated person who recommends to a customer the purchase, sale or exchange of any security shall have reasonable grounds to believe that the recommendation is not unsuitable for such customer on the basis of information furnished by such customer after reasonable inquiry concerning the customer's investment objectives, financial situation and needs, and any other information known by such broker or dealer or associated person.[3]

This rule was repealed in 1983 in light of legislative amendments eliminating the so-called "SECO program." The rule, however, is of considerable historical importance because it was the basis of a proposed similar

---

[3] 17 C.F.R. § 240.15b10-3 (1967).

rule by the Commodity Futures Trading Commission (CFTC) which will be discussed later.

Many stock exchanges have rules either specifying or strongly implying suitability requirements. The one most often cited is Rule 405 of the New York Stock Exchange:

> Every member organization is required through a general partner, a principal executive officer or a person or persons designated under the provisions of Rule 342(b) (1) [P2342] to
>> (1) Use due diligence to learn the essential facts relative to every customer, every order, every cash and margin account accepted or carried by such organization and every person holding power of attorney over any account accepted or carried by such organization. . . .

Rule 411 of the American Stock Exchange and similar rules of regional exchanges impose upon their members a duty to know and approve their customers by using due diligence to learn essential facts about the customers before accepting either their accounts or orders for them. It is interesting to note that such rules generally deal with all customers, all orders, and all accounts of the brokerage house and do not merely refer to securities customers, accounts, or orders.

Although many exchange and NASD rules apply also to stock option traders, it should be noted that the Chicago Board Options Exchange (CBOE) has clear and strong rules concerning suitability. Rule 9.9 reads as follows:

> Every member, Registered Options Principal or Registered Representative who recommends to a customer the purchase or sale (writing) of any option contract shall have reasonable grounds for believing that the recommendation is not unsuitable for such customer on the basis of the information furnished by such customer after reasonable inquiry as to his investment objectives, financial situation and needs, and any other information known by such member, Registered Options Principal or Registered Representative.
>
> No member, Registered Options Principal or Registered Representative shall recommend to a customer an opening transaction in any option contract unless the person making the recommendation has a reasonable basis for believing at the time of making the recommendation that the customer has such knowledge and experience in financial matters that he may reasonably be expected to be capable of evaluating the risks of the recommended transaction, and is financially able to bear the risks of the recommended position in the option contract.

Virtually all brokerage firms specify suitability rules in some internal documents. These may be in one or more manuals which may be labeled as operations, compliance, managers, or registered representative manuals. There are often internal interpretive memos or letters further dealing with suitability rules and procedures. Firms which have internal training programs almost invariably cover suitability at length. Firms that deal in stock options are obligated to have written rules of operation, many of which deal with suitability requirements, designed by a senior registered options principal (SROP).

There are an increasing number of disputes involving alleged options fraud and there are probably destined to be many more. Poorly trained or disreputable salespersons are often inclined to understate the risks of some option positions, such as uncovered short positions (particularly out-of-the-money option positions close to expiration dates), or such dangerous positions as uncovered short combinations (strangles). Brokerage firms are well-advised to supervise closely the establishment of options accounts and the types of positions established in them.

Futures

Determining the suitability requirements for the opening of futures accounts and for the solicitation of trades in them is especially difficult. One can hardly seriously maintain that the fiduciary duty of a full-line brokerage house ends at the entrance to their futures department and that all customers who pass through that entrance do so at their peril. Some brokerage personnel do profess that the lack of a specific CFTC regulation dealing with suitability means that there is therefore no suitability requirement for their customers in futures, but such a position to some has overtones of sophistry.

Brokerage houses that deal in futures are dealing largely with a group of customers who are destined to lose money, just as most such customers have always lost and always will. (One cynic maintains that a speculator who dies rich has died before his time.) The attraction, of course, is that the survivors have the opportunity to use highly leveraged capital to make large amounts of profit on a small capital base within a short time. The broker, in turn, has the opportunity to generate a substantial percentage of commission income from most of the traders, ultimate winners and losers alike, who usually have a tendency to trade often because of the inherent nature of the product in which they are dealing and the short-term strategies most often utilized. When these tendencies are combined with the representations of salespersons, many of whom recommend simplistic, invalid, or downright self-serving strategies designed primarily to create commission income, the mixture becomes explosive. Among the many clients who lose, some believe and more maintain that they were materially mislead concerning their chance of profiting. The salesperson usually maintains that any suggestions were reasonable, the relationship between possible rewards and risks were properly clarified, and that the complaining customer is just another sour-graper. The firm's compliance department most frequently concludes that the account and order forms were properly completed and accepts the salesperson's version of events at face value. Because some customers really are sour-grapers and sales personnel may in good faith give advice eventually leading to losses, it is not too surprising that complaints and formal action frequently occur.

Among the most usual assertions of the customer is lack of suitability and its frequent companion, churning, which is treated in Chapter 10. The firm then just as frequently asserts that there is no suitability requirement in the futures area because the CFTC chose not to pass any rule requiring suitability, or that the customer really was and is suitable, and the battle is joined.

Varying courts, hearing officers, and arbitration panels have taken different positions concerning this argument and some disagree with one another rather vehemently. The reader must understand, therefore, that any position taken here would be attacked by some, whether in good faith or for self-serving reasons.

There is certainly no question that suitability is an old and common requirement in the brokerage business. There is also no question that the CFTC made an attempt to adopt a rule in 1977 modeled upon the "know your customer" rule of the SEC then in effect. The proposed rule, 166.2, would have had the usual elements. It would have provided that commodity professionals must know their customers and that all trades recommended for customers or effectuated in discretionary accounts be suitable for the customers, in consideration of the risk of loss involved in the trade relative to the financial condition and trading objectives of the customers.

The proposed rule actually would have gone beyond the comparable SEC rule then in effect, because the latter evidently permitted securities professionals to issue recommendations to customers who declined to furnish suitability information if the professional made a good faith effort to know his customer. The proposed CFTC rule provided for no such latitude.

After hearings were held in five cities over a period of months and after absorbing both written and oral input from a large number of people who commented on the subject, the CFTC chose not to establish a suitability rule nor to establish a specific rule concerning the related area of churning. Its opinion was that the proposed new rules would only codify provisions already implicit in the antifraud provisions of the CEA act and the CFTC's rules, and that any codification might have the adverse effect of narrowing interpretations of existing antifraud provisions of the CEA Act. It was indicated that a suitability requirement might be enacted later if meaningful standards could be developed.

Strangely enough, despite the widespread and sometimes gleeful assertion by brokerage firm counsels that there are no suitability requirements because the proposed specific rule was rejected, there are none who assert that churning became permissible, although a rule (Rule 166.3) against that practice proposed at the same time was also rejected.

Customers who might have utilized a suitability rule to sustain a complaint can still maintain, of course, that they were mislead as to the degree of the risks in futures trading and that the misrepresentation was fraudulent in light of the widely held view that a broker is a fiduciary. In addition, the NFA has passed rules which bear on suitability.

Despite the ambiguity concerning suitability requirements, a position that accounts can be opened and trades recommended with no consideration of a customer's suitability is difficult to defend. Although the degree may vary with the circumstances, few would argue that a broker is not a fiduciary. The shingle theory has had few serious detractors. Many stock exchange rules and internal pronouncements of brokerage firms bearing on suitability deal with customers, not products. Above all, one should be able to rely upon common sense. The idea that a full-line brokerage firm must consider suitability in soliciting business in stocks, bonds, options, investment company shares, and limited partnerships, but not in futures which are the most highly leveraged, hence, riskiest product, approaches absurdity. One might visualize a door to a firm's futures department with the equivalent of a Dante warning sign over it admonishing "All hope, abandon, ye who enter here!" Unless the CFTC's industry partner, the NFA, is deemed to have filled the gap with its position on suitability, or unless Congress clarifies its legislative intent, the argument concerning this point seems destined to rage on, especially among those with something to gain or something to lose.

Limited Partnerships

Suitability requirements for limited partnerships are supposed to be taken especially seriously by those who solicit business in these vehicles.

Sometimes, however, the amount of effort that is assumed to have been devoted to determining suitability is overestimated merely because regulations mandate a suitability requirement and there are sometimes rather elaborate forms involving suitability which must be completed. Some salespersons make a diligent effort in this regard, whereas all too many treat it in a cavalier manner. The amount of money involved in many of these investments tends to be large, the risks are substantial, and there is a large amount of regulation with which to comply. Disputes concerning limited partnerships usually revolve around representations rather than suitability. All too often tax shelters have delivered losses equalling or exceeding those promised, but the income that was supposed to follow did not appear on time and sometimes did not appear at all. Sometimes, too, the attitude of the IRS toward favorable tax treatment differs from that anticipated in salespersons' representations or opinion letters. There are instances, however, when suitability is an issue, so it deserves at least brief treatment here.

Most financial institutions which include limited partnerships among their products require the opening of a standard customer's account with the attendant suitability requirements for the accounts themselves. In addition, however, partnerships sold to small numbers of investors may well have special requirements. Some of these are dictated by most individual states under their blue sky requirements.

The SEC regulates limited partnership private placement under many of its general provisions, but Rule 146 is of special interest. Although the rule was in in force only from 1974 to 1982, its provisions exemplified the thinking of the SEC, many individual states, and provides a good guide to trade custom and practice.

Consistent with most suitability requirements, the rule specified that the investor have enough understanding of financial and business affairs to evaluate the merits and risks of the investment. As is the case with most primary issues, furthermore, the buyer was to be provided with an offering circular. Somewhat less usual was the provision that investors who were not sufficiently sophisticated could employ an *offeree representative*. If either the representative or the representative and customer jointly exhibited sufficient sophistication, the customer could be deemed suitable. Offeree representatives were not to be employed by the issuer nor have any undisclosed connection with the issuer.

Many firms that solicit privately placed securities have devised suitability questionnaires which are approved by designated management or compliance personnel of the selling firm as well as by the issuer. These forms were designed to determine if certain specific requirements were met, such as designated levels of annual income, liquid net worth, and total net worth. Detailed questions to determine sophistication are often asked, such as age, education, marital status, retirement plans, and experience in financial areas, particularly involving previous investments in tax shelters. Other information might be required for such potential buyers as corporations, who may have special restrictions or who might be required to provide additional data. Some firms attempt to reduce suitability problems by requiring or forbidding certain sales practices. For example, they may forbid cold calling, require that mailed solicitations consist entirely or basically of the offering circulars themselves, and that sales meetings be held only with qualified potential buyers and not be open to the general public.

Changes in the tax laws and a consistently unfriendly attitude by the IRS have done much to eliminate the incentive to form limited partnerships for the primary purpose of sheltering income by providing deductions. There may well be enough investors interested in generating passive income to overcome previously incurred ordinary losses to encourage the establishment of a new breed of limited partnerships for this purpose.

Limited partnerships, for whatever purpose, are usually partnerships in which interests are sold directly or indirectly to limited partners by the general partner. The general partner knows more about the partnership than those solicited to become limited partners, and also has an incentive to get the highest price possible for the interests being sold. Sales representatives typically receive a sales credit consisting of a significant percentage of a comparatively high-priced item, so the incentive for both the general partner and for the sales representatives to sell the partnership units is high. If the incentive translates into overstating the financial and tax benefits and understating the attendant risks, the exposure of both the buyer and seller can be high. If a buyer is unsuitable for the investment, particularly if it is not publicly registered, and the seller knows of the unsuitability, such exposure increases exponentially.

CONCLUSION

There is considerable disagreement concerning suitability requirements in the finance business not only among the personnel directly engaged in the business, but also among various courts, attorneys, regulatory bodies, and arbitration panels. On balance, however, it appears wise for financial institutions to assume that there are minimum suitability requirements to be met by any individual or institution which may open an account. Special caution should be used where customers obviously have restricted capacity to act, such as corporations, minors, individuals with impaired physical, mental, or financial capacity, pension plans, or profit sharing plans.

If financial instruments are to be solicited for such accounts after they are opened, establishing suitability becomes even more important. Not only must the customer be suitable to open the account, but the transaction solicited must in itself be suitable for the customer. Failure to establish suitability may well be taken to be a violation of a fiduciary duty of the salesperson. If the customer loses money, the legal exposure of the salespersons may be quite high and may considerably exceed the amount of the customer's loss. There may even be an exposure in the cases of customers who make money, but allege that they would have made more in a more suitable investment. Cautious salespeople frequently place the burden of suitability primarily upon their firms by recommending only investments suggested by the firm's research department or by some outside source approved by the firm. Of course such salespeople should beware of improper adaptations of suggestions, such as applying a suggestion to buy a stock to an option or a futures position which may have quite different return and risk implications.

Suggesting that a cash account be converted to a margin account, or that money be borrowed from outside sources to increase leverage may prove hazardous to the salesperson as well as to the customer. It should also be remembered that suitability applies to the strategy utilized and not just to the instrument chosen. It is one thing, for example, to apply a negative opinion to a suggestion to liquidate a stock position and another to utilize the same opinion to justify a suggestion to sell short a stock or a call option.

If information concerning suitability is gathered primarily from the salespersons who will directly benefit from revenue received, supervisors of the firm are well advised not to be casual about routinely approving new accounts and monitoring changes in the customers' circumstances and the business done in such accounts. A fiduciary who controls an account might well be concerned with recommending changes in accounts to reflect material changes in economic circumstances, such as retirement, or the death of one of the holders of a joint account. Determination of suitability is an ongoing responsibility.

Merely completing forms does not fulfill salespersons' responsibilities to their clients. To avoid problems they should communicate in plain language any concerns they may have about the suitability of an account or transactions therein. Making a timely written record of warnings to clients can be of considerable value. In extreme cases, a salesperson might even require a client to prepare or sign a letter indicating that a position taken is in opposition to a salesperson's recommendation. Unless it is determined that the client lacked the capacity to act responsibly and the salesperson knew it or took advantage of it, such documentation should serve to protect salespersons and their firms.

7

Handling Accounts

The root of many serious problems, as already demonstrated, lies in the origination of the account itself. If proper care in establishing suitability standards is exercised, and proper documentation obtained at the outset, there would be fewer lawsuits and arbitration proceedings. Problems can also arise from a misunderstanding of the customer-broker relationship once the account has been opened. Charges of unauthorized discretion, excessive markups, and improperly entered orders are frequently made, often by inexperienced investors. Sometimes the charges reflect customer ignorance of the mechanics of order entry and execution. At other times, the charges may be caused by a mistake or, worse, by a violation of industry rules by the representative.

ORDER ENTRY

No customer of a brokerage firm loses money until an order is executed. Given this basic premise, customers should have at least a basic understanding of the difference between solicited and unsolicited orders, to say nothing of an understanding of the most common types of orders, such as market and limit orders. In fact, customers frequently know little of the process of order entry and execution. Even elementary comprehension of these functions would save many complaints.

Brokerage order tickets have a box or space where a registered representative must indicate whether an order was solicited or unsolicited. Some representatives routinely check "unsolicited" on all orders in the mistaken belief that this somehow protects them in case of a problem with the trade. Soliciting orders is what representatives are paid to do. It is the reason why most calls are made to customers. There may be some representatives so well established that they rarely do more than answer the phone and take orders, but their number is small.

In normal industry practice an order is solicited when it results directly from a representative's suggestion, even though it may not be on the initial call. For example, the representative phones the customer and recommends the purchase of 300 shares of Eastman Kodak, a security not the subject of any recent discussion between the two. The customer wants time to consider the investment and agrees to call back shortly. If the customer calls back within a reasonable time and places an order to buy Eastman Kodak, the order is solicited regardless of how the representative marks the order ticket. On the other hand, the passage of time may change the designation. A salesman needn't love Eastman Kodak forever at any price, and if significant time lapses or a substantial price change occurs, a later order to buy the shares may be unsolicited.

Some brokerage firms have internal policies prohibiting the solicitation of penny stocks and similar speculations. The usual policy is to accept only unsolicited orders from existing customers who are substantial and experienced enough to manage the considerable risks involved. In some cases the representative may tell other customers that a particular issue looks like a great speculation but also that his firm's policies prohibit recommendations to that customer. The representative may mark the order "unsolicited" although both customer and representative know the order to be truly solicited. Customers should not be party to a knowing breach of firm policies. The rules were established to prevent or limit losses which occur in disproportionate numbers with unseasoned speculative issues, especially low-priced ones. There are always a number of equally good choices that can be made without violating a broker's compliance policies.

When the idea for a transaction originates with the customer the order is unsolicited. Some customers develop all their own investment ideas and use the broker only for execution services. Most of these customers have since migrated to discount brokerage firms where trading costs are less. Others may make the decision to sell when the purchase had been recommended initially by the representative. For instance, a customer might have purchased shares at $50 on a recommendation that they might shortly rise to $60. When, however, the market reaches $55 the customer decides to take the profit. If the decision to liquidate starts with the customer, and the representative acquiesces in the decision, the order is probably unsolicited. If the representative actively concurs in the decision rather than simply following the customer's wish, the order should be marked solicited. The rule of thumb is that if orders fall in a grey area between solicited and unsolicited, they should be marked solicited.

Orders entered by a representative without prior discussion and confirmation with the customer are termed *discretionary*. The customer must authorize this type of trading in writing by submitting a signed power of attorney to the brokerage firm. Although the rule is well known, complaints alleging discretionary improprieties are among the most common received by the SEC and the self-regulatory bodies.

A typical situation involves the receipt of a trade confirmation by the customer when no order was placed. It is imperative that the customer question this at once, both by phone and in writing. Occasionally, a coding error may have routed another customer's trade to the investor. This problem should be easily fixed, and the customer should demand some form of written evidence that the correction has been made. Representatives who cannot seem to fix simple errors and make disparaging remarks about the incompetence of their firm's operations personnel are generally not to be believed. Frequently they are not taking the time to resolve the problem or else they are trying to camouflage a case of unauthorized discretion.

Sometimes the unauthorized trade may actually be profitable when the customer learns of it. The customer may then be tempted to allow the position to remain open without complaint. This is inevitably the wrong course of action. First, the position may quickly turn unprofitable; second (and more importantly), it may encourage the representative to try again. Sooner or later a sizable loss will result, and the customer's failure to complain previously will weaken her case before an arbitration panel or a jury.

Securities industry rules allow the representative to assume time and price discretion on the customer's verbal instruction (some futures exchanges do not permit this practice). The customer may consent to a request from the representative such as: "I'll watch your XYZ for you, and if it weakens any more, I'll sell it." Although permissible, this is a dangerous practice. There is little need to rely on a representative's judgment in such circumstances. If the customer wants to take action at a specific price level, either a limit or stop order can be entered immediately. This transfers the execution responsibility to an exchange specialist or trader by giving that person precise instructions. Indeed, some brokerage firms have had so many problems with the vague nature of time and price discretion that they prohibit its use as a matter of internal policy. The best overall rule from the customer's standpoint is always to enter orders with specific time and price directions. When this is done there is no second-guessing of the representative's judgment, and no allegations of churning—a situation which should be welcomed by both parties.

A form of quasi discretion sometimes exists when the customer rarely (or never) questions a representative's recommendation either as to the security or the action suggested. Because of a long-standing relationship, the customer may readily accede to any suggestion that he liquidate a current holding and buy some new security with the proceeds. Although the representative asks for, and receives, permission for all trades, the request is sometimes perfunctory at best. In itself such a relationship is neither good nor bad, although courts have held that it often constitutes control and is virtually discretion. One can presume that customers are under no obligation to remain with a representative who regularly loses money for them, or exposes them to uncomfortable risks. The real problem is that this type of relationship may be taken one step farther, so that instead of asking permission for each suggested trade, the representative starts reporting executions. When the call changes from: "I'd like to buy 500 ABC for you" to "I just bought you 500 ABC," the point of no return has been reached. The customer should at this point either close the account or authorize future trades in writing, in either case making written disavowal or approval of the existing account status.

A major source of error in the execution of orders lies in the actual writing of the order ticket. A common error is writing *buy* instead of *sell*, or vice versa. For example, a busy representative might be entering several purchase orders simultaneously when a sell order is received. It is quite possible for the new order ticket to be filled out like the others. This type of error is often discovered only after execution when the order clerk returns the executed copy to the representative. Industry rules require the representative to report any error immediately to the branch manager. Even if an accidental profit were to result, the customer should not be involved in the error correction. For example, instead of buying soybeans at 6.00 the representative sells them at that price. By the time the error is discovered the price has dropped to 5.90. The representative should not close out the position on his own even though a quick-turn profit might be made. Rather, the office manager should take the necessary action in the office's error account.

Misunderstandings over order entry and execution, like all human errors, will continue, but the careful customer can help reduce them. The customer should insist that the order be read back as soon as it is

written on the ticket by the representative. If this is done habitually, it
will eliminate the inadvertent error, such as *sell* instead of *buy*, 500
shares instead of 100, *at 25* instead of *at the market*, and so on. Representatives should likewise cultivate this habit, which is standard practice at some firms. A number of brokers and some customers now record
their phone conversations. This may make it easier to assign blame for
an order execution claimed to be faulty, but fixing the blame does not
necessarily recover lost money. If the error is prevented in the first
place, both sides gain.

TYPES OF ORDERS

A familiarity with the most frequently used orders should help all investors understand the markets better. Sometimes the failure to receive
an execution results in a substantial loss or missed opportunity. If that
loss is caused by the representative's negligence, the liability is clear,
although proving such and gaining restitution may be difficult. Some
complaints about order execution, however, stem from the investor's
lack of knowledge about the order entry process and industry rules
governing order execution.

The most common type of order is the market order. This order does
not specify a price. It must be filled at the best obtainable price when
presented at the point of execution, either an exchange trading post or
pit, or an electronic terminal manned by a trader. Although the order is
virtually assured of execution, the price received may be considerably
different from the price prevailing when the order was accepted.

Consider the following conversation between customer and representative:

Customer: What's the market at now?
Representative: December gold—last sale at $450; low today $449.50.
Customer: Buy me five contracts at the market.

The potential problem is apparent. By the time the order ticket is written, time stamped, transmitted to the exchange floor, and presented in
the trading ring, December gold might still be at $450 but might as
easily be at $440 or $460. The customer's order might be filled at any
number of prices. If the order was executed at $460, the high for the
day, the customer has no grounds for complaint presuming the order
was properly handled. On the other hand, he may feel victimized be-

cause the market when the order was written and the actual execution price were so different.

Representatives like market orders because they are almost always executed, thus generating commissions. There is much to be said for the use of market orders by the typical customer for whom finely tuned timing makes little price difference in execution. Representatives should make certain that customers understand that the last sale is not the market for an order just being written. Nor, indeed, is the next sale. The time between entry and execution may range from a few minutes to several. Representatives can save considerable time and good will by explaining the nature of the order in the first place. Even experienced investors do not always know what may appear to the representative as elementary order facts.

Next to market orders, limit orders are the most popular types. These orders specify a maximum price a buyer is willing to pay and a minimum price a seller is willing to accept. Customers should be aware that a trade reported at the limit price does not guarantee an execution. A limit order for an exchange traded stock will usually be placed with the specialist who enters it in sequence behind previously entered orders at the same price. Until the earlier orders are filled the customer's order must wait in line, sometimes for a considerable period. A limit order entered on a futures exchange is held by a floor broker as part of his *deck*, order tickets he is charged with executing. Although the broker will attempt to fill the order at the proper price or a better one, there are circumstances where an execution may not be possible. The price reporting system may indicate that an execution should have been obtained, but in a "fast market" reported trades may lag significantly behind actual pit executions. Here the customer must be aware that limit orders sometimes go unexecuted. The order cannot be filled at a price worse than the specified limit, but it runs the risk of not being filled at all.

Stop and stop-limit orders may provide useful protection for existing positions, either in cutting losses or in locking up profits. They can also be used to create new positions upon the piercing of support or resistance levels. Stop and stop-limit orders suffer from the same failings as market and limit orders, respectively. The main problem with them, however, is the overly optimistic promise of their utility made by some representatives. These orders may be useful, but they are not guarantees against loss. Suggestions that their use assures limited loss or locked-in profits should be discounted at once, as should any magic formula trading system. The simple fact is that no trading strategy can replace wise trade selection in a successful program.

TIME STAMPING

Federal law requires the time stamping of all securities and futures orders. Securities orders must be stamped at the time of transmission, which ordinarily means when entered by the order clerk—not when written by the representative. If the customer feels entitled to an execution because she saw apparently applicable trades printed on the exchange tape after the receipt of her order, the time stamped order ticket could be useful evidence. If the transaction took place on a securities or options exchange each trade is recorded in time sequence and printed in a daily publication called the *Fitch Sheets* (after publisher Emory B. Fitch & Sons). The NYSE also publishes its own version of all trades in NYSE-listed stocks, even if executed on other exchanges, or over-the-counter in the third market.

Futures orders must also be time stamped upon receipt by a futures commission merchant (brokerage firm), and an introducing broker, if any is involved in the receipt of the order. It is harder to pinpoint the execution time of futures orders than listed stock orders because the pit reporting system and execution method do not lend themselves to exact timing well. Prices and total sales during certain time periods, however, may be determined through computerized systems. Thus, if a customer wanted to know if Treasury bond futures traded at 97-24 between 1:00 P.M. and 1:15 P.M., this could be ascertained. Although not guaranteed an execution, the customer would have a good case if he could produce a time stamped order ticket showing an order to buy at 97-25 had been entered well before a trade took place at 97-24.

COMMISSIONS AND FEES

Brokerage firms are not eleemosynary organizations. The revenue derived from customer transactions is the primary reason for their existence. Some firms, especially the large national ones, earn money from many sources other than commissions—margin interest, trading profits, money management fees, and investment banking to name some. Others deal only in over-the-counter securities and rarely charge commissions as such. Their profits come from markups and markdowns, all but invisibly buried in the share or bond price. These are discussed in detail in the next section. Discount brokers rely almost entirely on commissions because they offer little to customers besides order execution service. Likewise with futures trading firms, whose capacity is mandated by federal law requiring all domestic futures transactions to be executed on a registered exchange.

Registered representatives employed by these firms are sales personnel. It is well for the customer to keep this firmly in mind. Representatives may be friends, trusted advisors, or even confidantes, but they derive their income from selling merchandise. The average established representative makes about $100,000 annually. Brokerage firms pay out varying percentages of commission revenues to representatives but an overall payout is probably about 35 percent. To earn $100,000, therefore, a representative must produce about $285,000 in gross commissions and sales credits. That sum is rarely produced by doing nothing more than answering the telephone and taking unsolicited orders.

There is nothing sinister in all this. One must simply realize that success in the brokerage business is usually characterized in terms of gross production, i.e., total revenues generated for the firm, and not by successful investment results or numbers of satisfied customers. Given this understanding one must also realize that there are times when representatives' desire to maximize their incomes must collide with the customers' desire to maximize investment return.

At most brokerage firms representatives earn more for selling proprietary goods than they do for executing orders on stock, options, or futures exchanges. There is a tendency toward recommending packaged products such as unit trusts, in-house mutual funds, variable annuities, and partnership units. Because these are often one-time purchases, representatives need an incentive to lock up money that might otherwise be turned over several times in a trading account. Sales charges range from 4.5 percent to over 9 percent of the money actually invested. This information is readily available in a prospectus or offering circular. The prospective buyer should read such documents carefully to learn if there are other charges, as is often the case. These typically include management, custodial, and redemption fees. Products offered by brokers are rarely unique, at least for long. A good product is quickly copied by the competition. The wise investor shops around to find the lowest sales charges. The NASD requires all members to maintain the same offering price schedule for mutual fund purchases, but some funds are available with no sales charge at all—the *no load* funds. With other investments, similar or identical vehicles are usually available at considerably different charges.

MARKUPS

Over-the-counter (OTC) transactions also provide a larger sales credit (per invested dollar) for the representative than he may earn from exchange transactions. Trades are customarily executed on a net basis, which means that customers are shown only the net execution price on their confirmations. Virtually all municipal, government, and corporate bond trades are so executed, as well as most OTC stock transactions. The dealer's profit is included in the price as a markup, much like the profit a car dealer makes. Rule 10b-10 of the SEC requires the amount of markup to be disclosed on certain OTC stock trades, but not on those done directly from a dealer's inventory, by far the most common method of OTC execution.

Markups on corporate securities transactions are governed by the NASD's *five percent* policy. Briefly, the policy states that unless unusual factors are present, markups (markdowns on customer sales) should not exceed five percent. For example, if a dealer buys stock at $20 per share and immediately reoffers it for sale at $21, his markup—or spread—is five percent. This allows the dealer a reasonable profit of $100 per $2,000 investment, considering not only the costs of doing business, but also the market risk that may force him to sell the shares at a loss rather than at the originally expected price.

There is, unfortunately, no way for the typical investor to discern whether a dealer is adhering to the policy. As noted, most customer confirmations for OTC transactions do not disclose the amount of the markup. Instead, they indicate only that the firm acted as dealer or principal, and the net amount due, e.g., "As principal we sold to you 100 shares Apple Computer Inc. at $37 per share—net amount due $3,700." If a customer is trading NASDAQ National Market System (NMS) issues he can compare his execution price with the newspaper reports on the following day. Complete listings are found in the *Wall Street Journal, Investors Daily,* and some other papers. If a stock was traded on the NMS, each day's high, low, and closing prices are shown, although they do not necessarily include markups that a retail customer might be charged. Active issues often have several market makers, and competition from these dealers tends to keep spreads narrow for such issues.

If a customer finds his execution price to be out of line with the reported prices he should question the representative immediately. Purchase prices above the day's high and sales below the day's low are not unusual or necessarily unethical. A price more than one-quarter or one-half point away from these figures for a typical customer order should be questioned. If the order was executed on an agency or brokerage basis, the execution price plus or minus the commission should approximate the newspaper report. Broker/dealers are not allowed to charge both a markup and a commission on the same transaction.

There is less competition between dealers for inactive OTC issues. Consequently, excessive markups become more likely. The problem is most acute with low-priced shares, especially penny stocks. Some issues are so obscure quotations cannot even be found in the newspaper listings. The usual source of prices for these shares is a daily publication called the *Pink Sheets*, which can be found in most brokerage offices.

Investors should be cautious of companies whose shares can only be found in the *Pink Sheets*. There are probably some largely undiscovered gems in these listings—tomorrow's Xerox or McDonald's. On the other hand, there is a much larger number of issues with little or no investment merit. It is difficult even for professional analysts to tell which of these are candidates for future growth. Unsubstantiated tips on these kinds of companies are best ignored.

Market makers are listed next to each issue in the *Pink Sheets*. It is usually not a good practice to buy shares when only one dealer is listed. If that dealer stops quoting the shares they may be difficult to liquidate. Customers should not deal with firms which claim to be the exclusive source of quotations and information for an issue. If genuine investment merit is present, the profit motive will impel other dealers to participate. The claim to exclusivity often involves manipulative pricing, where the market is simply what the dealer says it is. Some disreputable firms have developed schemes where a customer's shares are sold at a higher price than the customer's purchase price to another customer of the firm at a different branch office. The process is repeated, passing the stock from one branch office to another at progressively higher prices. Because of the profits resulting from the earlier transactions, there are usually a number of satisfied customers ready to play the next round. Of course, this daisy chain must come to a halt sooner or later, when the supply of greater fools is exhausted. The most recent purchaser buys at the end of the chain and acquires shares that can only be sold at much lower prices. In turn, earlier buyers of other issues will become victims. The practice is surely not investment. Rather, it has much in common with pyramid clubs or Ponzi schemes. The most interesting aspect of such schemes is their periodic reappearance and the apparently never-ending supply of new victims.

Municipal Bond Markups

Almost all customer trades in municipal bonds are executed on a net basis by dealers, which may be either securities firms or banks. The market is large but generally illiquid because of the large number of different issues available. Unlike NASDAQ or exchange listed stocks, municipal bonds are not actively traded once they are no longer recent issues. Many are immobilized in unit trusts, private portfolios, or trust accounts, leaving a reduced supply available for trading.

Offerings are made in the *Blue List*, an extensive daily publication featuring current inventory selections of various dealers. In addition, dealers may offer bonds via newspaper ads or from internal listings not available to the public. The retail customer may have considerable difficulty in evaluating the fairness of asking prices because of the way municipal prices are customarily quoted. Tax-backed general obligation bonds are usually quoted on a yield to maturity basis, whereas revenue issues are likely to be offered on a percentage of par value basis, like corporate bonds.

For example, a bond with a seven percent annual interest rate might be offered to yield 7.50 percent until maturity in 2010. The dollar price is then computed from the yield rather than vice versa. An offering at this yield would indicate to an experienced investor or trader a slight discount to par value, i.e., a price of something less than $1,000 per bond. An inexperienced investor, on the other hand, has little basis of comparison if the yield is quoted to her at 7.50 percent and the dollar price is said to be $1,100. With few readily available information sources, the customer is largely at the mercy of any dealer who chooses to be unethical.

Municipal bonds are exempt securities. This does not concern their tax status, but rather their exemption from most federal regulation governing the offering of securities to the public. This situation allows for a somewhat loose regulatory oversight of the industry. The Municipal Securities Rulemaking Board (MSRB) has indeed made a commendable effort to set ethical conduct rules and to see that they are enforced. The problem is that the enforcement procedure is difficult because of the number of dealers in the market. The municipal bond business to a certain degree resembles a cottage industry with hundreds of small dealers and banks offering bonds, in addition to the major dealers.

Although not profound, the best advice may be for the customer to deal only with an established securities firm or bank. Larger dealers have more customers, which in turn implies a greater level of sophistication, at least among some of those customers. This makes it more difficult for excessive markups to creep into the pricing structure. This provides no guarantee against excessive markups, but it probably minimizes the chance of the really outrageous 15–20 percent markups common in parts of the industry.

A FINAL WORD ON CHARGES

The services rendered to any investor by a broker are never free. Firms which advertise heavily the value of their advice and integrity on television or in the press attempt to recover some of their advertising costs through higher sales fees. The services provided by any one broker/ dealer are rarely so unusual that they cannot be duplicated elsewhere, possibly at lower cost. The message is not necessarily that one should deal only with the cheapest broker in town, but rather that one should shop around for services needed as well as for the best commission rates. The fact that a large firm offers dozens of different products and services is not relevant to the investor who requires only one or two. These services have a cost which is shared indirectly by all customers of the broker, whether they use them or not.

Of course, a large firm may offer certain services which the investor needs but are not available from smaller local brokers. If the choice comes down to selecting from among nationally known firms, a customer is likely to find that not only do their products look similar, but also that their fee schedules are quite alike. The persistent customer may be able to negotiate a commission rate (or a margin interest rate) below the broker's published schedules. Some firms allow the office manager latitude in making such adjustments for the customer who can demonstrate the ability to do substantial or otherwise desirable commission business. There is little, if any, negotiability in the charges for most packaged products.

Those whose activities are limited to occasional transactions should consider a discount brokerage firm. The services provided by these brokers are minimal but sufficient for the typical informed investor. There are also differences in discount commission rates. The customer should shop around farther if and when the decision is made to deal with a discount firm.

CHECKS

Paying for securities by check is the same as paying for merchandise by check, except, of course, that a broker may sell the securities if the check doesn't clear, whereas the merchant is left with legal remedies of repossession or other legal action. Common sense can prevent most problems. Customers should be aware that familiar dodges, like "forgetting" to sign a check, are treated as a failure to pay. The receipt of an unsigned or postdated check on the settlement date is not materially different to the broker from having received nothing. The same may be said for an apparently acceptable check that bounces.

Third party checks are usually not acceptable means of payment. Such checks are made payable to the customer, who in turn endorses them to the broker. Although such a check may be valid, the risk in collecting from a third party not also a customer is too great to be accepted. Under some circumstances, a U.S. government check made payable to the customer and properly endorsed might be acceptable, but most brokers discourage even such payments.

Checks issued by the broker may also be the source of problems. Brokers sometimes pay checks to customers from out-of-town, or even out-of-state locations. Banks ordinarily take more time to clear these checks than those of local origin. Naturally, this gives the broker the use of the customer's funds until the check clears. The customer may find that the funds are not available for several days after the check has been deposited in his own bank. Some major firms once made a practice of paying East Coast customers with checks drawn from West Coast banks, and vice versa. Customer complaints forced the abandonment of this particular practice, but the customer should continue to be vigilant about less blatant examples, such as checks drawn on banks in neighboring cities or states.

Occasionally customers ask brokers to issue checks that are in fact illegal. For example, a customer who maintains a joint account with his spouse may ask for a check made payable to his name only. Similarly, a request may be made to transfer securities from a joint account to an individual account, usually to meet a margin call. Any transfer from joint to single ownership, or any check from joint to single name, must be accompanied by the written permission of all parties involved. Were the broker to accede to these requests without written permission, it could be held liable for those funds.

ACCOUNT TRANSFERS

There are several reasons why a customer might wish to transfer an account to another brokerage firm. The customer might have reached a point of total incompatibility with the representative, or may have reached the end of her patience with operational difficulties. Another representative at a different firm may have made a persuasive presentation, or some friend or relative of the customer may have entered the brokerage business with a competitor.

If the investor's account is not actively traded, a transfer can be accomplished by signing a transfer of account form that any broker can provide. New York Stock Exchange rules require account transfer within five business days of the receipt of the transfer request. The customer, however, should normally not transfer an account if it is actively traded or has open positions, such as short sales, options, or futures, which may require speedy action. The potential for error or mismatched trades increases substantially if the customer enters an order while the account is in the transfer process. A better practice is to allow the account to wind down by closing existing positions when appropriate. An account can be opened with the new broker and gradually built up as positions are reduced with the former broker.

If a margin account is to be transferred, the customer should establish the interest rate before the transfer is initiated. This frequently ignored detail may lead to unpleasant surprises when the first monthly statement is received. Experience also indicates that correcting interest charges on previous statements is not easily done, either because the representative puts little time into following up operational difficulties or because the firm has little incentive to do so.

It is doubtful whether it is ever wise to transfer an account with open futures positions. The need for quick action is so probable that risking an error and the attendant complications of its resolution are too great to offset whatever benefits the transfer might provide. In addition, many brokers charge commissions on departing account positions on the grounds that the positions are being technically offset and reestablished with the new broker. When possible, the preferred course of action is similar to that described above for accounts with open short positions—close the open positions gradually and funnel the equity into a new account elsewhere.

CLOSING ACCOUNTS

When it becomes necessary to close an account, the customer has two options—one is simply to liquidate existing positions and have a check paid for the resulting balance; the other is to request delivery of the securities and payment of any remaining credit balance.

The first is rarely a wise course of action, but an impulsive customer may demand it as the ultimate show of displeasure with the representative or the brokerage firm. There are several problems with this action. First, unless the position consists of only a few issues, it is unlikely that the proper time to sell one is the proper time to sell them all. A precipitate liquidation may satisfy the customer's emotional needs, but probably isn't good investment strategy. Second, the liquidation of positions may raise immediate tax considerations for which the investor may not be prepared. Finally, commissions will be charged on the transactions. If the customer is determined to sell the securities anyway, the best course of action is to request delivery of the securities and sell them through a discount broker.

8

Margins

The use of the term *margin* in the securities business refers to the extension of credit by the broker to the investor, using the investor's securities as collateral. The usual, but not the only intent of this lending is to leverage investors' positions, allowing them to buy more securities with a given deposit than would be possible on a cash-only basis. Margin in the futures business, on the other hand, means something entirely different, although it too refers to deposits required of the customer. Because of this difference, this chapter is divided into two parts—the first part covering securities margin and the second dealing with futures.

SECURITIES MARGIN

Credit extension for the purpose of buying securities has a long and not particularly reputable history. The Great Crash of 1929 and its counterpart of 1987 were both exacerbated, if not precipitated, by overextended traders relying too heavily on future price appreciation to bail them out of risky positions. There are considerable differences between margin's contribution to the two debacles. Throughout the 1920s there was no federal control of credit extension for the purchase of securities. Brokers and banks could lend whatever they felt prudent. It was not uncommon to lend traders up to 90 percent of the value of their purchases, and indeed sometimes even more. Bucket shops actually reduced investing to an out-right bet on the market's direction. A good customer might initiate a position with no money down. When the position was closed out, accounts were settled. The trader received his net profit if successful, and paid up his net loss if he were not. It was not unusual in those days for shares to trade at high dollar prices. There were numerous stocks selling in the range of $300 to $400 per share, quite uncommon in the current American market. The reason for such prices was simple—few, if any, were actually putting up deposits of anything remotely like $300 per share. More likely, they were depositing something like $40 or $50 per share, an amount that would be wiped out in the event of a small decline in the stock price. Although a 10 percent decline in the stock price from $400 to $360 per share is not necessarily a catastrophe to a patient long-term investor who paid cash, the $40 per share loss completely wipes out the equity of one who had deposited just that amount. In order to protect themselves when this happened, brokers sold the undermargined shares, further depressing stock prices and in turn generating additional demands for increased margin as others became unsecured. The resulting snowball effect certainly added to the continuing decline.

In the Securities Exchange Act of 1934, Congress delegated the regulation of credit extension for the purpose of securities purchases to the Federal Reserve. Since that time the Federal Reserve has governed this activity through a variety of rules and regulations. The one most applicable to the typical brokerage firm customer is Regulation T, which limits the amount that may be loaned on securities collateral by a broker/dealer. A similar restriction, Regulation U, deals with loans obtained from banks in order to purchase securities.

Regulation T sets the maximum loan value that may be derived from using stocks as collateral. Thus, because Regulation T stipulates that equity securities have a 50 percent loan value, the investor may borrow only half the amount necessary to make a margin purchase and must deposit the remainder in either cash or fully-paid stock whose loan value is at least 50 percent of the purchase price. (Regulation T does not apply to nonconvertible debt securities, so deposits of these bonds receive more generous terms than stock deposits.) The regulation also covers short sales and requires the short seller to deposit the same amount of collateral as an equal value purchase would necessitate. Indeed, short sales of low priced stocks carry even higher margin requirements than those of higher priced shares because a small adverse price move incurs a large percentage loss, e.g., a $1 price rise is a 50 percent loss on stock sold short at $2 per share.

The Federal Reserve governors do not change the loan value

requirements often. The 50 percent level has been in effect since 1974. In the 1960s it had been as high as 80 percent, an indication of the Federal Reserve's displeasure with the speculation perceived rampant in the market at that time. In general the loan value is increased, i.e., the minimum deposit is lowered when the Federal Reserve desires to encourage equity investment, and raised to cool excessive speculation. The former usually happens after prolonged bear markets, and the latter often occurs near bull market peaks.

When a customer buys or sells short securities in a margin account he must pay promptly. Prompt payment is defined as *seven business days* following the transaction. The brokerage industry, on the other hand, requires payment within *five business days* because this is the standard settlement between brokers for most "regular way" trades. Thus, customer confirmations for typical trades involving corporate securities or municipal bonds prescribe a five business day settlement, even though the customer is allowed seven under Regulation T.

Customers who intend to pay for all purchases in full or sell only fully-paid securities may use a cash account. No financing is permitted in this type of account, and transactions whose potential loss are not limited to the cost of the securities, e.g., short sales and naked call writing, are prohibited. If the customer does not make full payment within the requisite period, the broker must cancel or liquidate the transaction. Unpaid securities are sold or undelivered securities are purchased at the current market price. If this procedure does not realize enough to cover the full amount of the original transaction, the customer is liable for the difference. The broker is entitled to use any of the customer's other assets in its possession to satisfy the claim. Assets in joint accounts or others where the customer's name is used in another capacity (such as custodian or trustee) may not be used.

If a customer has been sold out or bought in as the result of this Regulation T violation, the account is frozen, or blocked, for the next ninety days. During this period the customer must advance full payment in good funds—cash, federal funds, or a guaranteed check—before the broker may enter any orders on his behalf.

If the customer has a serious reason for not being able to pay within the specified time, a broker may request an extension from an exchange or the NASD, depending on where the transaction took place. Both customer and representative should understand that this is not an automatic process like filing for an extension of time for one's income tax return. Unless the reason cited is considered serious by the regulator, it may be rejected. Furthermore, extensions are costly to brokers which must extend their own funds to settle the trade with the other party before receipt of the customer's payment. Some brokerage firms dislike the practice so much that they have an official "no extensions" policy that is waived only for established customers on rare occasions. Others allow the branch office manager to set her own standards. In any event, no customer should expect, nor be led to believe, that extensions are easily obtainable and a routine procedure to be utilized at a customer's convenience. The representative must make sure that the customer understands that extensions are for use in emergency situations only, and even then cannot be guaranteed.

There is a simple way for a representative and customer to avoid extension requests and attendant problems, especially those which arise when the request is denied. When reporting the execution price to the customer, the representative should also report the approximate dollar amount and date due. The amount needn't be exact, as deficiencies of less than $500 may be waived according to Regulation T. The federal rule does not make prompt payment contingent upon the receipt of a written confirmation—it simply states not later than the seventh business day following the trade date. If the customer is allowed to await the receipt of a written confirmation before paying, a problem is sure to happen sooner or later. Brokerage firms usually mail confirmations on the day following the transaction. Given the two or three days needed by the Postal Service even for local deliveries, it is possible that the customer will receive the confirmation only two or three days before payment is due. Because mailing a check to the broker is at least as time consuming as the mailing of the confirmation, any delay could result in the customer's position being closed out, even when "the check is (literally) in the mail."

Margin Calls

Although there are two kinds of margin call—initial (Regulation T) and maintenance—most investors think of the latter when the expression is used. Regulation T calls are not surprises; maintenance calls usually are—and unpleasant ones at that.

Maintenance margin is intended to safeguard the broker, not the customer. In a margin account the broker is a creditor and the customer a debtor with a loan secured by the market value of her securities (or cash deposit if short). If the market moves against the customer the value of her collateral may decline to a point where it is less than the amount of the loan. This situation could have an adverse effect on the broker's capital. If enough undermargined customers were faced with a decline similar to that of October 19, 1987 the broker might well be put out of business.

The NYSE/NASD minimum equity requirement for long stock positions is 25 percent of the market value. For short stock positions the requirement may be 30 percent or even higher because of the greater risk. Because most stock positions start at an equity of at least 50 percent, the maintenance level cannot be reached without a substantially adverse price movement. Ordinarily, such a change might be expected to take weeks or months, but more recent events indicate that it could happen in a single trading session.

Brokerage firms generally insist on a higher minimum equity than the self-regulatory bodies, 30 or 35 percent being common house requirements for long positions. This increased margin not only provides extra protection, but also allows the broker to waive a house call when the circumstances merit it.

Maintenance calls must be met on demand. Brokers usually give the customer a day or two, possibly even three, to produce the necessary deposit which could be in either cash or securities. Brokers are free to accept whatever collateral they wish for maintenance purposes. Cash is always welcome. Securities do not have to be marginable, but they must be *marketable* because liquidation may be necessary to satisfy a subsequent call. Brokers usually do not accept deposits of issues with limited marketability, or else will accept them only at some fraction of their market value. For instance, many brokers will not accept a deposit of penny stocks to meet a maintenance call. In some cases, these issues have only one or two market makers. Because these market makers could abandon firm quotations without much notice, it is dangerous to rely on them for bids during a falling market. Similarly, some municipal bonds have a limited trading market and may be accepted only at a sizeable reduction from their current market price.

If the customer cannot, or does not wish to, make the deposit, the broker must sell sufficient long shares (or buy back sufficient short shares) to bring the account into compliance with the applicable maintenance regulations. In some cases this may be the best course of action for the customer, even though he may not admit such. The great speculator Jesse Livermore was reported to have held that a margin call was the only "sure tip" one would ever get from a broker. In other words, the market is telling the investor that he is wrong and answering a call with new deposits is often throwing good money after bad.

The customer should carefully monitor undermargined positions. With a little care she can anticipate the issuance of maintenance calls and possibly take remedial action under less pressing circumstances than a threatened sell-out. To gain some knowledge of her proximity to a margin call, the customer may use a simple formula to find where the maintenance level is reached and may then compare her current equity with that level. The point where the equity is at the minimally satisfactory level may be found by dividing the debit balance (the amount owed by the customer) by the complement to the given maintenance requirement. In the case of NYSE/NASD rules that complement is 0.75 (100 percent minus 25 percent). That is, if the customer took maximum advantage of Regulation T, she and the broker were 50–50 partners in the original purchase. Half of the funds to be paid to the seller were supplied by the customer's deposit and half by the broker's loan. Because the amount of the broker's loan is not affected by changes in market prices, the customer's equity bears the full brunt of adverse price changes. If the market changed such that the customer's equity had deteriorated to 25 percent, it follows that the broker's loan must constitute the other 75 percent. Hence, the formula: .75x (where x equals some unknown market value) = the customer's debit balance.

Suppose the customer had purchased 200 shares of XYZ Corp. common stock at $60 per share. If he makes the minimum 50 percent deposit he pays $6,000 of the $12,000 purchase price. The remainder is borrowed from the broker. Applying the formula, it can be seen that the maintenance level is reached when XYZ drops to $40 per share (.75x = $6,000; x = $8,000, or $40 per share for 200 shares).

Knowing the spot where trouble is likely and doing something about it are two different things. A decision to liquidate or wait for a rebound cannot be validated except by hindsight. Customers are not likely to get much help from their representatives. If the representative had not recommended a liquidation at higher prices, he is not going to tell the customer to sell when his equity has fallen materially. Correctly perceiving now less affluent customers as limited sources of future business, some representatives simply stop phoning, leaving the investors to their own devices. The story rarely has a happy ending. Indeed, the moral of the story for many is to avoid margin in the first place. If the investor develops a healthy fear of the unknown, he is well served.

Options Margin

Although options provide a measure of leverage even greater than may be achieved by margining stocks, trading them may be either much less risky or much more so. This seeming paradox derives from the fact that the *buyer* of a put or a call must pay the entire premium in cash. The trader's risk is limited to that amount, as the option can at worst expire unexercised. Premiums may range from as little as $12.50 to several hundred dollars. Profitable transactions with options are at least as difficult to achieve as with margined stock positions, and usually even more difficult. The buyer of options has, however, the advantage of knowing that he will never receive a margin call after the premium has been paid.

Selling options, on the other hand, may create much larger risks. The practice of writing covered calls is relatively conservative. This strategy consists of buying shares and immediately selling call options on them. If the share price rises, the calls are exercised and the stock is sold, earning the premium received as a profit. If the price declines, the risks are similar to those described earlier for buying stock. Covered writing may be done in either cash or margin accounts.

Selling uncovered calls is tantamount to selling the shares short. The margin necessary for these positions is computed by adding 15 percent of the stock's market value to the premium received. This amount is adjusted daily based on the new closing stock and option values. Should the market rise sharply during a trading session, the risk to the writer is substantial. This may occur simply through the volatile price swings that the entire market seems to be capable of, or through an unexpected tender offer for the shares from some potential acquisitor.

Even riskier is the practice of selling options on market indexes. These contracts are cash-settled options which reflect overall market movements. Some writers of puts on market indexes were forced to pay amounts in excess of their total equity (and indeed in excess of their net worth) during the market plunge in October, 1987. Margins had previously been set at the option premium plus 10 percent of the contract value, generally between $15,000 and $30,000, depending on the index. They have since been raised to 20 percent of the index value, at least temporarily, but considerable damage has been done to many traders already.

Writing uncovered options is a practice best left to professional floor traders and speculators capable of sustaining large losses. The deceptively small margins, even those increased after the market collapse, do not adequately convey the sense of risk that should be inherent in these positions.

Finally, one should note a peculiarity about settling options trades. Listed options have no loan value under Regulation T but are otherwise treated like any other security for settlement; settlement must occur within seven business days following the trade date. The various exchanges, however, have applied a more stringent next business day settlement for all options trades because members must post their own deposits on that day with the Options Clearing Corporation, the captive body through which all listed securities options clear. Thus, a customer who is a day or two late in payment may not have his position closed out, but may find he is charged interest for all days past the due date. As customary, some brokers may take a more rigorous approach and demand payment at the time of the trade or next business day at the latest.

FUTURES MARGIN

All futures trades are margin transactions. Futures margin, however, is conceptually different from securities margin. As previously described, securities margin is a downpayment on a purchase (or a short sale). The remainder of the purchase price is borrowed from the broker, making the broker the customer's creditor. The broker holds the margined securities as collateral and charges interest on debit balances.

Futures margin, on the other hand, is a good faith deposit—in effect a pledge by the customer that sufficient funds will be available to make or take delivery of the commodity in the contract should that ever come to pass. No money is loaned and consequently no interest is charged. Furthermore, there is no federal regulation of futures margin although events of October, 1987 rekindled off-and-on discussions about applying some form of uniform margin to securities and stock index futures. Minimum equity requirements are set for each contract on the exchange where it is traded. Brokerage firms often have house requirements in excess of these minimum levels.

Futures margins are smaller than securities margins, averaging about five to ten percent of the contract value. Margins for physical commodities are usually set in dollars or cents per unit of the contract, such as cents per bushel. For example, soybean margins might be set at 30 cents per bushel. Because there are 5,000 bushels in the contract, the required minimum deposit is $1,500. If soybeans were priced at $5.00 per bushel, this deposit would represent six percent of the $25,000 current contract value. Margin on financial futures contracts, on the other hand, is set in dollars per contract.

Exchanges normally raise margins in volatile markets. The Chicago Board of Trade, for instance, has changed margin requirements on various contracts dozens of times in the last decade, whereas the Regulation T minimum has not been changed since 1974. After the stock market fall of October 19, 1987, the Chicago Mercantile Exchange raised margins on the Standard & Poors 500 stock index contract from $10,000 to $20,000 for speculative positions. Even at the increased rate, margin was only about 17 percent of the contract's value of about $112,000. Had one bought comparable securities worth the contract amount, the required deposit would have been $56,000. It would appear that, at least in these and similar stock index contracts, this disparity may be narrowed by increased federal regulation of futures margin.

Low futures margins magnify both profits and losses, contributing to the impression that futures prices are inherently more volatile than stock prices—an exaggeration at the least. For example, assume a trader purchased a soybean contract when futures were trading at $5.00 per bushel and deposited $1,500 margin. If soybeans fell to $4.90 per bushel, the ten cent per bushel loss is two percent of the previous $5.00 market price. The contract value had fallen from $25,000 to $24,500—a $500 loss. Thus, the trader had lost 33-1/3 percent of his $1,500 margin on a decline of only two percent in the market price.

Maintenance margin is usually fixed at about 75 percent of initial margin. Continuing the example above, the trader could lose no more than $375 of his original $1,500 without being subject to a maintenance call. In the example, therefore, the ten cent drop would have generated an immediate maintenance call. On most exchanges a maintenance call requires the restoration of the equity to the original level. The trader must now deposit an additional $500, or his position will be liquidated. Note how this differs from securities maintenance margin where the equity need only be restored to the maintenance level.

Unlike securities transactions where Regulation T allows seven business days for the initial deposit, most brokers require the initial margin to be on deposit before the first order is accepted. Subsequent transactions depend on the amount of equity the customer may have at that time. Brokers must deposit their own margin for customer positions with the exchange clearinghouse not later that the opening of trading on the business day following the transaction. The possibility that the customer's initial equity could be wiped out on the first day is real enough for the broker to want sufficient equity on deposit before allowing any trades to take place.

Futures markets move very quickly. It is not unusual to see a particular contract open trading higher than the previous day's close, rally even farther, and then collapse and finish down by the maximum allowable trading limit. In a situation such as this it is seldom possible for the broker to dispatch a margin call with any reasonable hope that the situation will not have changed again by the time of its receipt by the customer. Occasionally the customer may receive a margin call when it is too late to take remedial action. Customers' positions are sometimes closed out before they have the opportunity to answer the margin call. At other times, the market may reverse by enough to pull the customer out of a maintenance violation after the telegram has been received, only to find that the next day the market has resumed its contrary trend with a vengeance. Customers then sometimes complain that had they been sold out (or bought in) at the time when the first margin calls were sent, they should have no further liabilities. Unfortunately for these customers, they have little to stand on. The standard commodities margin agreement allows the broker to liquidate a position whenever he deems necessary.

Futures margin calls can be met directly by the deposit of cash or U.S. Treasury securities. Deposits of other securities may be made to the customer's securities account if such exists. The ability to have both securities and futures accounts with the same broker is a material advantage to those who also own stocks, corporate bonds, or municipal bonds.

Futures exchanges customarily raise margin requirements when a contract becomes what is perceived as excessively active. When this happens, both initial and maintenance amounts are affected. Exchange rules vary. For example, on the Chicago Board of Trade if a contract rises or falls by the daily trading limit on three consecutive days in three different delivery months, the trading limit on the fourth day rises to 150 percent of the previous limit and margins are raised by a similar percentage. If a customer's position was properly margined before the increased level went into effect, she will not have to deposit more funds unless the changes throw her into a maintenance violation. Assume that the initial margin is $1,000 per contract and maintenance $750, and that the exchange raises the margin to $1,250 and $1,000 respectively. A customer whose equity was $900 was in compliance under the previous requirement, but is now in maintenance violation by $100 and will be called for additional margin.

Day trades do not have to be margined separately so long as any position open at the end of the day is properly margined. Again, brokerage firms may have more stringent policies and require sufficient excess equity to margin fully the initiation of any day trades. Because of the misleading appearance of a free ride, the customer may not realize the consequences of an unsuccessful day trade. Although the trade itself requires no margin, any loss suffered is subtracted from the account equity. A large enough loss could force the remaining equity below the maintenance level and generate a maintenance call substantially greater than the loss. Suppose, for example, that a customer's equity is $17,000. The initial requirement on his position is $20,000 and maintenance is $15,000. The customer loses $3,000 on a day trade, depleting his equity to $14,000 and creating a margin call to replenish the equity to the $20,000 original level.

Day trades are hazardous enough for professional floor traders, let alone retail speculators. There seems little reason, other than churning, that a representative ought to solicit or even encourage such activity from customers. Although most brokers give reduced commission rates for day trades, whatever savings may occur hardly justify the increased risk and unlikely long-term success of this activity.

Lower margins are permitted for some spread positions than those required for outright long or short positions. In a spread the trader has both long and short positions in the same, or related, futures. Profit or loss occurs because the price differential between the two contracts either widens or narrows. The assumption is that the prices for different delivery months or commodities will rise or fall in the same direction but at different rates. Thus, the profit or loss on the long leg will have a corresponding but opposite result on the short one. Initial spread margins are typically about one-third to one-half of the amount required for outright long or short positions.

Beginning traders should be wary of spreads. Although the low margins and supposed limited risks of some spreads may seem appealing, there is no guarantee that different futures prices will necessarily rise or fall together. Sometimes the trader has the doubly unpleasant experience of seeing her long position go down while the short position rises. Rather than reducing risks, spreads occasionally compound them. Risk is also increased when the trader is encouraged to take on more positions, because the lower margin allows more positions to be created than would ordinarily be possible with plain long or short positions.

Futures margin calls may be avoided entirely if the customer restricts his activities to the purchase of options. As with securities options, futures options must be paid in full; thus, risk is limited to the amount of the premium charged. The additional risks in trading options on futures, of course, is another matter entirely. Writers of futures options face risks similar to those trading uncovered securities options or the futures themselves.

9

Supervision

Professional management has never been a strength of the brokerage industry. Part of this results from the volatile nature of the markets themselves. This lends additional cyclicality to a business already linked to fluctuations in the business cycle. Given these peaks and troughs, long-term development of new products and market share is sometimes placed behind the need to generate earnings quickly. Although considerable lip service is paid to long-range planning, crisis management is endemic to the industry.

The major cause of this situation, however, is largely the industry's compensation system. With the exception of top management, the highest paid personnel in the retail securities or futures business are the salespeople. Unless a person is compelled by a driving ambition to manage, he is not likely to find the monetary rewards of management equal to those possible in sales. An experienced representative's earnings are at least equal to those of the typical salaried manager, and often much in excess of them. Furthermore, the successful salesperson is close to being his own boss. He generally sets his own working hours and vacation schedules. He also decides with whom he wants to do business, and, at least to a certain extent, how much he will earn. This does not mean the job is easy, for there is a considerable attrition rate among those who cannot meet the goals set for them by their employers. Among those who do succeed, however, the desire to manage often means giving up a client list built from much hard work, and taking on the problems of others—either customers of other representatives or the representatives themselves, a notoriously demanding group as a whole. In addition, there is the pressure from the home office to keep earnings up and problems down. Small wonder, then, that successful producers frequently shun invitations to become branch office managers.

Offices of large national firms are usually managed by a nonproducing (nonselling) manager. Branches of smaller firms are more likely to be managed by a producing manager—one whose sales commissions are likely to be among the largest in the office. This arrangement is also used in satellite offices of a large firm's main branch in the area.

The producing manager is bound to face conflicts of interest. Her own customers, and the branch's profits, may be placed ahead of the problems experienced by customers of other representatives. When a problem arises, this can be an unhappy situation for the customer of another representative in that office. Prospective customers should give careful consideration to this possibility before opening an account at an office with a producing manager. Not all such offices are poorly managed, and some such managers do a remarkable job of balancing priorities. In some cases, especially in smaller cities or towns, there may be no real alternative available to the investor. In general, however, when problems occur they are likely to be resolved more quickly and satisfactorily when the office manager gives all of her time to running the office, not just what is left over after managing her own accounts.

HIRING AND TRAINING

The process of selecting and training branch office managers ranges from lengthy formal programs at the home office, to a process so simple that the major change for the individual involved is moving into an office or receiving a more impressive business card. Unfortunately the primary criterion in the selection process for most candidates at all firms is gross production. There is some justification for this. A person chosen to hire, motivate, supervise, and reward sales personnel should know how to sell from firsthand experience. Only in this way can he appreciate the nature of the difficulties a representative faces and how to resolve them. It does not necessarily follow, however, that this experience equips one to manage. Many successful salespeople achieve their success without the talents required for good management: patience, attention to detail, adherence to policy guidelines. In fact, it is apparent that some succeed precisely *because* they lack these qualities.

The potential drawbacks of the producing manager have already been discussed. Because their employers can ill-afford to be without their production for any length of time, these persons often do not receive extensive management training. Their education may be largely on the job. This type of education is indeed often effective in the long run, but offers small consolation to the investor whose problems go unaddressed while the manager learns the job of simultaneously running the office and his own account book.

Management development programs at the large firms tend to be more formal. The candidates are often groomed for either branch office or staff positions, and are often not assigned until the conclusion of the program. The idea has considerable merit. By giving up their account books, these apprentice managers are freed from the daily tyranny of the market and the ticker tape. They are more likely to develop a management style that is relatively consistent with other managers of that firm. This, of course, is the intended corporate strategy. Managers become more or less fungible commodities, to be moved around the branch office system without causing serious disruption. As the financial services industry has consolidated into fewer and larger entities, this type of management becomes essential to maintain continuity. Branch managers are not likely to be allowed to develop the sort of local satrapy that was often the case when a manager was allowed to run an office for 15 or 20 years.

The chief drawback to this type of management from the customer's viewpoint is that managers are often shifted to newer and larger responsibilities as they progress up the corporate advancement ladder. They may be career managers but are not usually career branch office managers. Tenure at a branch may be only a year or two or even less. This is scarcely sufficient time to become thoroughly familiar with the representatives in the office, let alone their clientele. A manager who is a long-term resident of the area and who has detailed knowledge of customer backgrounds is better equipped to spot an unsuitable transaction or a developing problem than a manager to whom the customers are largely names or voices on the telephone.

NEW ACCOUNT APPROVAL

This important duty is often performed in a perfunctory manner. The typical new account form has spaces, which, if properly filled out, reveal customer information adequate to satisfy any reasonable standards of suitability. A totally accurate completed new account form, on the other hand, is a relative rarity. Managers should not tolerate partially completed forms and allow accounts to be opened with important data missing. Rather than making a cursory scan of the financial figures on the form, the manager should have an actual checklist (not just a mental one) to run through with the representative. This may take a few minutes more than a less rigorous procedure but may pay later dividends in trades not rescinded and lawsuits not filed.

Besides the standard personal, employment, and financial data to be checked, the manager should pay particular attention to the statement of investment objective. This item should never be left blank. Nor should the representative be allowed to enter broad statements like "speculation" for all customers. Presumably, some representatives feel that this objective is broad enough to encompass almost any strategy that may be later contemplated. Some customers may indeed be speculators, but the typical customer should not be considered a speculator in the normally accepted definition of that term. Accounts for elderly persons or those with limited resources should be carefully scrutinized to make sure that investment objectives are properly defined for their needs.

It is good practice not to approve a new account unless all required documents have been completed and accompany the new account form. For futures accounts the customer must submit a signed acknowledgment of the receipt of risk disclosure document. Other papers may not technically be required prior to the account opening but nevertheless should be obtained. These include joint account agreements, margin papers, options agreements, trust agreements, and corporate resolutions. An account should not be approved for discretionary trading until the signed power of attorney is in hand. The same may be said for any account requiring this document. Should an initial transaction be allowed with the power of attorney "to follow," one can generally assume two things will occur: (1) a large loss, and (2) a renunciation of all responsibility for the trade by the customer. Needless to say, the power of attorney will not follow.

ACTIVITY REVIEWS

One of the most important functions for which the office manager is responsible is the daily review of office trading activity. The review has two components—a review of all executed order tickets on the trade date and a review of the *blotter*, a computer run of all office trading activity on the previous day.

Discretionary orders must be plainly marked so that the manager can remove them from the executed order file for closer examination.

She must also initial each executed discretionary order ticket to indicate that she has approved it. It is important that orders are not simply initialed without close scrutiny. A number of major lawsuits against brokers have involved long-standing abuse of discretionary authority, not merely single transactions. Managers should check each purchase for suitability as well as for compliance with firm policies.

The manager should also examine carefully any order ticket which bears signs of erasure, alteration, or late entries or additions. Industry rules do not permit anyone but a manager or an authorized delegate to make changes in executed order tickets. The rule is designed to prevent arbitrary changes in designation by a representative who might favor more important customers over less important ones by allocating the most favorable execution prices to the former. Managers should also prevent representatives from entering incomplete order tickets bearing only their own sales or production number in addition to the securities information required. Upon receipt of the executed order tickets the representative can then direct the best executions to the most profitable account and take the less attractive prices into his own account, or allocate them to others. An important safeguard against this practice is to insist that the order clerk not accept any order ticket with incomplete information. Computer systems at some firms solve this problem automatically by rejecting any order without complete information.

Firms which provide hot lines for customers to phone orders in should establish procedures to insure that order tickets are written out immediately. Although some of these firms, often discount brokers, record incoming phone calls, they should take steps to see that orders are promptly transmitted to the order room or clerk in written form. This not only meets industry compliance standards, but also helps protect against errors caused by faulty, if well-intentioned, memory.

Each morning the office manager receives a computer run of her office's trading activity for the previous business day. This record, still occasionally referred to by its older term *blotter* or *trade blotter*, is the manager's most important tool in policing sales practices within the office. Except in very small offices, the manager is not likely to be familiar with each customer's activity at first glance. The blotter, however, gives her a means of investigating unusual or suspicious trades—those which merit further investigation.

Any unusually large transaction should be questioned. The manager should know from experience the size of typical customer orders in the office such as 300 shares of stock, $25,000 face amount of municipal bonds, or ten futures contracts. If a trade is out of line with these norms and the customer is not immediately recognizable as a large trader, the representative should be questioned about the customer. Possibly this might be a normal but infrequent trade by a substantial investor who may be active only a few times each year. It might also represent new resources available to a customer whose earlier trades were quite ordinary. This may have come about through an inheritance, a promotion or bonus, an insurance settlement, or some other event; but, if it allows for bigger and possibly riskier transactions, the manager should demand that the representative reevaluate the account for suitability. Buying and holding small lots is not the same as actively trading large lots, even if the securities are the same as those previously purchased. Does the customer appreciate the increased risks? Can he afford them? In other words, suitability can change with the investor's circumstances. A judgment rendered accurately when the account was opened may now be faulty, and it is the representative's duty to make certain that the customer's activity reflects changed circumstances. As circumstances change it is his further duty to note these changes in his customer information pages, a procedure often overlooked. The manager should insure that this process is indeed being conducted. Representatives are all too prone to treat an infusion of cash in the customer's account as a windfall that permits activity previously not effected solely because of lack of sufficient funds.

Another possible explanation is that the customer is using margin for the first time. For example, a customer may have purchased 400 or 500 shares of an investment grade stock periodically and paid for each purchase in full. Now he buys 1,000 shares of the same type of security in a margin account. Once again, the questions to be asked concern understanding the increased risks. In addition, the manager should determine if the representative had solicited the use of margin to increase the size of his order tickets and, consequently, his commissions. Does the customer understand the possibility of maintenance margin calls, and is she prepared to meet them? Movements in modern markets are so rapid that little or no advance warning of such calls is becoming commonplace.

Short sales should be investigated. The risks inherent in short sales of securities go beyond those acceptable to the typical customer. The manager should ascertain if the representative first established that the shares sold could be borrowed. This is not often a problem with actively traded shares of major corporations, but there are occasional shortages of loanable securities of smaller companies or those currently involved in takeover battles. If the broker cannot deliver the shares to the buyer on time, it might be bought in, forcibly closing the customer's position and subjecting him to the possibility of substantial loss.

Another area of scrutiny for the manager is the blanket recommendation. Many representatives go on campaigns of building large positions for their customers in a small number of securities. From the representative's viewpoint this is an efficient use of time. He need only track a few issues and may concentrate his efforts on developing a detailed knowledge of the company and its stock's trading pattern. This is unexceptionable. If, however, the representative recommends the same stock for *all* of his customers, it is likely that this security will not be suitable for them all. Even the most conservative of equities carries unacceptable risks for a customer whose primary concern is safety of principal. Thus, if the blotter shows that a representative has executed many orders for a number of different customers, the manager should question the representative regarding the suitability of this issue for so many customers. This is especially important when the issue is not well known or has not been recommended by the broker's research department.

A daily review of the blotter may reveal a customer becoming heavily concentrated in a single security or futures contract. Such positions can rapidly become dangerous if the market moves against the customer. A fully paid securities position, of course, has less risk than a margined one. An income-oriented investor might well have a large position in an investment grade public utility stock without creating excessive risk. On the other hand, if a customer were to put most of his liquid net worth into a single margined stock or futures position, one day's adverse price activity could produce large losses and may leave the customer with no means to answer a margin call. This situation could become more dangerous for the broker than for the customer. Upon discovery of such positions, the manager should contact the customer to establish why the position was established and how the customer intends to handle a possible unfavorable price change. If the position were solicited, a discussion with the representative is in order.

Day trades (buying and selling the same security or futures contract in the same trading session) should also be questioned. Like short sales, they are highly speculative and unsuitable for most investors. If unsolicited, the customer should have demonstrated prior ability to handle risky transactions. There are few circumstances where a representative should solicit day trades. Day trades look like churning even if this is not the intent. Even with futures where the trading pace is often more hectic than with securities, day trades should be discouraged because they rarely result in long run profits for public customers. Any representative who executes many of these trades on a regular basis is virtually a certain candidate for customer complaints.

Finally, the blotter review may turn up numerous trades in low priced penny stocks or similar activity in options so far out of the money as to be virtually worthless. Even if unsolicited, this type of activity rarely rewards the speculator, and indeed does little for the broker's profits either. Although an occasional flier might be permissible for the substantial investor who can afford to lose the entire investment, the smaller investor is better served by buying and holding odd lots of good quality stocks or mutual funds on a systematic basis. Representatives of reputable brokers should not solicit orders for low priced speculative shares or options, and managers should put a quick stop to any solicitation campaign involving such activity. Investors are usually well advised to avoid broker/dealers which offer only such merchandise.

Employee Transactions

Transactions by brokerage firm employees are also subject to review. Some brokers restrict investment activities of their employees, whereas others do not. Firms which are also investment bankers maintain a restricted list of securities which cannot be traded by employees because of the possibility that some of these employees might obtain inside information involving takeover attempts or significant changes in corporate business. Other restrictions may involve speculative activities such as day trading or some types of options or futures transaction. Most of these can be red-flagged or rejected through computerized order entry programs. Some brokers allow their employees to carry accounts with other brokers, negating this form of control. Industry rules require that employees obtain the written consent of their employer before opening an account with another firm. Also, the other broker must send duplicate trade confirmations and account statements to the employing broker/dealer. The examination of these reports may be delegated to the compliance department at the home office, but may be the manager's responsibility when branch employees are involved.

Aside from restrictions there are other reasons for the diligent manager to review employee trades. Representatives who trade actively for their own accounts are often not attending to those of their customers, supposedly their primary responsibility. Not only is active trading time and energy consuming, it may also create stress and emotional conflicts that diminish the representative's ability to give unbiased advice to his customers. When the representative owns the same positions as his customers these problems are magnified.

Representatives should be prohibited from "front running" customers' orders, i.e., making transactions for their own accounts ahead of their customers. For example, when a significant news announcement or a change in a research opinion is issued, the broker should notify his customers before executing any orders for his own account. This is sometimes the case when a research opinion is downgraded. Many representatives interpret an opinion change by a research analyst from "buy" to "hold" or "neutral" as tantamount to "sell," and they act accordingly. Most brokers have an internal restriction prohibiting employee transactions within, say, 48 hours of the change. Sometimes, however, the opinion change comes from an influential analyst from another firm and a "48 hour" rule cannot be applied. Nevertheless, managers should still be alert to representatives acting before their customers, as this may be a violation of a well-established legal principal called the law of agency.

ACCOUNT BOOK REVIEW

Representatives are required to maintain customer account record books. The usual method is to keep two sets of books. One set contains the personal and financial information for each customer, usually in the form of the new account document itself or a copy from a snap-out form. Each customer transaction is entered on this document or additional pages as necessary. The date and price of each transaction is entered in addition to the share, bond, or contract amount. Opposite the opening of a position is a space for recording its closing and any profit or loss realized.

The other set is maintained according to securities or futures positions as a cross reference. For example, assume a customer buys 100 shares of Citicorp. When executed, the trade, its date, and the execution price are entered into the first book. In the second set, the investor's purchase is recorded under Citicorp with all other customers who own this stock and deal with this representative (the representative should record the holdings of prospective customers also). With a system of cross references like this the representative can quickly locate all holders of a particular issue or position when quick action becomes necessary.

The manager should review these books with a representative on a regular basis. A quarterly review is generally satisfactory for ordinary accounts, whereas discretionary accounts and other active accounts should be reviewed more frequently, ideally at least monthly. These reviews allow the manager to observe customer trading patterns, and also to make more informed suitability judgments. If a customer's trading appears excessive given his financial resources and experience, the manager should contact the customer directly to discuss the conduct of activity in the account. Unfortunately, a more usual response is to mail the customer a more or less standard "happiness letter" which notes the activity, questions its appropriateness, but leaves further action up to the customer.

Margin accounts should also be scrutinized. First, some accounts may have been initially approved as cash accounts. If the customer has since filed margin papers it may now be possible to enter orders that were not initially contemplated when the account was approved. Margin accounts allow the customer to sell short and execute other risky transactions that the manager may have initially considered beyond the risk tolerance presented by this customer's profile. The manager should also check undermargined positions. Customers in jeopardy of receiving a margin call in the immediate future should be advised of precautionary procedures, such as liquidating some holdings, diversifying, or possibly buying options to protect the position, if appropriate.

CORRESPONDENCE REVIEWS

Managers are required to review both incoming and outgoing correspondence. This review is in some ways more important than reviews so far discussed because it deals with stopping potential future violations before they happen, rather than simply reacting to existing problems.

Incoming correspondence should be opened and scanned before distribution to representatives. Indeed, industry rules require this policy, so representatives should take care to have purely personal mail directed elsewhere. Customers may address written complaints to the representative directly. The embarrassing (or worse) situation that this might create may lead the representative to destroy the letter and hope that market action will bail him out of the current difficulty. Of course, it rarely does, and often gets worse. By intercepting these complaints, the manager may uncover problems before they get out of hand.

Incoming correspondence may also contain suspicious items, such as transaction checks made out to the representative instead of to the broker, or the broker's own checks to the customer endorsed in turn to the representative. Either of these irregular procedures may represent a serious problem in the making. For example, the checks may reveal an undisclosed (and unapproved) profit sharing agreement between the customer and the representative. They could also present the representative with the opportunity to misappropriate customer funds by depositing such checks directly to his personal account, bypassing the cashier.

Outgoing correspondence also presents several potential problems. First, and probably most important, the representative may be extolling the merits of a new issue which the firm is underwriting. Any written comment, no matter how apparently innocuous, on a security offering in registration is a violation of the Securities Act of 1933 and could subject both the representative and the broker to discipline from the federal authorities. The minimum penalty for such cases is usually disqualification from participating in the offering, a matter of some importance to the broker.

Representatives may also use inflammatory rhetoric to convince customers of the urgency of their recommended course of action. Phrases such as: "Gold is poised for a leap which should double its price," or "This company is a certain takeover candidate at prices considerably above current levels" are sometimes employed by overly exuberant or unethical representatives to enhance their recommendations. Managers should read all outgoing correspondence carefully to insure that this type of flamboyant language does not get into customer hands.

Representatives have also created their own tout sheets or mailed to customers reports by other brokers or services. Although not necessarily misleading, the effect of this type of solicitation may be to imply that it represents a recommendation by the broker itself. Numerous grossly exaggerated "research reports" have been mailed to customers who assume that they represent an official view of a reputable broker, when, in fact, they are nothing more than unauthorized hype.

COMPLAINTS

Customers are going to complain. Losing money is not pleasant. The nature of American society has become such that someone is almost always legally responsible for someone else's loss, no matter how apparently unconnected to that loss he may seem. Some customer complaints lack any real merit, but may be pursued anyway on the assumption that the broker would prefer to settle rather than become involved in an expensive lawsuit. Others are valid and will be settled one way or another, in court or out. These situations are dealt with in Chapter 18. The initial management response is at issue here.

All customer complaints should be considered serious when received. A written record must be made and placed in the office complaint file, which must be available for regulatory agency inspection. Representatives should be instructed to report all complaints to the manager, no matter how minor they may appear. Representatives should take no action on their own, such as selling out positions to eliminate margin calls or to prevent a customer complaint about what is seen as a poor execution or an unwanted discretionary order. The manager's handling of complaints requires considerable tact and diplomacy, even though the customer is sometimes complaining about something no one can control—the direction of the market. The most important step the manager can take is to contact the customer as soon after the receipt of the complaint as possible. This not only produces the feeling in the customer that someone really cares about his problem, it also helps uncover the full extent of the difficulty, which might not have been clear from the first report. Customers sometimes call in such a rage that it is difficult to tell just what their problem is. More than one customer has phoned threatening a lawsuit on the grounds that "You're all a bunch of crooks." The manager who can defuse this type of situation through patient, nonconfrontational questioning will solve some problems before they reach larger proportions.

Even if the customer's complaint appears groundless, the manager should instruct the representative to write a narrative description of the events for the office file and for the firm's compliance department. Should the situation deteriorate into a legal proceeding, the broker and the representative are better prepared to defend themselves with such a document. By addressing it to the firm's internal counsel it may be treated as a privileged communication and therefore not become available to the customer's lawyer.

CENTRAL MANAGEMENT

Customers do not frequently encounter home office management of large brokerage firms, any more than a car buyer encounters the senior management of General Motors. With smaller firms this type of access is still possible and sometimes useful. The national firms are divided into regions, such as Southwest or North Central, although some states or local areas have such a concentration of offices that they may be regions themselves, such as Florida or metropolitan New York City. Regional vice presidents or managing directors are in charge of the overall conduct of business in each area. Smaller firms, especially those with only a few offices, run all functions out of the home office, often with the president or chief executive tending to routine problems like customer complaints.

THE COMPLIANCE DEPARTMENT

Brokers operate under a web of regulation that makes it essential to have internal policies to avoid running into problems with the regulators.

These policies are developed and enforced by the compliance department. At small brokers this department might consist of a compliance director and a few clerical employees. At large firms it may comprise numerous attorneys, auditors, and support staff. The specialized nature of futures compliance usually calls for a separate department or branch of the compliance department, although with small firms this may not be necessary.

Every brokerage firm has (or should have) a compliance manual outlining policy. A copy should be available in each branch office. Internal policies must consider federal and state law, as well as the rules of the exchanges, the NASD, CFTC, and other self-regulatory bodies. It is customary to set internal levels at higher standards than those set by the regulators. This serves two purposes: (1) an additional margin of safety is created; (2) the compliance director can make exceptions in internal policy as appropriate and still not violate laws or regulations.

Branch offices are usually subjected to an annual compliance audit. Examiners from the home office compliance staff visit each office and review the office's adherence to the firm's compliance procedures. In addition, brokers are subject to surprise audits from self-regulatory bodies like the NASD or an exchange.

A vigorous and visible compliance director can set a tone of respect for the rules and an understanding of why such rules are for everyone's mutual benefit. In firms where the compliance director serves as little more than a scold, a climate of laxity often develops. Rules are not taken seriously. Finding ways to bend or evade them becomes more important than finding ways to sell or trade ethically.

A customer with a complaint or a question that is not addressed adequately at the branch office level should try the compliance director next. This officer is more likely to give a direct response (although not necessarily what the customer wants to hear) and may resolve the complaint more expeditiously than through other channels. Indeed, compliance officers may be among the more understanding home office employees that a customer is likely to encounter.

CREDIT AND TRADING LIMITS

Much like banks, brokers must be careful not to extend excessive amounts of credit. With stock margin accounts, of course, Regulation T restricts the customer's credit to no more than 50 percent of the purchase price of eligible securities. Industry maintenance margins require the customer to have a minimum equity of 25 percent of the market value, and many brokers have even higher requirements. Although a precipitous drop in price could reduce the value of the collateral to less than that of the loan principal, such situations have not been frequent, and brokers have not lost money often for this reason.

Short positions in either securities or options, or any futures position, on the other hand, create quite different problems. The potential loss is much greater with these positions than with long positions. The possibility that a customer may not be able to meet a maintenance call exposes the broker's capital to substantial risk. It has therefore become customary for most brokers to assign position limits to large traders who take short securities positions or who trade futures, either long or short.

A credit review committee generally decides how many futures contracts a trader may control. Its analysis is usually based on financial reports such as those prepared by Dun and Bradstreet, Inc., TRW Credit, or Hooper Holmes. A customer might, for example, be authorized to have a net long or short position of 25 or 50 contracts. The representative should keep a close watch on accounts which approach these limits so that she will not enter orders that violate them. She may then be forced to liquidate positions by the compliance department, potentially causing losses for the customer, to say nothing of the ill will engendered.

Any large trader of naked options or short stock positions should be evaluated for creditworthiness in the same manner. Several major brokerage firms suffered huge losses in October, 1987 when customers were unable to answer margin calls on naked stock index or other put options they had written. These traders were allowed to take positions that were beyond their means because it was felt that "another 1929" wasn't likely. Indeed!

The Wall Street Journal (December 2, 1987) carried in a feature article stories of the misfortunes of these investors. One case cited a retired civil servant who lost a $54,000 equity and was being sued by the broker for an additional $318,500. In another, a 76-year-old retiree lost $360,000 in a trust account for his daughter and grandson. The suitability issues raised are apparent. What were retirees without significant sources of new income doing in the options market in the first place? Were the risks explained and understood? Suitability considerations aside, a rigorous credit committee review should never have permitted these customers to carry the 40 to 50 short puts that did the damage.

For very large options or futures traders there are additional position limits mandated by the regulatory bodies. No investor (or any group acting in concert) may acquire an options position on the same underlying security greater than a specified amount. The limits range from 8,000 contracts (100 shares each) downwards, on the same side of the market. *Same side of the market* positions are defined as: (1) long calls and short puts, and (2) short calls and long puts. The largest limits are applied to the most actively traded securities or those with the largest capitalization.

The CFTC imposes contract limits for speculators in some futures, mostly the agricultural ones regulated by its predecessor, the Commodity Exchange Authority. Some exchanges have also set their own limits on certain futures. In either case the intent is different from the credit standard which the brokers stress. The options and futures limits are directed against those who might use these derivative vehicles to manipulate the price of the underlying security or commodity. Bona fide hedging accounts, i.e., commercial users of the underlying commodity, are exempt from the futures position limits, provided their position is justified by their cash market needs.

REGISTRATION

All brokerage industry sales personnel must be registered. This process involves accounting for educational background, employment for the preceding ten years, and any criminal convictions. Applicants must also be fingerprinted. The registration required depends on the type of business being contemplated. The typical stock brokerage registration candidate will be registered with the NYSE, the NASD, the options exchanges, and any states in which he does business. A futures representative must be registered with the CFTC as an Associated Person and also with the National Futures Association and/or various exchanges. Successful completion of examinations is required for both securities sales and futures trading.

Managers should be sure that their sales personnel are properly registered. With the overlap between the industries, it is possible that orders might be entered in good faith but still violate rules because of lack of proper registration. For instance, a full securities registration allows the salesperson to trade options on actual stock indexes, but not options on stock index futures or the futures themselves. There are also a variety of securities examinations less rigorous than the blanket Series 7 general representative test. These qualify one for only a limited number of products—one covers only mutual funds and variable annuities, another qualifies for municipal bonds, etc. Here again a salesperson may be registered, but not qualified to offer a specific product. A salesperson could, for example, be registered to offer municipal bonds, but not municipal bond mutual funds or unit trusts.

Salespersons who are not properly registered may create serious difficulties for brokers. It may well mean that all transactions they enter into are either illegal or rule violations, no matter what good faith the representative may have shown. The danger to the broker is that any trades these representatives have made may have to be rescinded. If the lack of proper registration had not been noted for several months, or even years, the potential for loss is large. Despite this clear danger, proper registration remains one of the weak links in the compliance chain at many firms.

10

Churning—Real and Imagined

Churning is frequently alleged by customers who believe they were deceived because their accounts were manipulated by their brokers. Those who represent clients in courtrooms and before reparation and arbitration panels allege churning almost as often. Yet those who use the term are often unable even to define it accurately, much less prove its existence. Sometimes opposing expert witnesses testifying in good faith argue vehemently as to whether an account in fact was or was not churned. Given the real complexity of the term, the possible existence of churning must continue to be determined on a case-by-case basis and cannot be reduced to something which can be easily identified by a checklist of quantifiable conditions.

ELEMENTS OF CHURNING

Churning, like such other nightmares of definition as *security* or *futures contract*, can easily be described by listing its broad necessary conditions. Basically it occurs when someone who is in control of another's account engages in trading of excessive frequency, volume, or both. The frequency is deemed to be beyond that justified by the size and character of the account and therefore is without regard to the customer's needs, desires, and objectives. There is obviously a close relationship between the terms *churning* and *suitability* in that a transaction made for the benefit of the churner might not be suitable for the customer.

Some might argue that there are three necessary conditions for a churned account: self-serving motivation of the churner, excessive trading, and control. Although this is the position taken here, there are others who might argue that only the last two elements need be proved because the first is so clearly present or absent. Obviously a broker who bases a trade upon his own self-interest is acting at the least in reckless disregard for the best interests of his clients.

It should be noted that churning does not require long-run losses in an account. Although a profitable account is less likely to result in a dispute, excessive trading may damage a client by reducing the level of profit that might otherwise have been attained. It should also be noted that the churner, like the customer, prefers profits. Accounts that grow can be churned for longer periods and on grander scales. The churner no more wishes to destroy a client's account than any other parasite wishes to destroy the subject upon which it feeds.

Motivation

A person might well choose to overtrade his own account because of poor judgment or lack of discipline, but he cannot be deemed to be engaged in churning. That must be done by a third party and that party must be self-serving. In short there must be a breach of fiduciary duty, and this requires a fiduciary acting improperly.

If the churning is done by a broker's salesperson, the motive is generation of an unreasonable amount of commissions or sales credits. This serves to increase the take-home pay of the salesperson and may help her achieve other perceived benefits such as job security, status, or fringe benefits. It also increases the revenue of the brokerage firm itself. Because the acts of a salesperson can easily be deemed to be ratified by the firm because of customary supervision requirements, damages resulting from churning are almost always assessed against the firm as well as against the salesperson who actually entered orders.

If the trading is done by a third party, such as an investment advisor, the third party must personally benefit one way or another from commission generation if the account is to be deemed churned. He might, for example, be given office space, equipment, payments toward expenses, or referrals of other accounts. Barring such direct benefits, if he trades so frequently that it is not reasonably possible to overcome the high cost of trading, he might be faulted for a breach of fiduciary duty, misrepresentation concerning the viability of his trading method, or negligence, but not churning. The latter requires that the churner benefit directly from sales revenue.

Whether one trading another's account is motivated by a desire to churn it or not is generally so clear and obvious that few cases are determined on this basis. Most discussion here, therefore, centers on the other two elements—excessive trading and control.

Excessive Trading

It is excessive trading that calls to mind the very term *churning* or *churning up* an account. It is so obvious, in fact, that many people make the mistake of considering churning and excessive trading as synonymous terms, when actually the latter is merely one necessary element of the former.

It would appear that the establishment of excessiveness would be quite simple, but this is not the case. Excessive trading appears to be quite obvious when a large number of trades takes place in too short a period, but when an effort is made to quantify the excessiveness the matter becomes somewhat less obvious. How many trades are necessary to constitute a large number? What period is to be considered short and what period is to be selected in the first place? How does one reconcile volume with velocity? If an account is abused by causing it to trade 100 shares of stock 100 times, is it less abused by causing it to trade 10,000 shares of stock in one transaction if that amount is abusive for the account? What considerations should be given to trading strategies utilized and the types of financial instruments traded? Some trading styles and instruments result naturally in more commission generation so activity that is judged to be clearly excessive in one case may be deemed reasonable in another.

To complicate matters further, various courts, arbitration panels, and administrative judges have handed down diametrically opposed opinions in matters in which it is virtually impossible to identify any real differences. Lawyers looking for comforting precedent can find almost anything they like. Even those who engage sophisticated expert witnesses discover that they too may analyze an account and in good faith reach varying conclusions.

Sometimes excessiveness is defined in terms of a pattern occurring over time. Obviously a pattern requires a number of trades, but this leaves the other problems suggested above, that is, defining how many trades are too many, determining the period during which an account was churned, deciding how to deal with a small number of trades which are in themselves too large, and accounting for trades involving different kinds of financial instruments or, worse yet, a mix of them.[1]

Cases involving stocks, bonds, options, and commodity futures have attempted to utilize varying quantitative standards but these differ among the various instruments and even in different cases involving the same one. Some judges and arbitrators have taken the quite reasonable position that the word *excessive* should be taken at face value and that only one trade can clearly be considered excessive if it is one too many.[2]

This point may be of increasing significance in commodity futures disputes if the front-end load which a small number of firms have borrowed from the mutual fund industry becomes increasingly popular. In such cases, a broker takes a large amount of money from an account when it is opened and characterizes that money as something other than a commission. It then behooves the broker to make as few trades as possible and to establish only small positions so the remainder of the funds is unlikely to be lost quickly. The broker can then maintain that the account was not churned because the trades were so small and infrequent.

It should be stressed that the real evil of excessive trading by a churner is not the number of trade tickets but rather the unjustifiable erosion of the customer's capital by trading costs. A small number of trades with large commissions can destroy a customer just as surely as a large number of trades with small commissions. A front-end load is a cost of trading and has the same effect as a commission regardless of what it is called. The customer who faces the nearly impossible hurdle of overcoming annualized trading expense of 50 percent to 100 percent of his trading capital finds small comfort from the fact that he has made only one or two transactions. Perhaps this type of villainy might be designated as *negative churning* until someone thinks of a better name for it.

In the case of stocks, the most frequently used standard of excessiveness is capital turnover, which was established in an administrative case.[3] This relates the dollar purchases in an account to its average equity on an annualized basis. The mathematical inputs may be daily,

---

[1] Many cases deal with this subject. A sampling includes Miley v. Oppenheimer & Co., 637 F.2d 318, 327 (5th Cir. 1981); Mihara v. Dean Witter & Co., 619 F.2d 814, 821 (9th Cir. 1980).

[2] *See* Quigley v. Dean Witter Reynolds, Inc., CFTC Docket No. R79-306-79-451; Piskur v. International Precious Metals Corp., CFTC Docket No. R80-1186-81-142.

[3] *In re* Looper and Co., 38 S.E.C. 294, 297 (1958).

weekly, or monthly depending on the amount of time which can be reasonably devoted to the analysis. Suppose, for example, that an account was deemed to have been churned for a period of three months and that it would be deemed fair to use monthly data. The equity at the beginning of each month is added to the equity at the end of the month and divided by two to yield the average equity for that month. Assume that the average equity the first month proves to be $10,000; $8,000 the second month; and $6,000 the third. Assume further that purchases were $6,000 the first month; $5,000 the second; and $4,000 the third. Capital turnover the first month is $6,000 divided by $10,000; or .6. Similarly, the turnover the second month is .625 and for the third month, it is .667. The total for the three months is 1.892 which, multiplied by 4, yields an annualized figure of 7.568. Dividing the total purchases of $15,000 by the average monthly net equity of $8,000 and annualizing the result would yield a similar solution.

Analysis to this point leaves many problems unresolved of which three are especially important. One of these involves the standard of excessiveness to be applied. Generally speaking, most authorities would consider an annual turnover of two to be indicative of active trading, four to be an inference of excessiveness, and six to be presumptive.[4] It must be stressed, however, that accounts with turnovers of under two might be reasonably deemed to be excessively traded, and those with turnovers of more than six may be considered to have been traded reasonably. Not only the financial instruments but the strategies employed must be considered if the analysis is to be fair.

The second of the three problems most frequently faced has to do with the amount to be considered capital. It might seem obvious to begin with the account itself. If, however, a client deposits a given amount, but indicates that additional funds are earmarked for trading that can be provided if and when necessary, the capital is best considered to be the total amount available. Similarly, if it is indicated that only part of the money in an account is to be risked in a trading program, then only that part of the account is best considered to be the capital. Another problem is created by the use of margin. Is the capital the client's equity or the total amount utilized, including the money borrowed from the broker? In every case, the best answer would appear to be the total client equity designated for trading, but support can be found for almost any position one wishes to take.

The third major question involves the trading period to be considered

---

[4] Stuart C. Goldberg, *Fraudulent Broker-Dealer Practices* (New York: American Institute for Securities Regulation, 1976), 2-42, 2-43.

in a fair analysis. Should it be the entire period during which an account is open or only the period during which the account is considered to have been churned? The period selected often has a great influence on the turnover figure computed. Here, again, support can be found for almost any position, but the most reasonable would seem to be that most accounts are churned for only part of the time during which they are open. The most common pattern is for modest activity during an early period while the client may be making some money and gaining trust and confidence in the broker. The account is then churned as long as assets and trust allow. Following that, there is a period, sometimes extensive, during which the broker is hoping that the client will quietly go away, whereas the client may be talking extensively to an advisor or lawyers and trying to figure out what went wrong. Including the early period of confidence building and the late cooling off period in a turnover analysis warp the conclusions reached.

Another approach to determining excessiveness involves commissions generated, which provide the motive for churning. Obviously, commissions can be compared with beginning capital or with average capital to compute a cost-equity ratio. This would appear to be a rather straightforward approach, but here, again, there are usually enough possibilities of variable inputs to make case-by-case analysis by experts necessary. The question of how much capital is involved has already been discussed. But how much is the cost of trading? Commissions, of course, need only be totaled, but how does one consider principal (net) trades involving markups or markdowns? These may or may not be disclosed or discoverable. If known, consideration should be given to the fact that the registered representative, who is usually presumed to be the churner, may be paid a higher percentage on such net trades than the percentage paid on agency transactions, and this influences his motivation to churn.

If the customer utilizes margin, the capital borrowed clearly allows greater purchases and, hence more commissions. The borrowed money, however, also involves the payment of interest which may also be considered a cost of trading. The interest seldom generates any direct income for the registered representative, but does generate income for the brokerage firm and may therefore increase the income of management. Like commissions, interest may encourage management to tolerate churning. The question remaining is whether the cost of trading should include only commissions and sales credits or should it also include interest? The fairest approach would seem to favor the inclusion of the interest, but there are those who would argue against it.

Even when the data utilized are deemed to be reasonable, the question of a fair standard remains. Where a 50 percent annual cost-equity ratio might be considered appalling in a dispute involving stocks or bonds, it might be considered marginal in an options case and quite reasonable in a case involving the active trading of futures positions. The cause of the problem in setting standards revolves around the differences in trading strategies and motivations of the investors.

Most of those who trade stocks and bonds are inclined to trade in and out as seldom as possible, but rather prefer to buy and hold portfolios perceived to be well selected. Periodic culling might result in some capital turnover but the figure would be low. There are, of course, some customers who enjoy short-term trading or who even perceive this to be the best way to trade, but it is rarely the first choice of professionals attempting to maximize capital.

Futures contracts and options trading are more difficult to analyze for excessive trading because these instruments have short lives and therefore more frequent trading is common. Traders who have faith in programs which provide many short-term signals and knowingly follow such programs, may find it difficult to complain later about being wronged by the commissions generated. This, of course, does not mean that such customers may not have a well-founded complaint if they learn that the outlook for success in a program was exaggerated before it was entered, that there was a significant departure from a strategy that had been accepted, or that commissions are unusually high and are paid only because of the customer's ignorance.

Analysis of strategies in options trading is necessary on a case-by-case basis. Frequent trading may well be unavoidable, but excessive trading is avoidable. Liquidating positions, for example, just before expiration of an out-of-the money option may be quite unreasonable when it is considered that a commission is involved, whereas no commission is generated when the option is simply allowed to expire. Rolling up (or down) and out may be justified in some cases but not in others.

As in all churning cases, excessive trading is not just measured in terms of the number of transactions but rather in trading costs generated. It is necessary, therefore, to consider the number of instruments traded in each transaction and the commissions charged. If commissions per contract charged to an unsophisticated controlled customer are more than for a sophisticated customer whose account is traded in the same manner, a suspicion of churning may be greatly increased. Likewise, it is productive to compare accounts controlled by a suspected churner with other accounts which she handles but does not control, with her personal account, and with other accounts in the same firm handled by others. In a dispute, the firm will usually allege that other accounts must not be disclosed because of a confidentiality privilege, but usually such evidence is admitted with a proviso that customer identifying material be blocked off.

If the correct data to be utilized in an analysis of excessiveness could be provided here and accepted for all types of brokerage accounts along with quantitative standards, a tremendous amount of litigation time could be saved. To date, no government agency nor legal scholar has succeeded in developing a generally accepted statistical standard. Unfortunately, all that is possible is to point out that excessive trading is a necessary ingredient to churning, but the determination of excessiveness still requires a laborious examination of the account involved, the financial circumstances and trading objectives of the client, the nature of the trading techniques utilized, and the specific types of costs involved. After all, a churner is not interested in establishing an obvious trail.

Control

If an account is determined to be churned it must be controlled by one who benefits from the churning. This, of course, cannot be the customer. If a broker utilizes discretion granted by a power of attorney over an account, control may be assumed. If a customer uses the broker only as an order taker there clearly is no control. The middle ground presents the greatest difficulty in determining whether or not an account has been churned.

It is common for a salesperson and a customer to discuss the merits of a trade before it is made. Sometimes a customer initiates both a contact and the idea for the nature and size of a proposed transaction and the salesperson contributes only some casual comments. In other cases, the salesperson initiates the contact, suggests a transaction and the customer accepts both the proposed position and its size. This creates a situation involving *de facto* control, and it is on this point that a substantial number of churning disputes rise or fall. As is true in the matter of excessiveness, de facto control must usually be decided on a case-by-case basis.

If a customer accepts all trades suggested by a broker, rejects none, and initiates no trades of his own, de facto control is probable. If a customer rejects many trades and suggests many of his own, de facto control is improbable. But where is the dividing line? Most experts would agree that de facto control is present if a salesperson upon whom a customer relies suggests most trades and the customer rejects few, but they might differ on the definitions of *most* and *few*.

The tendencies toward dominance and diffidence in the personalities of the broker and customer must also be considered. Further muddying the water is the tendency of some courts to conclude that customers cannot be considered to be controlled if they have the capacity to pass on the merits of a suggestion whether or not they choose to do so. It is not clear whether those who take this approach mean that customers have sufficient native intelligence to understand what they are doing, or whether capacity involves both intelligence and some degree of sophistication. It also seems to ignore the fact that people of intelligence and related experience may choose to place their affairs in the hands of someone they trust because they prefer to spend their time and energy elsewhere. If their accounts are abused by the fiduciary, many would argue that control by the latter should not be precluded merely because the customer could have understood the abuse if she diligently monitored the trading, when it is clear to the broker that the customer's attention was elsewhere or that the customer was relying on incomplete or misleading information. Various jurisdictions have yet to reach consistent conclusions on this point. It would hardly seem reasonable to conclude, however, that the only accounts that could be deemed to have been churned would be those in which the broker utilized discretion under a power of attorney, unauthorized discretion, or the client is a blockhead.

THE FINGERPRINTS

Given the difficulty of determining whether an account was controlled and, if so, whether it was traded excessively frequently requires expert analysis of its trading history. The account analyst, like fingerprint and handwriting experts, seeks a number of points large enough to be significant. Although no one of these signs may be necessary or sufficient to prove that an account was churned, the presence of a preponderance of them is generally enough to prove a reasonable probability that churning took place.

Those who churn securities are concerned with their maximum income on each trade, so the compensation formula of the broker must be considered. If the salesperson's payout is especially large for such transactions as new issues or over-the-counter principal trades, an unjustifiably high percentage of such trades should be noted. Switching or quickly liquidating mutual funds with no apparent good reason where a large load is involved is certainly questionable. Soliciting the purchase of several funds in amounts just below favorable breakpoints is almost impossible to justify. The same is true with exchanges of one security for another of similar quality and value.

In the case of futures, frequent trades of extremely short duration are typical in churned accounts. Day trades are especially noteworthy. Although the broker will usually maintain that such trades involve smaller commissions on individual trades, it is also true that day trades frequently involve no call for additional margin and that a practice of day trading almost never results in profits in the long run for other than professional floor traders. Although individual commissions are smaller, the total commissions generated over time may be quite large and are almost impossible to justify by the limited profit potential of day trades. If an account has suffered substantial overall losses but contains a large number of day trades, most of which are profitable, churning is implied. It would appear that the broker who controls such an account liquidates profitable day trades to gain his commission and avoid tying up capital which can be utilized for additional trades. If a trade shows a loss at the end of a day however, a churner might retain the position for a brief period hoping to avoid realizing losses which might alarm the customer. Naturally, if the market cooperates by converting the loss to a profit, the position will be liquidated at a break-even level or with a small profit.

Churned option accounts are usually characterized by frequent day trades and by unjustified switching to similar options but with different maturities or strike prices. Some churners are fond of selling covered calls and then buying in the call on small declines in value with the intent of reselling them if the opportunity presents itself. Others like to sell uncovered combinations and trade whichever side shows a small profit, thereby leaving the client with an increased risk on the side showing a loss.

Also common is a tendency to establish or liquidate positions shortly before expiration in cases where market action or exposure does not indicate the wisdom or necessity for doing so. Positions established shortly before expiration will result in tying up capital for only a brief period. Positions liquidated near expiration yield a commission, albeit a small one, whereas no commission is charged on an option which expires. It should be emphasized, however, that in some cases, the establishment or liquidation of option positions near expiration are justifiable.

Some characteristics of churned accounts are common regardless of the investment instruments involved. Trades which result in losses tend to be held longer than those which result in profits. The average size of losses tends to be larger than the average size of profits. Both of these are caused by the tendency of the churner to liquidate profitable trades quickly and reinvest the capital elsewhere in order to generate another commission. Losing trades tend to be held in order to avoid alarming the customer. Customers who do not watch the market closely are unlikely to notice losses until positions are liquidated and they actually receive a confirmation, if then. Further complicating matters is a tendency for some churners deliberately to confuse their customers. One device is to suggest that communications from the brokerage house be ignored in favor of communications directly from the salesperson summarizing trading results. Such communications may provide information in misleading ways such as showing only the results of positions which have been profitably closed, while ignoring substantial equity losses on open positions. Others may be sent only after successful periods. Some are even more blatant and provide results which are nothing short of pure fiction. Customers, of course, could check their confirmations and monthly statements, but it is not unusual for them to place trust and confidence in their brokers and believe assurances that any adversity is temporary or has been overcome by favorable developments subsequent to the statement date. Brokers or house attorneys will frequently then assert that acceptance of the mail ratified any abuses that took place.

A common fingerprint is a pattern of in-and-out trading. Recommending that a position be liquidated after a brief period only to be replaced with a position in a similar investment is difficult enough to justify, but reentering a long position at a higher price or a short position at a lower price shortly after an identical position has been liquidated is much more difficult. Individual cases, of course, might be justified by newly acquired information, but more frequently the salesperson maintains that he has developed a "proprietary" timing device enabling him to take advantage of short-term market fluctuations. It is, of course, not possible for the customer (nor, most likely, the salesperson) to validate the effectiveness of the timing device. A consistent practice of in-and-out trading for customer accounts is rarely profitable except for the broker.

Some cynical salespersons even engage in *cross trading;* that is, selling and buying the same stocks, usually on a principal basis, from one customer's account to another. Sometimes this is even accompanied by trading such positions at ever increasing prices to give their customers the illusion that their advisor has a highly developed ability to select investments rather than a highly developed ability to manipulate markets.

Traders have long debated the question of whether it is wiser to add to open positions as the market goes their way or when it goes against them, but churners seldom have any difficulty with this point. They much prefer to average against the market. This is just one more excuse to exit a profitable trade quickly while postponing losses. If the price direction of the losing position reverses after its size has been increased, the churner will exit somewhere near the breakeven point and search for new positions elsewhere. If the losing position gets too large, he will tend to avoid realizing the loss as long as possible, exiting only when capital is too impaired to continue trading, meanwhile buying and selling other positions as frequently as possible. As a result, the churned account sooner or later will consist of a large open loss which has been carried for an unusually long period.

Churners are quite fond of related positions such as spreads in futures and spreads, straddles, and combinations in options. Some such positions are well-intended and thoughtful and others provide problem areas other than churning, but churners have some special favorites.

In futures, a frequent ploy is the use of a spread to buy time. For example, a client may have a serious open loss in a long position of December silver, the price of which has gone down and seems destined to head lower still. Rather than simply liquidating and taking the loss, the churner recommends a short position in September silver. This has the effect of freezing the position, but avoids having to realize the loss. The customer can then take some new positions before the loss on the spread is taken. Of course, there is always the hope that one side of the spread can be liquidated early one trading day (preferably the winning side at the moment) and that the other side will miraculously recover before the margin clerk gets too unpleasant, but such hopes are rarely realized.

An additional abuse is accomplished through the establishment of spreads with an extremely low risk of loss. This sounds quite attractive but the attraction lessens when it is realized that a spread which offers only a small chance for loss offers at best an equally small chance for a profit, but does provide a rather large commission relative to any profit which may be possible.

Spreads, straddles, and combinations in options also vary widely in their abilities to yield profits and losses. Most abuses in options involve unsuitability, fraudulent representations, omissions, or concealments, but trading in options is also popular among churners. Sometimes, as in futures, churning is done by establishing high-cost positions which are unlikely to yield much profit or loss. At other times related positions are established with one side held to provide some profit or reduce loss while the other is rolled into new maturity months or strike prices. Although a long-run profit is almost impossible to realize, the churner can generate substantial commissions as long as the market trades in a reasonably narrow range.

It is especially common to find unusually large losses just before the death of the account. The churner delays realizing such losses until the last possible moment while making other trades in the hope of recovering some capital or, at the least, generating a few more commissions before the end comes. When the last positions are finally liquidated, almost invariably yielding large losses, the account is allowed to remain dormant as long as possible while it is hoped that the customer quietly disappears. It is also common during this last stage for communications between the customer and salesperson to diminish or disappear. The salesperson by this time has given up hope of inducing his customer to deposit additional money into the account and prefers to avoid or at least delay confrontation. If nothing else is accomplished during this lull before the storm, the churner may later maintain that the customer has ratified the trading by his silence or that the account was not really churned because the commissions were not too large considering the total time that the account was open.

DEFENSES AGAINST CHURNING

For a broker accused of churning, the best defense is simply to provide clear evidence that the account was not churned. Because it is almost impossible to assert successfully that the broker did not benefit from the generation of commissions or sales credits, such evidence usually takes the forms of denying that the account was controlled by the broker or that activity was excessive in light of the customer's objectives or the trading strategy utilized.

If it is maintained that trading was not excessive, the broker simply indicates that such usual ratios as capital turnover, trading cost to initial or average equity, or summaries of the fingerprints are below the levels generally presumed to indicate churning in previous cases or the literature. If the numbers are high, a successful defense might result from establishing the fact that the trading strategy employed naturally leads to apparently unreasonably high ratios and that this fact was explained to the client and was understood. Computerized futures and options programs may fall into this category, but if the costs generated are so high that they cannot be reasonably overcome, the account might well still be deemed to have been churned even though the mechanical aspects of such a program were accurately explained. As usual, a paper trail to prove what was represented may be of great value to the broker if the

paper trail did not result from misrepresentation, lulling, or blind reliance by a customer who obviously was paying little attention to what
was being signed. The same may be said of recorded telephone conversations. Mere existence of a self-serving tape may not protect a broker who
clearly obtained a tape from a confused or misled customer who was
coerced or browbeaten into providing it.

A more usual and more effective defense generally is the indication
that control was not held by the broker. Obviously this is almost impossible if the broker utilizes a formal power of attorney or uses discretion
without authority. It should be noted that the use of "informal" (unauthorized) discretion is even more insidious than the abuse of formal
authority. Brokerage firms usually devise procedures to maximize supervision of accounts they know to be discretionary. By avoiding a
record of discretion, the churner also avoids this higher level of supervision. If there is communication before every transaction an account
might well still have been churned, but if a substantial number of ideas
were initiated or rejected by the customer it would be difficult to allege
churning successfully.

Even if all trades were solicited by the broker and accepted by the
customer, one might maintain that the customer was not controlled if he
had the capacity to understand the trading. Whether capacity refers to
basic intelligence, sophistication, or the availability of sufficient time
and energy to exercise judgment is not all that clear. Relying only on a
customer's capacity to defend against churning is a somewhat fragile
defense.

Even if churning is deemed to have taken place, the broker may still
base a defense on ratification or estoppel based on failure to mitigate. A
customer who did not know what was going on originally may be deemed
to have become reasonably educated after receiving enough confirmations, statements, and other correspondence, or after filing a tax return
summarizing trading results.

Many brokerage houses have an internal procedure further designed to protect themselves from allegations of churning, or, least, to
discover any problem at an early stage. This consists of mailing letters
to customers whose accounts are unusually active in terms of scale or
frequency of trading thanking them for their business and asking them
to sign and return a copy of the letter indicating their understanding
and acceptance of the handling of their account. Such letters are
termed *activity letters* but are sometimes informally called *happiness
letters* and by some more cynical as *suicide letters*. It is more difficult to
sustain a complaint after one or more such letters has been acknowl-
edged. It is not, however, impossible if the letter itself was obtained

through fraudulent reassurances by the salesperson that all is really well or that the letter is just so much more red tape and should be routinely signed and returned.

At the point where a reasonable person would have understood what had happened the customer might well be deemed to have ratified the churning by accepting it. Even if he does not ratify the churning to that point, the broker might well maintain that the customer had enough warning of abuse and has a duty to complain and to demand that trading be halted. Failure to do so might cause any damages to end at the point where a reasonable person would call a halt. The alternative, of course, would be a customer allowing his account to be churned, planning to accept the results if favorable and demand damages if not favorable. Under such circumstances there is no formula to indicate how much time is reasonable. It rather depends upon the relationship between the broker and the customer, what representations are made, and to what degree they may reasonably be relied upon.

The customers' defenses against churning are rather clear. Basically they need only take the time and energy to observe, question, and gain an understanding of what is happening in their accounts. They need not grant trading authorities nor accept unauthorized trades. Confirmations and statements can be reviewed and questions can be asked. Activity letters and income tax returns deserve more than a cursory glance and a signature.

Many customers, however, will choose not to monitor closely what is being done in their accounts on a day-to-day basis but rather prefer to place their trust and confidence in their brokers, much as they do in their physicians, dentists, attorneys, or accountants. This will allow those salespeople whose hunger for revenue exceeds their ethical standards to take advantage of such customers by telling them not to worry about the red tape and make-work paper, but rather just to have faith and confidence and all will be well sooner or later.

REMEDIES FOR CHURNING DAMAGE

The common measure of damages in churning cases is based upon the unjust enrichment of the broker who has churned the account. This approach requires the return of trading costs for the trading done throughout the period during which the account was deemed to have been churned. Such costs may include commissions, sales credits, fees, and interest charged on debit balances.

Sometimes the measure of damage may be determined to be the out-of-pocket loss suffered by the client. The loss suffered is sometimes defined as merely the difference between the amount invested before the period deemed to have been abusive and the amount, if any, remaining at the end. Alternatively, it may include opportunity costs if they are clear. A customer, for example, may be induced to liquidate a conservative portfolio of stocks to enter an options or a futures program which results in losses and is later determined to have been tainted by churning. An award might then be based not only upon the customer's actual loss for the period but also whatever increase would have taken place in his former portfolio. If losses are restored it is generally necessary to provide convincing evidence that the losses would not have taken place if the account had not been churned. This may not be too difficult when a client formerly held a conservative portfolio of stocks which was rarely disturbed. All that is necessary is to compare the market value of the original portfolio on the various significant dates and take dividend income into consideration. Sometimes the customer is even restored to the greatest value reached by the portfolio within a reasonable time after discovery of the damage done by the churning. If the figures and evidence of fraud are clear enough, an award may include both return of trading costs and restoration of trading losses, while allowing the customer to retain any profits that were achieved.

It is sometimes considered reasonable to make an award including benefit of the bargain. A customer may have had a history of investing only in high-quality stocks and bonds. Although there is no specific portfolio to use as a measurement, it may be reasonable to utilize an index measuring stock or bond market returns during the period in question to determine what might have been achieved had his program not been interrupted.

If the customer had previously engaged in speculative trading in options or futures, it might be more difficult to secure the return of more than just the cost of trading. It is quite difficult to prove that results would have been profitable in such trading if the account had not been churned because losses by aggressive speculators are so frequent anyhow.

If the circumstances are sufficiently egregious as to indicate clear evidence of fraud, negligence, or violation of the antifraud provisions of state security laws, it is possible that the churning may even be considered to be a sufficient basis for the award of punitive damages. Because this is intended to punish by definition, such an award may be many times the amount of any out-of-pocket loss suffered by the client. If the damage is to be assessed against the brokerage firm itself, it is necessary that the management of the firm must be found guilty of participating in the act. This generally requires proof that the firm as a controlling person hired the churner and then allowed the damage to occur by participating in or approving of and ratifying the acts of the churner. This usually happens when supervision is lax, as when managers approve all orders in a cursory manner, no matter how outrageous, or do not check them at all, fail to examine monthly statements, or fail to follow up a firm's activity reports.

In some cases, often after receiving complaints from one or more customers of a brokerage firm, the SEC itself files a complaint against the firm based upon allegations of churning. It is possible that such a procedure can result in criminal as well as civil sanctions. This, of course, might satisfy a customer's desire for retribution but may not benefit him economically.[5]

A FINAL THOUGHT

Hundreds of brokerage firms with thousands of registered representatives deal with millions of customers. So long as brokers profit from the generation of commissions, some of those customers will be cheated by some of those brokers, and churning will be one of the favorite abuses used.

Brokerage houses cannot eliminate exposure to damages from allegations of churning, but they can sharply reduce it if they are willing to forego some commission and interest income. Discretionary trading should be allowed only under rare circumstances, if at all. Where it is allowed, supervision should be rigid. Someone other than the registered representative should contact customers with active accounts at intervals, and the customers' informed satisfaction should be made a matter of record. This is especially true during bull markets when rising markets might conceal churning from casual observation because customers are still able to make some money or lose little enough to accept their fates quietly. This should go beyond mere happiness letters. Training and retraining programs should stress such matters as the danger of unauthorized discretion and the necessity for making sure that customers are really kept informed of strategies suggested

[5] For a detailed discussion of damages resulting from churning including many case references, see Hyman, *Churning in Securities: Full Compensation for the Investor*, 9 U. Dayton L. Rev. 1–29 (1983).

for their accounts and are given an accurate and clear record of the results.

Customers should not sign documents in haste, and certainly not in blank. If a salesperson suggests or implies that documents need not be read or that time is not available to answer questions, it might be wise to seek out a salesperson with better judgment.

Although a salesperson is a fiduciary bound by high standards and stands in a stronger position than those with whom they deal, customers should still be able to demonstrate that they used at least a reasonable degree of common sense and diligence before placing trust and confidence in a virtual stranger.

The mere signing of documents or acceptance of mailed documents do not provide an automatic presumption of authorization or ratification, but they do make it more difficult for a customer to allege later that he was ignorant, controlled, or both. Caveat emptor hardly applies in a fiduciary relationship, and a customer who was defrauded has a right to redress. Lawsuits, reparation proceedings, and arbitrations, however, are seldom rewarding economically or emotionally for any of the disputing parties. Like most battles, they are better avoided than fought.

Part Three
Compliance

11

Documentation:
A Detailed Look

Customers opening brokerage accounts are usually presented with a number of documents to sign. As is often the case with documents of any kind, the papers are usually signed after a cursory glance. Of the many possible mistakes one can make in investing, few are as preventable as the mistakes made in signing documents not understood, or in agreeing to actions of which one does not approve.

NEW ACCOUNT FORMS

Each brokerage firm has its own new account document, although in essence these forms are much alike. The basic information required was discussed briefly in Chapter 5. The customer is not usually asked to sign any documents to open a cash account in a single name, and thus may never see the new account form itself. In light of the Supreme Court ruling in the *McMahon* case, it appears that more customers will be asked to sign arbitration agreements in order to conduct cash business with a broker.[1] Previously, arbitration agreements often were incorporated in

---

[1] Shearson/American Express, Inc. v. McMahon, 107 S. Ct. 2332 (1987).

margin or options agreements. (The nature of the arbitration process is discussed in Chapter 14.) If a customer does not wish to subject potential disputes to arbitration, he should either refuse to sign an arbitration agreement or cross out the portion of any document that requires the submission of all disputes to binding arbitration. The broker, of course, may refuse to open the account if the customer does so, but at least the customer will not be compelled to give up his right to sue in the event of a serious problem with the broker.

A broker is prohibited by CFTC rules from rejecting a futures account because the prospective customer refuses to sign the arbitration agreement. The broker, however, may choose not to open the account for a variety of other reasons even though the arbitration issue may be the crucial one.

A sample new account form is reproduced in Figure 11–1. The customer's full name should be entered on this form together with those of any joint tenants or co-owners of the account. Sometimes a customer may wish to carry an account under a code name or number to preserve a certain measure of privacy. This may be accomplished by submitting a letter to the broker acknowledging the ownership of the account and responsibility for the conduct of business in it. Customers should understand that this does not create the equivalent of a Swiss bank account. The confidentiality derived from this account relates primarily to the name which appears on account records, trade confirmations, and account statements. Because such items are routinely handled by a variety of different persons, it would otherwise be difficult to assure that confidential information would not leak out. A law enforcement or tax official with proper authority may obtain these records simply by requesting them from the broker. Removal of the records from the broker's office, on the other hand, usually requires a court order, but duly authorized officials ordinarily have little difficulty in obtaining one.

The customer should provide both his home and business address. A post office box may be used as a mailing address, but only if the broker has one or both of the other addresses in his records. From a practical standpoint, using a post office box as a mailing address may be unwise unless the customer either receives no regular mail deliveries, or has the ability to check the box regularly. The possibility of an erroneous confirmation or a margin call sitting unnoticed in a post office box for several days is a chilling thought.

It is not necessary to record the customer's exact age or birthdate in most cases. It might, however, be appropriate where the customer is clearly young, e.g., a college student. The dangers of conducting business with a minor were noted in Chapter 5. The best defense against these

MANAGEMENT GROUP — The Management Group for an account is the party who is managing the funds for the account. The Management Group name and number can be obtained by looking at a related mnemonic on the Quotron. Please place the name and number of the Management group in the appropriate boxes on the front of this form.

TYPE OF BUSINESS (of Management Group)

A	Mutual and Hedge Funds	F	Investment Advisor
B	Savings Bank	GM	Municipal Operating Funds
HM	Mortgage Corp/Mortgage Sub	GP	Municipal Pension
HS	Savings and Loan	GS	Supra National Government Agency
HU	Credit Union	HF	Federal Bank/Agency
CA	Commercial Bank	IU	Corporation-Treasurers/Operating Fund
CP	Com'l Bank — Portfolio Dept	IB	Partnership
CD	Com'l Bank — Dealer Dept	IP	Corporate Pension
CT	Com'l Bank — Trust/Advisory	IH	Union Pension
CF	Merchant/Universal Bank	J	Foundation
CC	Central Bank	JA	Charity
CZ	Universal Bank US Branch Sub	JB	University
DA	Insurance Co/Insurance Sub	JC	Hospital
DC	Insurance Co/Casualty	JD	Religious Group
DL	Insurance Co/Life	ZZ	Miscellaneous
EU	Broker Advisor/Broker-Advisor Sub		

CUSTOMER TYPE CODES

01 Individual	10 Trust	17 Estate	48 Joint Account
03 SB Employee			

LEGEND OF SECURITY TYPES FOR STANDING DELIVERY INSTRUCTIONS

1 — C = Corporates	C — CD = Certificate of Deposit
2 — M = Municipals	B — BA = Bankers Acceptance
3 — S = Stocks	W — AW = All Government Wireables
4 — CW = Commercial Paper Wireable	(TN,BL,TB,AG)
6 — D = Government Definitive	N — TN = Treasury Notes
7 — MP = Muni Project Notes	L — BL = Treasury Bills
8 — EC = Euro CD	T — TB = Treasury Bonds
9 — CG = Canadian Govt. Issues	A — AG = Government Agency
H — GF = GNMA/FHLMC	G — G = All Gov't Except Wireables
E — E = Euro bonds	(D,CP,CD,BA,GF)
Y — Y = Yankee bonds	5 — DI = D.A.T.E.S.
M — AM = All Government Money Market	K — K = CATS
(CP,CD,BA)	Q — Q = Muni Project Notes Wireables
P — CP = Commercial Paper	R — R = FHLMC PC Wireables
	U — U = Zero Coupon Treasuries

TRANSACTION TYPES	B OR S = BUY OR SELL	BS = BUY AND SELL

DELIVERY CODE

1 SOR	4 COD Broker
2 COD Cust	5 COD Draft
3 COD Bank	

FIGURE 11-1 Sample new account form.

INDIVIDUALS — GENERAL SECURITIES NEW ACCOUNT REPORT

(Including: Partnerships, Joint Accounts, & Unincorporated Associations) **Please PRINT or TYPE all data.**

Branch	Account Number	Salesperson's Number	Date	OSS Account Number	Social Security Number

PART 1 PRIMARY NAME & ADDRESS

Name	United States Citizen? ☐ Yes ☐ No State of Domicile
	If No. ____ Specify Country
	Individual (s) Authorized to Trade
Attention	
	Trading Restrictions
Address	
City State Zip	

May we identify you to an Issuer upon request as beneficial owner of it's securities? ☐ Yes ☐ No   Initials:

PART 2 DUPLICATE CONFIRMATIONS

1. Name	2. Name
Attention	Attention
Address	Address
City State Zip	City State Zip

PART 3 STANDING DELIVERY INSTRUCTIONS   (Enter Security Type & Circle Appropriate Fields - Refer to Reverse Side)

Set 1 Security Type	Transaction Type	Delivery Code	Set 2 Security Type	Transaction Type	Delivery Code
	B S BS	1 2 3 4 5		B S BS	1 2 3 4 5

PART 4   Refer to Reverse Side for Definitions and Codes.

Mnemonic	Name of Management Group	Management Group Number (Leave blank if new)

Customer Type	☐ Cash ☐ Margin ☐ Credit (Repo/Reverse/TBA)	Type of Business (of Mgt. Group)

I.D. Institution Number	I.D. Agent Bank Number	Custodian Client Number
Interested Party 1	Internal Account Number (1)	Interested Party 2	Internal Account Number (2)

PART 5

Customer's Age	Occupation	Name of Employer	Check if Sal , Inc Employee ☐
Nature of Duties	Earned Income	Number and Ages of Dependents	Investment Objective
Annual Rental, Dividends, Interest Income	Estimated Net Worth	Estimated Liquid Assets (Cash, Securities)	Life/Health Insurance
Board Member of Public Company	Controlling Position in Public Company	Referral	

If individual is married, complete the next line.

Name of Spouse	Occupation	Name of Employer	Type of Business	Earned Income

PART 6

Is an Investment Advisor, Counselor, Attorney, or any other person, with authority, phoning in instructions for this account
☐ YES   ☐ NO   (If YES, the next line must be completed)

Name & Address of Authorized Party	Type of Power ☐ Limited ☐ General
	Individual(s) Handling Account

Signature of Registered Representative	Salesperson's Name	Date
Approved	Accepted	
Sales Unit Manager / Registered Principal	Compliance Officer / Registered Principal	

2113 (DOC) REV 11/84   **BRANCH OFFICES:** Retain the GOLD copy and forward all other copies to the Documentation Department

White - Documentation Dept. / **Green** - I.D. Control / **Canary** - Internal Audit Dept. / **Pink** - Branch Office / **Gold** - Branch Office Temporary

FIGURE 11-1 (continued)

problems is to request a copy of the birth certificate where reasonable doubt exists about the customer's age. A common error on the representative's part is not to ask the age question at all, creating the potential for considerable problems.

The customer's occupation must be revealed. The reason for this requirement is twofold: (1) the nature of the employment may give the representative a better understanding of the customer's investment sophistication; and (2) some types of employment require the prior written consent of the employer. For example, employees of banks and insurance companies must obtain the consent of their employers to open margin accounts with brokers who are members of the NYSE. Curiously enough, officers and directors are exempt from the rule, although logic might indicate that a bank president is more likely to create a large problem for the broker than a bank teller who might try to make up trading losses by dipping into the deposit drawer.

Concerning the relationship between employment and investment sophistication, one should not make overly generalized conclusions about sophistication based on the customer's job. Professionals such as accountants and lawyers may (or may not) be relatively knowledgeable about certain forms of investment, but their incomes and duties typically give them the opportunity to invest and gain experience. This opportunity is less frequently available to clerical employees. This does not mean that such persons cannot invest successfully, but that the representative should be careful about recommending to them situations which involve excessive risk for the inexperienced. The investment funds may have been generated from a one-time event, such as an inheritance or an insurance settlement. In such cases safety of principal is usually the paramount consideration, although some customers (or their representatives) may desire to try to multiply that sum quickly.

The customer's marital status must also be indicated on this form, even if the spouse's name does not appear on the account. Also, if the spouse is employed, the name of the employer must also be furnished. The self-regulatory bodies are concerned that transactions that might be prohibited by the employer of one spouse might be camouflaged in the other's account. Thus, if the customer's spouse works for a bank, insurance company, or other brokerage firm, permission of the spouse's employer must be obtained for some accounts, even though the account does not belong to that spouse. Where a clear separation of the source of funds and investment decisions can be demonstrated, some brokers waive the requirement.

An accurate statement of the customer's annual income and net worth is important. Like employment, income and net worth are not foolproof guides to the knowledge and risk tolerance that the customer brings to the account, but these facts help establish a suitability profile. The customer should give these facts freely without undue regard for privacy. The representative should enter them as reported by the customer. Guesses or estimates of earnings based on appearances or a particular occupation are sometimes wide of the actual mark and should not be used.

One of the most important pieces of information is also one of the most abused. This is the statement of investment objective. The representative should not be allowed to fill this in without consulting the customer, although this is sometimes done. In many cases, the representative takes down the account data over the phone, and the customer responds to the representative's questions. If the question about investment objective is never posed, the customer may not even know it is to be provided. A representative should not be allowed to enter broad statements like "speculation" in the hope that this will cover any recommendation he might make. A 65-year-old retiree of substantial means may enjoy an occasional speculative fling, but it would be unusual if speculation were the primary investment objective for such a customer. By the same token, speculation may be appropriate for a young investor who has time to recoup the losses that are inevitable in aggressive investing, but should not be used as a blanket endorsement for the use of high-risk instruments or trading tactics which the investor may not understand.

Options New Account Forms

Many brokers use a separate new account form for options trading (Figure 11–2). The customer information requested is essentially the same as that found on a regular new account form. However, industry rules covering the need to obtain the information are more stringent than they are for most other securities accounts. In addition to the data already specified, the representative must seek to obtain the following customer information:

Net worth, exclusive of equity in principal residence

Liquid net worth (cash and securities)

Dependents

Investment experience

The representative is required to ask for this information and is further required to note any refusal by the customer to provide the requested data. The customer must be provided with either a copy of the new

OPTIONS NEW ACCOUNT REPORT

TO BE COMPLETED BY NEW ACCOUNTS DEPT.

Branch	Account Number	Salesperson #	Salesperson's Name	Date	Account Short Name

PART 1 (Mandatory For All Accounts)

Name & Address of Account   **(Circle One)** Mr.   Mrs.   Miss   Ms.

Management Group

Business Telephone

Accounts Needed: – ☐ DVP Stock ☐ Cash Option ☐ Margin ☐ Short Margin

Customer Type

☐ Corporation ☐ Individual ☐ J/T Ten WROS ☐ J/T Ten in Common ☐ Partnership ☐ Bank

☐ Trust ☐ Estate ☐ Omnibus ☐ Other: _____

Type of Business - If the account is | United States Citizen? ☐ Yes ☐ No   If No. _____ Specify Country | State of Domicile | Tax Identification Number

May we identify you to an Issuer upon request as beneficial owner of it's securities? ☐ Yes ☐ No Initials:

PART 2 (For Individuals) If customer refuses to give information, check here

Customer's Age	Occupation	Name of Employer	Social Security Number
Nature of Duties	Earned Income	Number & Ages of Dependents	Investment Objective
Annual Rental, Dividend, Interest Income	Estimated Net Worth	Estimated Liquid Assets (Cash, Securities)	Life/Health Insurance

If Individual is Married, Complete the next line:

Name of Spouse	Occupation	Name of Employer	Type of Business	Earned Income

PART 3 (Mandatory For All Accounts)

How was account Acquired? ☐ Investment Advisor ☐ Solicitation ☐ Cold Call ☐ Personal Friend

☐ Variation of existing account; If so, which one? _____

☐ Referred to _____ by: _____ Other: _____

PART 4 (Mandatory For All Accounts)

Is an Investment Advisor, Counselor, Attorney or any other person, with authority, phoning in instructions for this account?
☐ Yes ☐ No   (If YES, the next line must be completed)

Name & Address of Authorized Party	Type of Power Limited ☐ ☐ General	Individual (s) Handling Account

PART 5 (Mandatory For All Accounts)

Commercial/Savings Bank References	Average Balances	Issuer of Escrow Receipts/Guarantee Letters

Does or Did Customer have Accounts with Other Firms?

☐ Yes ☐ No Name of Firms: _____

Restrictions on Options Activities

Has Customer ever Written or Purchased

	Options?	Stocks?	Bonds?
	☐ Yes ☐ No	☐ Yes ☐ No	☐ Yes ☐ No

SEND DUPLICATE CONFIRMATIONS AND STATEMENTS TO:
Margin Department   Compliance Department   Option Sales Department

PART 6 (Mandatory For ALL Accounts)

Signature of Registered Representative _____ Date: _____

Approved: _____ Registered Option Principal or Branch Manager   Branch: _____   Accepted: _____ Registered Option Principal or Managing Director/Officer

BRANCH OFFICES: Retain the pink copy & forward all other copies to the New Accounts Department.

White - Customer Approval / Canary - New Accounts Department / Pink - Branch Office / Gold - Compliance / Margin Departments

FIGURE 11-2 New account form for options trading.

account document or an extract revealing this information. She is instructed to review the document and correct any errors regarding her situation. The document is to be signed and returned to the broker within 15 days of the approval of the account for options trading. The customer must also sign and return an options agreement to the broker within the same period. The documents are often consolidated on a single form, with the options agreement printed on the reverse of the new account document. Should the customer fail to return the agreement within the 15-day period, her account is restricted to closing transactions only. That is, the customer is then allowed only to offset existing positions, not create new ones. Some firms demand that all necessary documents be completed before the customer is permitted any options transactions at all.

The options agreement contains standard language obligating the customer to observe the rules of the various options exchanges and the NASD. It also requires the customer to be in compliance with the industry's position and exercise limits. The limits are so large that they offer little restraint except to institutional customers. Some agreements also contain a statement that the customer has been provided with a copy of the Options Clearing Corporation Disclosure Document, the explanatory booklet required under the provisions of the Securities Act of 1933.

A perusal of this document is extremely important. In it the risks of options trading are clearly delineated. The most commonly employed options strategies are defined, and the potential problems that may arise from their use is also discussed. The document should be read prior to the commencement of options trading, not as an afterthought. All too often, by the time this is done the customer may have already found out about the inherent risks by unpleasant first hand experience.

Margin Accounts

Almost any type of customer account can also be opened as a margin account. The customer is required to sign a margin agreement (Figure 11–3), which is also called a customer's agreement or a hypothecation agreement. This agreement is fairly standard, and a form used by one firm is likely to be similar, if not identical, to ones used by others. As always, a close scrutiny of this form by a customer prior to signing is important. Many customers are unaware of the leeway given to brokers by the typical form. For example, from paragraph 7 it is clear that the broker can sell the customer out (or buy him in) without notice of any kind. This sometimes comes as a rude shock to the customer long after the account has

CUSTOMER'S MARGIN AGREEMENT

In consideration of your accepting one or more accounts of the undersigned (whether designated by name, number or otherwise) and your agreeing to act as brokers for the undersigned in the purchase or sale of securities, options on securities and futures the undersigned agrees as follows:

1. All transactions under this agreement shall be subject to the constitution, rules, regulations, customs and usages of the exchange or market, and its clearing house, if any, where the transactions are executed by you or your agents, and, where applicable, to the provisions of the Securities Exchange Act of 1934, the Commodities Exchange Act, and present and future acts amendatory thereof and supplemental thereto, and the rules and regulations of the Securities and Exchange Commission, the Board of Governors of the Federal Reserve System and of the Commodity Futures Trading Commission in so far as they may be applicable.

2. Whenever any statute shall be enacted which shall affect in any manner or be inconsistent with any of the provisions hereof, or whenever any rule of regulation shall be prescribed or promulgated by securities exchanges or commodity contract markets, the Securities and Exchange Commission, the Board of Governors of the Federal Reserve System and/or the Commodity Futures Trading Commission which shall affect in any manner or be inconsistent with any of the provisions hereof, the provisions of this agreement so affected shall be deemed modified or superseded, as the case may be, by such statute, rule or regulation, and all other provisions of the agreement and the provisions as so modified or superseded, shall in all respects continue to be in full force and effect.

3. Except as herein otherwise expressly provided, no provision of this agreement shall in any respect be waived, altered, modified or amended unless such waiver, alteration, modification or amendment be committed to writing and signed by a member of your organization.

4. All monies, securities, commodities or other property which you may at any time be carrying for the undersigned or which may at any time be in your possession for any purpose, including safekeeping, shall be subject to a security interest or a general lien for the discharge of all obligations of the undersigned to you, irrespective of whether or not you have made advances in connection with such securities, options, commodity futures or other property, and irrespective of the number of accounts the undersigned may have with you.

5. All securities and commodities or any other property, now or hereafter held by you, or carried by you for the undersigned (either individually or jointly with others), or deposited to secure the same, may from time to time without notice to me, be carried in your general loans and may be pledged, repledged, hypothecated or rehypothecated, separately or in common with other securities, options, commodity futures or any other property, for the sum due to you thereon or for a greater sum and without retaining in your possession and control for delivery a like amount of similar securities or commodities.

6. Debit balances of the accounts of the undersigned shall be charged with interest, in accordance with your usual custom, and with any increases in rates caused by money market conditions, and with such other charges as you may make to cover your facilities and extra services. Although calculated daily interest expense is charged to the account(s) monthly. Thus, unless each monthly interest expense is paid immediately the account(s) will be charged with interest on interest; that is, compound interest pursuant to terms of the accompanying Truth-In-Lending Statement.

7. You are hereby authorized, in your discretion, should the undersigned die or be adjudicated incompetent or should you for any reason whatsoever deem it necessary for your protection, to sell any or all of the securities, options, commodity futures or other property which may be in your possession, or which you may be carrying for the undersigned (either individually or jointly with others), or to buy in any securities, options, commodity futures or other property of which the account or accounts of the undersigned may be short, or cancel any outstanding orders in order to close out the account or accounts of the undersigned in whole or in part or in order to close out any commitment made in behalf of the undersigned. Such sale, purchase or cancellation may be made according to your judgment and may be made, at your discretion, on the exchange or other market where such business is then usually transacted, or at public auction or at private sale, without advertising the same and without notice to the undersigned or to the personal representatives of the undersigned, and without prior tender, demand or call of any kind upon the undersigned or upon the personal representatives of the undersigned, and you may purchase the whole or any part thereof free from any right of redemption, and the undersigned shall remain liable for any deficiency; it being understood that a prior tender, demand or call of any kind from you, or prior notice from you, of the time and place of such sale or purchase shall not be considered a waiver of your right to sell or buy any securities and/or options and/or commodity futures or other property held by you, or owed you by the undersigned, at any time as hereinbefore provided.

8. The undersigned will at all times maintain margins for said instructions to the contrary shall be recognized or enforceable.

FIGURE 11-3 Margin agreement.

9. In case of the sale of any security, option, commodity futures, or other property by you at the direction of the undersigned and your inability to deliver the same to the purchaser by reason of failure of the undersigned to supply you therewith, then and in such event, the undersigned authorizes you to borrow any security, commodity, or other property necessary to make delivery thereof, and the undersigned hereby agrees to be responsible for any loss which you may sustain thereby and any premiums which you may be required to pay thereon, and for any loss which you may sustain by reason of your inability to borrow the security, commodity, or other property sold.

10. At any time and from time to time, in your discretion, you may without notice to the undersigned apply and/or transfer any or all monies, securities, options, commodities and/or other property of the undersigned interchangeably between any accounts of the undersigned (other than from Regulated Commodity Accounts).

11. The undersigned agrees to provide financial information requested by you and the undersigned understands that an investigation may be conducted pertaining to its credit standing and to its business.

12. It is understood and agreed that the undersigned, when placing with you any sell order for short account, will designate it as such and hereby authorizes you to mark such order as being "short," and when placing with you any order for long account, will designate it as such and hereby authorizes you to mark such order as being "long." Any sell order which the undersigned shall designate as being for long account as above provided, is for securities then owned by the undersigned and, if such securities are not then deliverable by you from any account of the undersigned, the placing of such order shall constitute a representation by the undersigned that it is impracticable for him then to deliver such securities to you but that he will deliver them as soon as it is possible for him to do so without undue inconvenience or expense.

13. In all transactions between you and the undersigned, the undersigned understands that you are acting as the brokers of the undersigned, except when you disclose to the undersigned in writing at or before the completion of a particular transaction that you are acting, with respect to such transaction, as dealers for your own account or as brokers for some other person.

14. Reports of the execution of orders and statements of the accounts of the undersigned shall be conclusive if not objected to in writing, the former within two days, and the latter within ten days, after forwarding by you to the undersigned by mail or otherwise.

15. Communications may be sent to the undersigned at the address of the undersigned given below, or at such other address as the undersigned may hereafter give to you in writing, and all communications so sent, whether by mail, telegraph, messenger or otherwise, shall be deemed given to the undersigned personally, whether actually received or not.

16. **This agreement and its enforcement shall be governed by laws of the State of New York and its provisions shall be continuous;** shall cover individually and collectively all accounts which the undersigned may open or reopen with you, and shall endure to the benefit of your present organization, and any successor organization, irrespective of any change or changes at any time in the personnel thereof, for any cause whatsoever, and of the assigns of your present organization or any successor organization, and shall be binding upon the undersigned, and/or the estate, executors, administrators and assigns of the undersigned.

17. The undersigned, if an individual, represents that the undersigned is of full age, the undersigned is not an employee of any exchange, or of any corporation of which any exchange owns a majority of the capital stock, or of any corporation, firm or individual engaged in the business of dealing, either as broker or as principal, in securities, options, commodity futures, bills of exchange, acceptances or other forms of commercial paper. The undersigned further represents that no one except the undersigned has an interest in the account or accounts of the undersigned with you.

Very truly yours,

Witness _____   _____
                                                                        (Signature)

Dated, _____   _____
                                                                        (Signature)

_____   _____
(City)   *(State)*   *(Signature)*

CUSTOMER'S LOAN CONSENT

Until you receive notice of revocation from the undersigned, you are hereby authorized to lend, to yourselves or to others, any securities held by you on margin for the account of, or under the control of, the undersigned.

Very truly yours,

Dated, _____   _____
                                                                        (Signature)

_____   _____
(City)   *(State)*   *(Signature)*

Witness _____   _____
                                                                        (Signature)

1122 (NA) Rev. 10/87

FIGURE 11-3 *(continued)*

been opened and traded actively. To cite one dramatic situation, events of October 19, 1987 necessitated numerous such actions by brokers, and yet customers felt unfairly treated despite the fact that they agreed to be bound by these policies.

The customer should also note the separate signature required on the brief customer's loan consent. There is little reason why the margin investor should object to signing this document even though he usually derives no benefit from doing so. On the other hand, refusal to sign may make the account unacceptable to some brokers, who earn considerable income from loaning securities to others.

Federal law requires that all margin customers be furnished with a truth-in-lending statement which describes how interest on debit balances is to be computed. The rate charged to customers is typically based on the broker loan, or call money, rate. This rate is published daily in *The Wall Street Journal*, the *New York Times*, and some other newspapers. The published rate is often a range like $7^1/2 - ^3/4$ percent. Customers are usually charged this base rate plus some additional percentage, an extra one-half percent being the customary minimum rate. The size of the debit balance often determines the margin rate. Customers with large debit balances qualify for the lowest rates, and those with smaller debits are charged higher rates. Margin debits of less than $10,000, for example, may be charged two or more full percentage points above the broker loan rate. In fact, many brokers are actually able to obtain margin funds at rates cheaper than the broker loan rate by issuing commercial paper or using other financing techniques like repurchase agreements. Needless to say, little if any of such savings find their way to the investor.

POWERS OF ATTORNEY

When investors assign the right to transact business in their accounts to others, they must sign a power of attorney (Figure 11–4). A customer should never give, nor a representative accept an order from someone other than the account principal without having the signed power of attorney in hand. The form illustrated is a limited power of attorney, or trading authorization. This is the more common of the two forms used for this purpose. The less common variation is the full power of attorney. The limited power allows trading decisions to be made by a third party but does not allow for the withdrawal of funds, which is permitted by the full power. The limited power is often signed in favor of an investment advisor or a registered representative. When it is made out to a registered representative, the account is called *discretionary* in industry terminology.

TRADING AUTHORIZATION LIMITED TO PURCHASES AND SALES OF SECURITIES AND COMMODITIES

To ....

(Name of Firm Addressed)

....

(Address of Firm Addressed)

Gentlemen:

The undersigned hereby authorizes .... (whose signature appears below) as his agent and attorney in fact to buy, sell (including short sales) and trade in stocks, bonds and any other securities and/or commodities and/or contracts relating to the same on margin or otherwise in accordance with your terms and conditions for the undersigned's account and risk and in the undersigned's name, or number on your books. The undersigned hereby agrees to indemnify and hold you harmless from and to pay you promptly on demand any and all losses arising therefrom or debit balance due thereon.

In all such purchases, sales or trades you are authorized to follow the instructions of Mr. .... in every respect concerning the undersigned's account with you; and he is authorized to act for the undersigned and in the undersigned's behalf in the same manner and with the same force and effect as the undersigned might or could do with respect to such purchases, sales or trades as well as with respect to all other things necessary or incidental to the furtherance or conduct of such purchases, sales or trades.

The undersigned hereby ratifies and confirms any and all transactions with you heretofore or hereafter made by the aforesaid agent or for the undersigned's account.

This authorization and indemnity is in addition to (and in no way limits or restricts) any rights which you may have under any other agreement or agreements between the undersigned and your firm.

This authorization and indemnity is also a continuing one and shall remain in full force and effect until revoked by the undersigned by a written notice addressed to you and delivered to your office at ...., but such revocation shall not affect any liability in any way resulting from transactions initiated prior to such revocation. This authorization and indemnity shall enure to the benefit of your present firm and of any successor firm or firms irrespective of any change or changes at any time in the personnel thereof for any cause whatsoever, and of the assigns of your present firm or any successor firm.

Dated, ...

....
(City)   (State)

Very truly yours,

....
Witness

SIGNATURE OF AUTHORIZED AGENT:

....

FIGURE 11-4 Authorization of power-of-attorney.

Customers should give considerable thought to opening a discretionary account, or to converting a regular account into a discretionary one. The built-in conflict of interest that is inseparable from discretionary trading is such that the customer should not sign the power of attorney unless he has complete trust and confidence in the representative.

If the power is made out in favor of an investment advisor caution is again in order. The designation *registered investment advisor* may be obtained by virtually anyone who has applied to the SEC, completed the appropriate documentation, and paid the requisite fee. Before delegating authority, the investor should meet the advisor personally and discuss thoroughly the investment strategy to be employed. Aggressive strategies involve active trading by definition, and this type of activity is sure to generate large commission expenses in addition to the management fees due to the advisor. Although the power of attorney does not give the holder the right to enter into blatantly unsuitable activities, there have been numerous cases where the customer has later complained about excessive activity and been denied full (or any) restitution on the grounds that the adviser or the broker was merely following an aggressive strategy under proper authorization. The adviser may claim that the activity is inherent to the strategy being followed, and that the losses suffered were the results of misjudging the market in good faith, something for which no one can be faulted.

FUTURES ACCOUNTS

These accounts require more comprehensive documentation than is necessary for the typical securities account. All customers opening new accounts must receive a copy of the risk disclosure document as required by rule 1.55 of the CFTC (Figure 11–5). In addition, the more comprehensive options risk disclosure document must be supplied to those who intend to trade options on futures. Other necessary documents include the bankruptcy disclosure document (CFTC rules; Figure 11–6), the Transfer of Trades statement (Chicago Mercantile Exchange rules), and the National Futures Association risk disclosure document concerning linked markets. The last named document indicates that the customer may not be afforded full protection of the Commodity Exchange Act if he executes orders on foreign exchanges linked with domestic exchanges, but not governed by United States law or practice.

As with securities related documents, each of these papers should be read thoroughly before any agreements are signed. If anything is not clear, the customer should ask questions. If the disclosure document is

RISK DISCLOSURE STATEMENT

THIS STATEMENT IS FURNISHED TO YOU BECAUSE RULE 1.55 OF THE COMMODITY FUTURES TRADING COMMISSION REQUIRES IT.

THE RISK OF LOSS IN TRADING COMMODITY FUTURES CONTRACTS CAN BE SUBSTANTIAL. YOU SHOULD THEREFORE CAREFULLY CONSIDER WHETHER SUCH TRADING IS SUITABLE FOR YOU IN LIGHT OF YOUR FINANCIAL CONDITION. IN CONSIDERING WHETHER TO TRADE, YOU SHOULD BE AWARE OF THE FOLLOWING:

(1) YOU MAY SUSTAIN A TOTAL LOSS OF THE INITIAL MARGIN FUNDS AND ANY ADDITIONAL FUNDS THAT YOU DEPOSIT WITH YOUR BROKER TO ESTABLISH OR MAINTAIN A POSITION IN THE COMMODITY FUTURES MARKET. IF THE MARKET MOVES AGAINST YOUR POSITION, YOU MAY BE CALLED UPON BY YOUR BROKER TO DEPOSIT A SUBSTANTIAL AMOUNT OF ADDITIONAL MARGIN FUNDS, ON SHORT NOTICE, IN ORDER TO MAINTAIN YOUR POSITION. IF YOU DO NOT PROVIDE THE REQUIRED FUNDS WITHIN THE PRESCRIBED TIME, YOUR POSITION MAY BE LIQUIDATED AT A LOSS, AND YOU WILL BE LIABLE FOR ANY RESULTING DEFICIT IN YOUR ACCOUNT.

(2) UNDER CERTAIN MARKET CONDITIONS, YOU MAY FIND IT DIFFICULT OR IMPOSSIBLE TO LIQUIDATE A POSITION. THIS CAN OCCUR, FOR EXAMPLE, WHEN THE MARKET MAKES A "LIMIT MOVE."

(3) PLACING CONTINGENT ORDERS, SUCH AS A "STOP-LOSS" OR "STOP-LIMIT" ORDER, WILL NOT NECESSARILY LIMIT YOUR LOSSES TO THE INTENDED AMOUNTS SINCE MARKET CONDITIONS MAY MAKE IT IMPOSSIBLE TO EXECUTE SUCH ORDERS.

(4) A "SPREAD" POSITION MAY NOT BE LESS RISKY THAN A SIMPLE "LONG" OR "SHORT" POSITION.

(5) THE HIGH DEGREE OF LEVERAGE THAT IS OFTEN OBTAINABLE IN FUTURES TRADING BECAUSE OF THE SMALL MARGIN REQUIREMENTS CAN WORK AGAINST YOU AS WELL AS FOR YOU. THE USE OF LEVERAGE CAN LEAD TO LARGE LOSSES AS WELL AS GAINS.

THIS BRIEF STATEMENT CANNOT, OF COURSE, DISCLOSE ALL THE RISKS AND OTHER SIGNIFICANT ASPECTS OF THE COMMODITY MARKETS. YOU SHOULD THEREFORE CAREFULLY STUDY FUTURES TRADING BEFORE YOU TRADE.

FIGURE 11-5   Risk disclosure document.

BANKRUPTCY DISCLOSURE STATEMENT

THIS STATEMENT IS FURNISHED TO YOU BECAUSE RULE 190.10(c) OF THE COMMODITY FUTURES TRADING COMMISSION REQUIRES IT FOR REASONS OF FAIR NOTICE UNRELATED TO THIS COMPANY'S CURRENT FINANCIAL CONDITION.

(1) YOU SHOULD KNOW THAT IN THE UNLIKELY EVENT OF THIS COMPANY'S BANKRUPTCY, PROPERTY, INCLUDING PROPERTY SPECIFICALLY TRACEABLE TO YOU, WILL BE RETURNED, TRANSFERRED OR DISTRIBUTED TO YOU, OR ON YOUR BEHALF, ONLY TO THE EXTENT OF YOUR PRO RATA SHARE OF ALL PROPERTY AVAILABLE FOR DISTRIBUTION TO CUSTOMERS.

(2) NOTICE CONCERNING THE TERMS FOR THE RETURN OF SPECIFICALLY IDENTIFIABLE PROPERTY WILL BE BY PUBLICATION IN A NEWSPAPER OF GENERAL CIRCULATION.

(3) THE COMMISSION'S REGULATIONS CONCERNING BANKRUPTCIES OF COMMODITY BROKERS CAN BE FOUND AT 17 CODE OF FEDERAL REGULATIONS PART 190.

FIGURE 11-6   Bankruptcy disclosure document.

required by CFTC rules, the broker must obtain the customer's signature acknowledging both receipt of the document and the fact that it has been read and understood. It ill behooves a customer to sign such acknowledgments without actually having read and understood the warnings contained therein. A later complaint that the risks were not appreciated earlier, i.e., before losses have occurred, is substantially diluted in force if the broker then produces this signed statement claiming otherwise. The representative opening the account should not be allowed to present these documents to the customer as mere formalities to be signed with just a glance, if that.

CONFIRMATIONS

All securities and futures transactions must be reported to the investor with a written confirmation. This confirmation is generally mailed to the customer on the business day following the trade and may not be received until several days later. A detailed review of confirmations is essential for any investor and absolutely critical to the active trader, particularly the futures trader.

The executing broker/dealer must report the following on a securities confirmation:

Security

Price

Agency or principal execution

Commission (if agency transaction)

Fees or taxes deducted

Place of execution (OTC, which exchange, etc.)

In addition, some types of principal transactions require the dealer to report the amount of the markup charged. Large retail firms generally report the markup as the equivalent of a comparable commission for an exchange transaction at that price. In most cases, however, OTC executions are reported on a net basis. Thus, for almost all bond purchases and sales, as well as the majority of OTC equity trades, the customer receives only an indication that the executing firm is acting as dealer and the net price.

It may appear elementary, but the first item to note is the actual receipt of the confirmation. Brokers are obligated to mail these promptly, and delays longer than those customarily attributed to the mail should be questioned. Tardy mailing on a regular basis may suggest an operations problem with the broker and could be an early warning of later processing problems. In such a case the customer might consider the transfer of her account to a firm with more efficient processing. More dangerous, perhaps, is the unethical practice of not mailing confirmations to customers because the execution price may be different from that reported to the customer, or worse, because the confirmation reports a trade not authorized by the customer. There have been a number of reported situations where a registered representative, with the collusion of clerical employees, has arranged for confirmations to be sent only to himself or to an address where he alone could collect the mail.

Presuming nothing of this nature is involved, however, the customer should still scrutinize confirmations. A purchase reported as a sale (or vice versa) can result in a substantial loss if not quickly corrected. Even though the customer may not be at fault, the resolution of mistaken reports or executions is often time-consuming and expensive. Reports of the wrong numbers of shares or bonds should also be dealt with quickly. One should not assume that such errors are self-correcting, as they rarely are.

Customers are sometimes confused by the standard terminology employed in confirming trades. For example, when a firm has acted as dealer for a purchase, the confirmation typically reports: "As principal, we sold to you _____" (Figure 11–7). Seeing the word *sold* the customer may think there has been an error, when in fact there has been none. Likewise, the lack of a commission charge may lead inexperienced investors to think that the confirmation contains an error of omission (one, however, that they are unlikely to bring to the representative's attention). In fact, the markup on such trades is almost always larger than a brokerage commission involving the same dollar amount.

Exchange-executed sale orders also carry a small SEC fee (three cents per $100), which is also charged if a listed stock is sold in the OTC market. Because the fee is not charged on ordinary OTC trades, customers sometimes question the reason for the deduction. The fee is actually the primary source of funding for the SEC, which is empowered to collect it under the Securities Exchange Act of 1934.

Options orders should be carefully checked for the proper notation of *opening* or *closing* transactions. A customer with a long position must enter a *closing sale* order to reduce or eliminate that position. For example, if the representative had mismarked the order ticket, the confirmation may reflect an *opening sale*, creating a simultaneous long and short position in the option instead of closing out the original position. Such

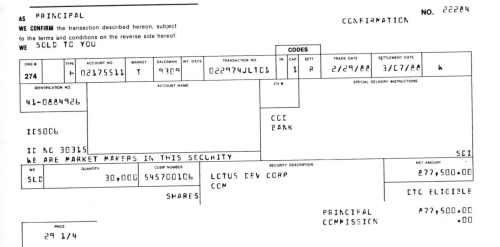

| AS | PRINCIPAL | | | | | | | | | | | | CONFIRMATION | | NO. 22284 |

WE **CONFIRM** the transaction described hereon, subject to the terms and conditions on the reverse side hereof.

WE SOLD TO YOU

						CODES					
ORG #	TYPE	ACCOUNT NO.	MARKET	SALESMAN	INT. DAYS	TRANSACTION NO.	TR	CAP	SETT	TRADE DATE	SETTLEMENT DATE
274	H	02175511	T	9309		022974JLTC1	1	R		2/29/88	3/07/88	h

IDENTIFICATION NO. 41-0884926

ICS006

IC NC 30315

WE ARE MARKET MAKERS IN THIS SECURITY

ACCOUNT NAME

CH #   CCI PANK

SPECIAL DELIVERY INSTRUCTIONS

SCI

WE	QUANTITY	CUSIP NUMBER	SECURITY DESCRIPTION	NET AMOUNT
SLD	30,000	545700106	LCTUS CEV CORP CCM	877,500.00

SHARES

PRICE 29 1/4

CTC ELIGIBLE

PRINCIPAL   877,500.00
CCMMISSION   .00

FIGURE 11-7 Sample confirmation.

errors can compound themselves quickly if not soon caught because an unintended short position may receive an exercise notice calling on the customer to satisfy the exercise with either a cash or securities deposit.

If shares are exchange-listed the customer may compare his execution price with the trading range for that stock as shown in a comprehensive financial newspaper like *The Wall Street Journal* or *Investor's Daily*, or the business section of the *New York Times*. Errors in such reports are not frequent, but any sale price below the day's reported low or purchase price above the day's reported high should be questioned. Because odd lot executions and those made using the NYSE's SuperDOT or similar automated systems may be executed on a bid or offer price instead of a sale, some execution prices may fall outside the day's range by 1/8 or 1/4 of a point, but should not be further distant from the indicated range.

It is more difficult to ascertain the execution price exclusive of the markup in many OTC transactions. This is particularly true with municipal bond orders and those for low priced or obscure shares not listed in the NASD's *National Market System*. If the investor is a sizable buyer of municipal bonds, he should examine a copy of the *Blue List* which is available in most well-run branch offices. Although the specific bonds the customer seeks may not be quoted, there are usually a number of issues of similar quality, coupon, and maturity. A reasonably accurate estimate of comparable prices can be obtained from this source. Exact price comparisons should not be expected, but if the customer suspects an excessive markup, a good arguing point might be so established. This is not to suggest that one should question every municipal execution price; it may not be worth the trouble. On the other hand, an informed customer quickly becomes known as one who will not accept any price without question. This demonstration of knowledge (as opposed to the carping of the chronic malcontent customer) may lessen the chances of an excessive markup.

ACCOUNT STATEMENTS

Customers with securities accounts must be sent a statement of account for any month in which there has been an entry in the account. An entry includes any transaction, receipt of a dividend or an interest payment, interest charges, or any cash or securities deposit or withdrawal. If no entry has been made, a statement must be sent at least quarterly so long as a cash or securities position remains in the account.

As with all documents connected with securities accounts, account statements should be examined with diligence. The statement shows all account activity during the period it covers. Sometimes customers become confused with the dates of securities transactions as they appear on the statement. Brokerage statements generally reflect *settlement* dates of trades, not the date of the execution of the order. Thus, for typical "regular way" stock or bond transactions, the trade date is actually five business days (a normal calendar week) prior to date shown on the statement. Transactions that occur near the end of the month, therefore, may not appear because they settle in the following month and will appear on that month's statement. The reason for this seemingly perverse practice is quite logical. Money and securities from trades do not enter into or exit from the account until the settlement date. From an accounting viewpoint they remain in the account until delivered out or received in.

Suppose, for example, that a margin customer sells a securities position on the last business day of the month. His stock will appear long in the account for another week, and he will be charged interest until the proceeds of the sale offset part or all of his debit balance five business days later. Consequently, the customer will receive an interest charge on his statement for the first week of the next month and may feel this is unfair, the securities having been sold before the month began.

Aside from routine (but important) reviews for the proper crediting of dividends and interest, customers should examine carefully all transaction reports and compare them with confirmations. An entry not corresponding to the customer's records should be reported at once. An occasional key punch error in the data entry process may result in the report of a trade executed in a different account. On the other hand, it may also reflect an unauthorized discretionary trade by the representative. Such questions should not be left to resolve themselves. If the position or monetary result of the action has not been corrected by the receipt of the next monthly statement, the customer should phone the office manager (*not* the registered representative) and follow the phone call with a written complaint. The customer should demand a *written* acknowledgment that the account entry was made in error and will be corrected on the next statement.

The customer should also check cash credit balances and be watchful for unauthorized cash withdrawals. Although the practice is not common, it happens with a frequency disturbing enough for customers to be vigilant. If a representative or a clerical employee diverts money or securities from a customer's account to his own, the matter may become a criminal one involving theft. A suspicion that this is happening should be reported at once.

As a general rule, customers should not leave significant credit balances with a brokerage firm unless a reasonable rate of interest is paid. Brokers are not obligated to pay interest on credit balances, but some will do so if the customer insists. A number of firms, including all the large national retail ones, offer a "cash management" or "sweep" account which automatically rolls cash credit balances into a money market mutual fund. If credit balances are placed in such funds they are less accessible to those with no right to them. In addition the customer can earn a rate of return comparable to that available on money market securities, and usually somewhat greater than that which can be earned on money market deposit accounts offered by banks.

If the customer has a margin account he will sometimes notice different interest rates charged for certain periods within the month. As noted earlier, brokers base their lending rates on the broker loan rate. This rate changes periodically, and the revised rates are applied to customer debit balances as the rates change.

Statements for options accounts carried on margin must provide additional information. If there are open options positions as of the settlement date, statements must provide mark-to-market prices and the market value of any other security positions in the account. The total market value of all securities and the margin account equity must also be revealed. The statement must bear a legend requesting the customer to advise the broker promptly in the event of any material change in investment objective or financial situation. Unfortunately, this warning is usually printed in fine print boilerplate language on the back of the statement. Although it is likely that few customers take the time to do so, those so affected should notify the broker. Failure to do so may weaken a later charge of unsuitability. If, for example, the customer claims that the types of transactions once undertaken in the account are now unsuitable because of lessened ability to bear risk, the broker will be able to produce copies of statements bearing this legend and note that the customer did not inform it of any change in circumstances.

Options customers should also examine transactions for the proper opening and closing designations (Figure 11–8). As previously noted, errors in option order entry can create problems which are unusually difficult to rectify. These problems are often magnified by the fact that "regular way" settlement of options trades is one business day, and by the possibility that options may either expire or be exercised. Resolution of errors after either of these events has occurred is more difficult than the correction of errors involving existing positions. A detailed review of both confirmations and statements can help prevent minor errors from becoming major problems.

CUSTOMER ACCOUNT NO 017 665738 203 PAGE 22 OF 102

STATEMENT PERIOD		FINANCIAL SUMMARY		YTD INCOME SUMMARY
BEGINNING	10-01-87	1194090.64CR	356381.96CR	
ENDING	10-30-87			
SOC SEC I D NO				

DATE	BOUGHT RECEIVED OR LONG	SOLD DELIVERED OR SHORT	DESCRIPTION	TICKER SYMBOL	TYPE	PRICE OR ENTRY	AMOUNT CHARGED	AMOUNT CREDITED
			OPENING TRANSACTION					
10-15-87		40	CALL JOHNSON JOHNSON		1	8 1/4		323[illegible]
			APR 085					
			OPENING TRANSACTION					
10-16-87	40		CALL JOHNSON JOHNSON		1	1/4	1060.00	
			OCT 090					
			CLOSING TRANSACTION					
10-16-87		10	CALL KERR MCGEE		1	2 1/4		2204.92
			JAN 045					
			OPENING TRANSACTION					
10-16-87	10		CALL KERR MCGEE		1	1/8	140.00	
			OCT 045					
			CLOSING TRANSACTION					
10-15-87		35	CALL LILLY ELI		1	5 7/8		20404.31
			JAN 090					
			OPENING TRANSACTION					
10-15-87	35		CALL LILLY ELI		1	1/16	271.25	
			OCT 095					
			CLOSING TRANSACTION					
10-15-87	8		CALL LITTON		1	1/16	62.00	
			OCT 100					
			CLOSING TRANSACTION					
10-16-87		4	CALL LITTON		1	4 5/8		1831.93
			DEC 095					
			OPENING TRANSACTION					

2574 (CR) Rev. 4/86

SEE REVERSE SIDE FOR IMPORTANT INFORMATION CONCERNING THIS STATEMENT

PLEASE RETAIN THIS COPY FOR YOUR INCOME TAX RECORDS

FIGURE 11–8 Sample statement.

EQUITY

OPEN	25,039.93CR
CLOSE	25,129.13CR
T-BILLS	

ACCOUNT BALANCES

TYPE	OPENING	CLOSING
1-REG. FUTURES	36,833.90CR	31,343.62CR
4-REG. OPTIONS	2,278.43CR	1,298.61CR
TOTAL	39,112.33CR	32,642.23CR

GAIN/LOSS

FUTURES/FGN CURR

UNREALIZED	MARCH	4,192.00 LOSS
REALIZED	MARCH	5,193.45 LOSS
REALIZED	YR-TO-DTE	9,015.74 LOSS

OPTIONS

REALIZED	MARCH	4,663.62 GAIN
REALIZED	YR-TO-DTE	11,269.82 GAIN

RFC

REALIZED	MARCH	5,193.45 LOSS
REALIZED	YR-TO-DTE	9,015.74 LOSS

IRS WITHHOLDING MTD YTD

VARIOUS CHARGES

	NFA ASSESSMENTS	OTHER FEES	TAXES	INTEREST	DELIVERY CHARGES
MARCH	1.72	11.65			

CASH ACTIVITY

TYPE	DATE	DESCRIPTION	AMOUNT
1	03 21	TRF TO SEC L0905137	296.83
		TOTAL CASH ACTIVITY	296.83

TYPE	P&S DATE	DESCRIPTION	BOT	SOLD	TRD DATE	TRD PRICE	DIFF	P&S COMMISSION	TAX	NFA-ASSESS	OTHER	FEES	REALIZED GAIN/LOSS
1	03 01	CT MAY88 SUGAR 11	1		11-03-87	757.00		IRS REPORTABLE					
				1	03-01-88	805.00	537.60CR						
		**** TOTAL ****						60.00	.28	2.25			475.07CR
1	03 08	CT APR88 SWT CRUDE	1		01-15-88	1658.00		IRS REPORTABLE					
			1		03-04-88	1700.00	ASN						
			2	2	03-08-88	1538.00	2,820.00						
		**** TOTAL ****						120.00	.56	5.40			2,945.96
1	03 17	BU MAR88 SOYBEANS	5		03-17-88	620		IRS REPORTABLE					
				5	02-18-88	550	3,500.00 ASN						
		**** TOTAL ****						60.00	.28	1.00			3,561.28
1	03 17	BU MAY88 SOYBEANS	5		02-02-88	611 1/2		IRS REPORTABLE					
				5	03-17-88	629 1/2	900.00CR						
		**** TOTAL ****						60.00	.28	1.00			830.72CR
		******* TOTAL REALIZED GAIN/LOSS FOR MARCH											5,193.45

FIGURE 11-9 Sample statement of account.

OPTIONS ACTIVITY

TYPE	DATE	BOT	SOLD	DESCRIPTION	TRADE PRICE	PREMIUM	COMMISSION	TAX/OTHER	NFA	NET
4	03 15		1	CALL CME LIVE CATTLE APR88 STR PR 640.00 EXPIRES 03/25/88 ASSIGNED	300					
4	03 25		1	PUT CME LIVE CATTLE APR88 STR PR 660.00 EXPIRES 03/25/88 EXPIRED						916.11
4	03 11	1		PUT CEI GOLD JUN88 STR 440.00 EXPIRES 05/13/88 CONT SIZE 100 OZS	880.00	880.00	35.20	.75	.16	
4	03 15	1		CALL NY SUGAR 11 MAY88 STR PR 10.00 EXPIRES 04/08/88 CONT SIZE 11200 LBS	4.00	44.80	17.50	1.25	.16	63.71

OPTIONS ACTIVITY

TYPE	DATE	BOT	SOLD	DESCRIPTION	TRADE PRICE	PREMIUM	COMMISSION	TAX/OTHER	NFA	NET
4	03 04		1	CALL NYM SWT CRUDE APR88 STR PR 17.00 EXPIRES 03/04/88 EXPIRED	82.00					
4	03 04		1	PUT NYM SWT CRUDE APR88 STR PR 17.00 EXPIRES 03/04/88 ASSIGNED						

**** TOTAL OPTIONS ACTIVITY 979.82

YOUR OPEN POSITIONS

TYPE	DATE	QUANTITY LONG/SHORT	DESCRIPTION	TRADE PRICE	MARKET PRICE	UNREALIZED GAIN/LOSS	MARKET VALUE
1 ASN	03 15	1	CT APR88 LIVECATTL	6400	7490	4,360.00	
4	02 02	1	CT MAY88 SUGAR 11	875.00	888.00	168.00CR	
4	02 04	1	CALL CBT SOYBEANS MAY88 STR PR 6.25 EXPIRES 04/23/88	18	33	IN THE MONEY	1,650.00
4	02 25	1	PUT CBT SOYBEANS MAY88 STR PR 6.25 EXPIRES 04/23/88	17 1/2	4 3/4	1,425.00	237.50
4	11 24	1	CALL NY SUGAR 11 MAY88 STR PR 8.00 EXPIRES 04/08/88	74.00	90.00	IN THE MONEY	1,008.00
4	12 18	1	CALL NY SUGAR 11 MAY88 STR PR 9.00 EXPIRES 04/08/88	69.00	12.00	985.60	134.40
4	02 01	1	PUT NY SUGAR 11 MAY88 STR PR 9.00 EXPIRES 04/08/88	82.00	26.00	IN THE MONEY	291.20

****** TOTAL UNREALIZED FUTURES/FGN CURR GAIN/LOSS 4,192.00
****** TOTAL MARKET VALUE 3,321.10
****** ACCOUNT NET WORTH 25,129.13CR

FIGURE 11-9 (continued)

Futures Accounts

Virtually everything so far discussed concerning securities accounts is applicable to futures accounts. The main differences between the accounts are: (1) futures accounts have no settlement date in the securities sense because the funds involved are margin deposits, not payments for the transfer of ownership; and (2) futures accounts must display a profit and loss (p&l) figure every time a position is closed out. Although futures statements may appear more difficult to comprehend than securities account statements, they provide more information in readily understandable form about the current account status (Figure 11-9). A customer examining the monthly p&l reports should have a good understanding of what her success or lack thereof has been. There have been recurring cases of customers "suddenly" discovering that their account equity was virtually wiped out, despite the fact that they have been receiving monthly statements explaining the deteriorating situation for months, or even years.

Because the typical securities investor is not likely to be very knowledgeable about futures trading, statements should be reviewed in detail with the representative (or some other informed party) upon receipt. Putting the statement aside as incomprehensible and resting on the representative's assurance that all is fine opens the door for catastrophe.

12

The Customer's Responsibilities

All problems between brokers and their clients cannot be prevented. Each side, however, can take steps that can materially reduce the number of disputes or reduce the damages of those which are not prevented.

This chapter will suggest some attitudes and actions that can help customers avoid trouble and better handle that which they could not avoid. Many customers who are aware of the fiduciary duty owed to them by their brokers rely upon it for protection too heavily. A pedestrian hit by a truck in a crosswalk finds small comfort in the fact that he had the right-of-way.

EXPECTATIONS

Substantial problems arise simply because customers expect more from a broker than can actually be delivered. It is not uncommon for customers to indicate that they are primarily interested in safety of principal, but also wish to increase substantially their income or capital despite the widespread understanding that these goals are conflicting and mutually exclusive. There is nothing wrong with participating in such speculative instruments as common stocks or futures, but a customer would have to be quite naive to enter markets in such instruments if safety were really a primary objective.

Of course sometimes inflated expectations result from a salesperson's unreasonable representations, but even in such cases, informed customers may recognize them as unreasonable. It is not unusual for customers to ask financial salespeople what returns can be expected from a particular investment, or by following an investment strategy. Salespeople accommodate them by indicating results that might be expected. Evidence may vary from a long-term validated track record to vague assurances by salespersons based on their long but undocumented experience, or even on pure conjecture. The differences among these is not great because none are really worth much anyhow. Reputable sellers of financial products are among the first to warn that for many reasons (some are discussed below) satisfactory past performance is no guarantee of satisfactory future results. Even when disclaimers are made customers have a tendency to take projections as promises or guarantees of favorable results.

Those who enter the financial markets should not lose sight of some basic truisms. Probably most important is recognition of the fact that if potential investment returns are high, accompanying risks are at least as high and probably are higher. This does not mean that a customer who chooses to seek high returns along with the high accompanying risk is making a mistake. Such customers, however, should beware of naive or unscrupulous salespeople who assert that high risk need not accompany high expected returns, and that they have a means of offering high returns with relatively little or even no risk. Customers who choose to rely upon such assertions should at least suggest that they be placed in writing and become quite cautious if offered an excuse why such written assertions cannot be provided.

It should also be noted the market is either efficient or close enough to efficiency to make financial success difficult. (See Chapter 1.) The customer therefore should be wary of representations that the research department of a given firm has an outstanding record of outperforming the overall market over an extended period. Even if figures that are presented are accurate, they may be highly misleading. Raw figures of successful performance might be offered covering periods during which the market was strong and in which the results of investments chosen at random would look equally good. A small firm might have specialized in investments in a particular industry during a period when that industry outperformed the market. The individual who made the selections might have recently left the firm or have suffered a recent breakdown of his mental faculties. In a word, some track records are based on false figures.

Some are misleading because of their self-serving choices of date or failure to consider all variables leading to successful performance. Some
cover too short a period to be meaningful. None, however, are predictive
and all respectable firms will assert that in the form of a disclaimer
(hedge clause). This should not be taken to mean that many firms would
not like to offer ideas which would provide profits to their customers. It is
merely that the market absorbs information too rapidly to permit firms to
prepare and distribute a timely report of an overvalued or undervalued
opportunity. It should also be noted that many research departments are
maintained to serve customers who insist on asking questions concerning potentially great opportunities or for expert forecasts on market
direction. Disappointing results which frequently follow might well have
been caused more by the unreasonable questions asked than by the
equally unreasonable answers provided.

Many of the same comments apply to representations made by
salespeople concerning their own ability to outperform the market, or
their own firm's research. Some salespeople indicate that they have
devised effective proprietary technical methods, have valuable personal contacts, unusually effective trading techniques, or esoteric
strategies that will inevitably lead to outstanding gains for their
clients. Any effort to get descriptions of these in writing will usually
result in assertions that this is not possible for any of a number of
reasons. If anything is actually written, any forecasts will usually be
either far less attractive or will be accompanied by the ubiquitious
hedge clause which will say in effect, that nothing written is to be
relied upon so far as expectations are concerned.

Losses resulting from trades based upon unreasonable projections
by a broker's personnel might well be recoverable. Nevertheless it is
far better to avoid the losses than to rely on expensive time-consuming,
stressful disputes after the fact.

CHOOSING A FIRM AND THE REGISTERED REPRESENTATIVE

The intelligent selection of a brokerage firm is much like the choice of a
physician, dentist, attorney, accountant, or anyone else rendering a professional service. Professionals who are basically honest and reliable have
good reputations. Those who lie and cheat eventually become known for
doing so. The potential customer therefore is well advised to ask informed people about their experience with brokerage houses, and in general terms what their experience has been. It is strange that people who
are reluctant to dine in a restaurant because they know little or nothing

about it will place their lives' savings with financial firms based on an advertisement or unsolicited telephone calls.

Even if a firm is basically reliable, there are certain to be wide variations in the quality of its sales personnel. There may be great differences in experience, attitudes toward service, intelligence, and integrity. The best firms often find themselves in trouble with their clients because of actions taken by their salespeople ranging from misjudgments to downright dishonesty. The firm may suffer great losses because the salespeople who caused the problems said things or did things in the name of the company that should not have been said or done, particularly if the company is deemed to have been deficient in its training or supervisory practices.

Customers should expend some time and thought in selecting the salesperson as well as the firm. For those who prefer full-service firms, it is not required that one deal with the person who happens to answer a telephone or is referred by a receptionist. It is not unreasonable to request an interview with the office manager to help select a salesperson who can best serve the needs of the customer. If a manager will not take the time to help develop satisfactory relationships with new customers, it is likely that the wrong firm was chosen by the customer in the first place.

It is not unusual to rely upon a friend to recommend a brokerage firm with which she has had a favorable relationship. Even such a personal recommendation does not eliminate the need for one to investigate further and make one's own decision. The objectives and interests of one client might lead to a satisfactory relationship with a salesperson; a client with different objectives and interests or a different personality might have an unsatisfactory relationship with the same salesperson.

OPENING THE ACCOUNT

Customers who open accounts at a brokerage house are given one or more documents to read and sign. They also provide information for other documents to be completed by salespersons for the firm's records. It is all too common for customers to read the forms casually or not at all, ask few or no questions, provide misinformation on those that are submitted, and not obtain and preserve a copy of the forms. Unless they are rushed through the process or told that the forms are actually meaningless red tape, they may find later that failure to read or understand a form is not a good defense if a dispute develops. It could have been read and questions could have been asked.

Financial markets have been operating for a long time. Entering the market a few minutes sooner at the expense of understanding what is signed can be an extremely expensive purchase of time. It is wise to make certain that one understands the implications of each form signed. If a form requires more than one signature it usually means that it covers more than one subject, and is in effect more than one form. Margin agreements, risk disclosure agreements, arbitration agreements, powers of attorney, and other documents are discussed in detail in Chapters 5 and 11, but the point here is that they should not be executed lightly. If a signature indicates that the signer certifies that what is on the documents has been read and is understood, the need for understanding such documents is even greater than usual. If one is uncomfortable with the implications of some of the documents, it is worth the time to discuss them with a sophisticated but disinterested third party before trading begins.

Information given for the personal information form should be accurate. Financial information and trading experience should not be understated or, even worse, overstated. It is difficult enough for a brokerage firm to obey the rules requiring that solicited positions be suitable. Providing the firm with misleading information makes its task even more difficult. Making one's objectives clear and accurate is still more important for the same reason.

Customers should be given and should preserve copies of everything signed. Even if they were originally signed in some haste, documents can be read more carefully before they are filed away. Warnings of risk in options and futures accounts should be absorbed and taken seriously. If documents are not clear, questions should be asked before, rather than after, trading begins.

Special thought should be given to the signing of a power of attorney (trading authorization) which allows a representative of a brokerage firm to act for a customer without prior consultation. If a customer is difficult or impossible to contact, such a document sometimes may be desirable, perhaps for a brief period, but it should never be granted lightly. If a long-term satisfactory relationship with a salesperson has developed and the trading strategy utilized requires speed or follows easily identifiable and clear signals, trading authorizations may be justified. Even under such circumstances problems may still result. Given enough market adversity the most satisfactory relations may become quite unsatisfactory.

It is wise for a new customer to inquire as to the nature of the types of orders that might be utilized and the information presented in trade confirmations and statements that will be received when trading begins. Questions can be asked about credit rules, dividend and interest procedures, or anything else of interest. Problems based on miscommunication and lack of understanding are all too common. Many can be forestalled.

Some trading strategies are quite difficult to absorb and all written communications cannot be comprehended by all customers, but an effort should be made to achieve maximum clarification. Customers should read forms and booklets given to them and ask questions. Salespersons should give oral and written information to their new customers and not try to create the illusion that the brokerage procedures and trading strategies are so esoteric that they are beyond the grasp of any mortals except for brokerage house personnel.

A general rule for customers might well be: "If you don't understand it, don't do it, and if you feel you must do it anyhow, get it in writing."

AFTER TRADING BEGINS

The role to be played by the registered representative should be made clear before trading begins. If a customer wants to make her own decisions, the salesperson need only act as an order taker and service the account in a mechanical sense. The customer has a right to assume that orders are placed promptly and accurately and are followed up conscientiously. Account status reports should be available and should be accurate. It is reasonable for a customer to ask what her market and credit positions are. If her salesperson is unavailable, someone else should be able to service her needs promptly. If the customer desires to be kept informed by telephone of market events, order executions, or account cash and equity balances, this should be done accurately and promptly. Of course, if the customer's account is small enough and the market is active enough, there might be different conceptions of what is reasonable.

When the salesperson participates in the decision-making process, the possibility of problems becomes much greater. There is no guarantee that opinions rendered by personnel of brokerage houses are any better than those of anyone else, but there is no question that such opinions should be reasonably based. If such opinions are based upon the output of the firm's research department, they may not necessarily be worth much, but it is generally reasonable for a salesperson to communicate such opinions. If the salesperson is relying upon such sources as his own technical analysis or upon his own published or personal sources, he had better have some justification for relying upon them. A customer has a right to assume that opinions are informed and if a salesperson has no confident opinion that he will frankly say so. The customer, however, should have no illusion that the salesperson or his firm have market information or judgment approaching infallibility. Sometimes unreasonable answers are given in response to unreasonable questions. It is primarily the salesperson's responsibility to make certain that orders are clear. If a customer initiates an order, however, it is good practice to have the salesperson read it back to make certain that a buy does not become a sell, quantities and prices are correct, and any special instructions are clear. As always, taking accurate and contemporaneous notes is wise. Customers who generally follow their broker's advice have every right to assume that information is accurate and opinions are reasonably based and given in good faith. Customers who largely direct their own trading, however, hardly have the right to blame their broker after the fact for anything that might go wrong.

After a trade has been made, it is usual for brokerage firms to mail a confirmation to the customer. The latter all too often does not take the time to make certain the confirmation is correct, but merely files it or throws it away. It is wise to check the confirmation for accuracy and then file it. If there is an error of any kind, the broker should be notified promptly and a dated record kept of when the broker was called and what was said. If a salesperson appears to be avoiding a solution, a complaint should be made to management, preferably in writing and sent by certified mail. Such action might reduce the chance of the broker later alleging that any wrongdoing was ratified by the customer or that the customer delayed action too long after discovering a problem. When the monthly statement is received it is good practice for the customer to check the confirmations against it to make certain that all trades and money transactions made during the statement period appear properly and that no items appear on the statement that do not belong there. Again, any errors should be reported promptly and a record kept of the communication. If an adjustment does not appear promptly, a follow-up request should be made by letter.

It is usual for brokerage houses to mail *activity letters* to customers from time to time. Such letters are sent to customers who maintain especially active accounts as measured by the frequency or size of trading or by commissions generated. The letters usually request the customer to respond if any problems are perceived or to confirm that she is satisfied with the handling of her account, which is why it is sometimes called a *happiness letter*. If a customer is satisfied, she need merely sign and return the copy as requested. If, however, the letter suggests that trading is unusually active and if the account is controlled by the salesperson, the signed copy should not be given quite so freely. If it appears later that the account was traded abusively, the brokerage house will utilize the approved activity letters or failure to complain when invited to do so as an indication that the customer was satisfied with the handling of the account. Unless the customer was pressured, misinformed about the nature of the transactions in the account, or rushed into signing such letters, they may well be an effective defense.

IF PROBLEMS ARISE

The nature of a problem may help direct a customer toward an effective resolution. Routine errors involving confirmations or statements should be handled by the salesperson. Examples of such errors involve missing or erroneous confirmations, erroneous entries on statements, and failures to indicate receipt of stock certificates or checks within a reasonable time. If the salesperson does not succeed in correcting such problems promptly and satisfactorily, the customer can then speak with the local branch manager not only to correct the problem but also to assign a new salesperson with more concern for his customers.

Problems that involve the salesperson may be more serious. Examples include rendering unreasonable opinions, offering false or misleading information about investment instruments or trading strategies, churning the account, trading without authorization, handling orders improperly, inducing customers to trade in a manner which is unsuitable and inconsistent with an agreed upon trading strategy, or even absconding with the customer's money or securities.

In such cases any effort to arrive at a satisfactory solution usually begins with the local manager, assuming that he is not the cause of the problem. A customer could write a letter explaining what she perceives to be wrong and request that a reply be made by a given date. The letter itself should be sent certified with a return receipt requested to memorialize the time of the complaint. It is also possible to telephone or visit the manager, in which case notes should be made of when the contact was made and what transpired. If it is desired to bypass the manager, or if the manager does not act to resolve the problem, the customer can write to the firm's president. Here again, it is wise to use certified mail.

If the customer perceives herself to be seriously damaged or mistreated, it may be desirable to seek out counsel at an early stage. Letters written by a layperson may be less effective than those written by a professional. Sometimes what is said in such letters may even later be used successfully against the writer.

Customers may also reduce their chance of achieving satisfactory resolution of claims by acting too slowly. They may be deemed to have ratified actions simply by waiting too long in some cases, or by continuing to trade with the same broker. They may also be accused of failing to mitigate damages by acting too slowly. At the worst, they may run afoul of statutes of limitations if their disputes are ultimately arbitrated or tried in a court.

An attorney or other representative to be utilized in an arbitration should be selected carefully. The previous discussion concerning the experience and competence of brokers applies equally to counsel. They differ considerably in experience, competence, and cost. In legal disputes brokerage houses use either internal counsel or outside counsel who tend to specialize in financial disputes. A customer's counsel who is not usually involved in litigation or who has little experience in financial instruments may be at a serious disadvantage, particularly if she does not utilize competent co-counsel or an experienced expert witness.

Some customers represent themselves at reparations hearings, arbitrations, and even in courts. Although this may reduce expenses, most such customers do not handle their own cases too well and should take this course only if the amount of damage involved is too small to justify professional help.

SUMMARY

Nothing can be done by a customer to prevent all problems in the financial arena, but some knowledge and common sense can reduce their number and the damage resulting from them.

Most personnel of brokerage houses are honest and ethical, but some are not. Brokerage house revenue is derived from activity and not customer profits. Salespeople do not really know where markets are going, although too many are more than ready to render baseless opinions. Accordingly customers are well advised not to place their trust blindly in people they hardly know. They should keep in mind that advice might be given in good faith but might also be self-serving, baseless, or downright false. They should not consider opinions to be guarantees.

Documents should be read before they are signed, and certainly before trading begins. Being rushed into signing forms or being assured that they are meaningless are common danger signs. If something is not clear, questions should be asked and answers should be offered graciously. Salespeople who make assurances concerning profits or control of losses should be asked to put the assurances in writing. As a minimum the customer should write a letter to the broker indicating her understanding of any such assurances.

Communications from the broker should be reviewed and filed. Discrepancies should be reported promptly and a written record should be maintained of any such reporting. If serious problems are suspected, the customer should compose for her record a narrative of the events surrounding the problem. Time quickly dulls one's recollections of events which might later make satisfactory resolution more difficult or even impossible. If competent advice from an advisor such as an attorney or consultant is sought, it should be secured as quickly as possible.

13

General Rules and Their Sources

DEMYSTIFYING THE LEGAL ANALYSIS

The object of this chapter is not to make the customer or broker an expert in the law, but to illustrate how general everyday principles apply to the relationship between customers and brokers. Brokers, for example, could avoid creating unhappy customers by adhering to the simple rule of employing the utmost in good faith, honesty, full disclosure, and fair dealing with their customers. In the discussion of the general rules which follows, there will be virtually no rule which does not encompass these basic principles. For customers, the rules should be clear when viewed in this light and combined with common sense. If a customer didn't understand the risks of a transaction, then there may have been a failure of the full disclosure principle. Attorneys who are not familiar with the securities laws are often guilty of abandoning their training when confronted with what appears to be a securities law case, when principles of general law would apply nicely (at least in the preliminary analysis of a client's case). For all concerned, it is best to start with basic principles, then look to the securities laws for specific rules which may apply.

As an overview, the general rules which apply to brokers are no different than in many other relationships. A person injured in an auto accident due to the negligence of another, for example, is in no different situation than a customer whose broker has negligently failed to execute an order which has caused a loss. A customer whose account has been churned may view churning as analogous to embezzlement, theft, or fraud in other contexts. Brokers who fail to disclose material facts (usually about the risks of a transaction) may be likened to a real estate broker who fails to disclose that the home a client wishes to purchase is built over a nuclear waste site.

Criticism of the analogies and the technical analysis of the customer's potential legal claims is possible, but the point is that customers, brokers, and even attorneys should not throw away their common sense in viewing possible breaches of the rules. If it walks like a duck, acts like a duck, and flies like a duck, it probably is a duck. Woodrow Wilson, in a speech in Washington on February 26, 1916, said: "Justice has nothing to do with expediency. Justice has nothing to do with any temporary standard whatever. It is rooted and grounded in the fundamental instincts of humanity."[1] The proof of the fundamental basis of the law is illustrated by the fact that heretofore most disputes have been settled in court cases before juries.

A Los Angeles attorney well known for his representation of customers makes the following salient point in his closing arguments before a jury regarding its role in deciding apparently complex legal cases:

> When mankind wants to do the mundane things like measure the depth of the ocean or chart the stars, that is when mankind hires its experts.
> When civilization wants to do something really important, that is when it employs 12 people like you who know nothing about the law. Just such a thing was done, if I recall correctly, by the founder of Christianity, 12 ordinary people off the streets.[2]

If there is one thing which is remembered about this chapter it should be that if 12 ordinary citizens from any community can decide complex cases (involving churning, suitability, options and futures) then brokers, customers, and even attorneys should begin their analysis of any dispute by employing their own common sense. If a broker has to ask whether the opening of an account is suitable for a retired person

---

[1] Burton Stevenson, *The Home Book of Quotations*, 10th ed. (New York: Dodd, Mead & Company, 1967), 1028.

[2] With permission of Timothy Sargent, Esq., Bodkin, McCarthy, Sargent & Smith (Los Angeles).

whose life savings are going to be used for highly speculative investments on the broker's recommendation, then it is likely the nonexpert
jury will have the same question and will answer it based upon their
good, common, everyday sense of what is right and what is wrong.

Common sense should be the guide for brokers and customers. Let
the attorneys attempt to discern the fine points, and keep your eye on
general principles and moral standards as a guide.

THE RULES ARE CONSTANTLY EVOLVING

The relationship of stockbrokers and their clients is one which has been
developing as long as some people have acted as agents for others. Before
there were written rules, brokers acted upon custom and trade practice.
Once exchanges were organized, these customs and trade practices were
encompassed by exchange rules. And, eventually, legislators established
special statutes covering brokers and securities transactions. Prior to
1933, the law pertaining to stockbrokers had three general sources: the
common law, exchange rules, and the state statutes related to securities
transactions.

One of the early attempts to describe the rules for stockbrokers and
customers was made by Charles H. Meyer in *The Law of Stockbrokers
and Stock Exchanges,* published in 1931 and now sadly out of print. Mr.
Meyer's introduction to his book wrestles with some of the same problems as are discussed herein.

> The body of the law relating to brokers who deal in securities on
> exchanges is derived from three sources: (1) judicial decisions, (2)
> statutes, (3) exchange rules. The authoritativeness of the first two of
> these sources is obvious. The third is of nearly equal importance by rea-
> son of the judicial sanction which it has been accorded. The rules of an
> exchange constitute a contract between the members of the exchange.
> They enter into and form a part of every purchase and sale made on the
> exchange. As between the members of the exchange, therefore, they
> have the force of law. They are binding also, subject to qualifications
> which we shall discuss in the text of this volume, on non-members who
> entrust their business to members for execution. . . .
>
> A word of caution is in order as to the status of the case law pre-
> vailing in this country at the time of the writing of this volume. Al-
> though the broad general doctrines of stockbrokerage law may be
> regarded as fairly well established, there remain many questions, some
> of which arise quite commonly, which are not yet wholly settled.
> . . . Moreover, this branch of the law is to some extent still in a state

of evolution. The tendency of our courts is to keep their decisions in conformity with the necessities of modern business and to progress as business progresses. This aim, if it be the aim of the courts, has perhaps not been wholly achieved. Nevertheless, new principles are being developed, and old ones are being amplified or qualified and at times even discarded. Adjudicated decisions must be read in the light of this progress. There is much room for new law, and new law is constantly in the making.[3]

A classic example of a rule in the process of evolution from custom and practice to exchange rule to legislation is the concept of suitability discussed in Chapter 6. The unwritten custom and practice of brokers was that a determination of suitability was the duty of the broker; it eventually became a rule of the NASD when it adopted Article III, Section 2 of its Rules of Fair Practice, and may or may not become a statutory rule.

THE CONCEPT OF DUTY

The rules established by case law express the common sense rules applicable to brokers. The most basic of these rules concern the duties of brokers that result from the relationship they establish with their customers.

To the customer or broker, the legal concept of duty may be unintelligible. Before discussing the general rules, a legal definition of the term *duty* is offered.

> *Duty.* A human action which is exactly conformable to the laws which require us to obey them. Legal or moral obligation. Obligatory conduct or service. Mandatory obligation to perform.
>
> A thing due; that which is due from a person; that which a person owes to another. An obligation to do a thing. A word of more extensive signification than "debt," although both are expressed by the same Latin word "debitum." Sometimes, however, the term is used synonymously with debt.
>
> Those obligations of performance, care, or observance which rest upon a person in an official or fiduciary capacity; as the duty of an executor, trustee, manager, etc.
>
> In negligence cases term may be defined as obligation, to which law will give recognition and effect, to conform to particular standard of

---

[3] Charles H. Meyer, *The Law of Stockbrokers and Stock Exchanges*, (New York: Baker, Voorhis & Co., 1931), 1–2.

conduct toward another. The word "duty" is used throughout the Restatement of Torts to denote the fact that the actor is required to conduct himself in a particular manner at the risk that if he does not do so he becomes subject to liability to another to whom the duty is owed for any injury sustained by such other, of which that actor's conduct is a legal cause. Restatement, Second, Torts Section 4. [Citations omitted.][4]

The general rules discussed in this chapter provide guidelines concerning the types of duties owed by brokers to their customers. Brokers who recommend trading programs which end up losing money for their clients may or may not be responsible for the losses. A broker's legal liability depends upon whether the broker has breached any duties owed to a customer required by the common law, statutes, exchange rules, or custom and trade practice.

AGENCY LAW

In exploring the various duties of brokers to their customers, the focus will be on those duties involving the purchase or sale of a security (or futures contract) for a customer. The status of a broker in the purchase or sale of securities is that of an *agent*, acting on behalf of a *principal* (the customer), in placing the customer's order.

As an agent in a contractual relationship with a customer, the broker must act pursuant to the instructions of the customer. Specific examples of breaches of a broker's duties as an agent would be unauthorized trades, entering orders for quantities in excess of or less than the client's instructions, or at different prices than instructed. In each case, the wrongdoing is simply that the broker breached the duty to follow the customer's instructions. Problems, thus, are abundant when the customer's instructions are unclear, when the broker assumes the customer wishes to trade on margin, and when a broker is unclear about changes in margin requirements.

The Fiduciary Nature of the Relationship

Where the client depends upon the broker's advice or is solicited to purchase a security, additional duties are imposed upon the broker by the fiduciary nature of the relationship. The additional duties required by a fiduciary relationship can be generically described as involving the

---

[4] Black's Law Dictionary, 5th ed. (St. Paul, Minn.: West Publishing Co., 1979), 453.

salesperson's utmost in good faith, honesty, full disclosure, and fair dealing relative to his clients.

Exactly when this fiduciary relationship is imposed is an area of legal dispute. Some view virtually every transaction entered into by a broker for a customer as involving a fiduciary relationship. For example, in *Twomey v. Mitchum, Jones & Templeton, Inc.,*[5] the court countered the defendant's contention that the relationship between the customer and the broker was not a fiduciary one because it had not been described as such in the pleadings.

> This argument completely disregards the following principle: "Confidential and fiduciary relations are, in law, synonymous, and may be said to exist whenever trust and confidence is reposed by one person in the integrity and fidelity of another. . . ."[6]

At the other end of the spectrum, the existence of a fiduciary relationship may only occur where the broker is in de facto control of the investment decisions for an account.[7] Whether characterized as fiduciary obligations or simply as professional duties of a stockbroker, the analysis begins with what duties are owed. Overviews of the broker's duties are sometimes expressed in court decisions.

> Duties associated with a non-discretionary account include: (1) the duty to recommend a stock only after studying it sufficiently to become informed as to its nature, price and financial prognosis. . . . ; (2) the duty to carry out the customer's orders promptly in a manner best suited to serve the customer's interests. . . ; (3) the duty to inform the customer of the risks involved in purchasing or selling a particular security. . . ; (4) the duty to refrain from self-dealing or refusing to disclose any personal interest the broker may have in a particular recommended security. . . ; (5) the duty not to misrepresent any fact material to the transaction. . . ; and (6) the duty to transact business only after receiving prior authorization from the customer. . . .
>
> Of course the precise manner in which a broker performs these duties will depend to some degree upon the intelligence and personality of his customer. For example, where the customer is uneducated or generally unsophisticated with regard to financial matters, the broker will have to define the potential risks of a particular transaction carefully and cautiously.[8]

[5] 262 Cal. App. 2d 690, 69 Cal. Rptr. 222 (1968).
[6] *Id.,* 708.
[7] Leboce, S.A. v. Merrill Lynch, Pierce, Fenner and Smith, 709 F.2d 605 (9th Cir. 1983).
[8] Lieb v. Merrill Lynch, Pierce, Fenner and Smith, 461 F. Supp. 951, 953 (E.D. Mich. 1978).

The duties described by this court decision are only a partial list of the possible duties which stem from the generic rule that a broker must deal with a customer with the utmost in good faith, honesty, full disclosure and fair dealing. Thus, the use of the general rule offers a guideline to specific violations. Churning, obviously, violates all of the requirements of good faith, honesty, full disclosure and fair dealing.

Reasonable Basis for Recommendations

Whether described as a fiduciary duty or simply as a professional duty of a stockbroker, there appears to be no dispute that when a broker makes a recommendation, there must be a reasonable basis for doing so. Rule 472-40(1) of the Constitution and Rules of the New York Stock Exchange provides:

> A recommendation (even though not labeled as a recommendation) must have a basis which can be substantiated as reasonable.

In *Hanly v. S.E.C.*, the court stated: "A securities dealer occupies a special relationship to a buyer of securities in that by his position he implicitly represents he has an adequate basis for the opinions he renders."[9]

AVOIDING NEGLIGENCE

The duties of a stockbroker are important in determining whether a broker is guilty of negligence or not as a matter of law. Negligence is one of the most widely used concepts in law, and the key to negligence is the concept of duty. It is the breach of a duty owed to another, which results in damages caused by the breach, which leads to legal liability.

A broker must perform her duties to clients using due skill and care. Due skill and care of a professional exceeds the standard of care that is required of nonprofessionals, which is termed *ordinary care*. Thus, the broker must meet the standard of skill and care which is commensurate with her profession.

> Inherent in every agency relationship is the agent's obligation to use the skills and diligence necessary to protect the client's interest. . . . "every agent must possess a competent degree of skill to enable him to perform the duties he assumes, and if he undertakes such duties without the

[9] 415 F.2d 589, 596 (2d Cir. 1969).

requisite skill, or is guilty of negligence . . . he is liable in damages,"
quoting 3 Ohio Jur.3d *Agency* §104 at 161–162.[10]

Professor Louis Loss of Harvard University describes the elevated standard of care of brokers by reference to the "shingle" theory: "[T]he theory
is that even a dealer at arm's length impliedly represents when he hangs
out his shingle that he will deal fairly with the public."[11] Meyer's views
and the shingle theory may only express a common sense transactional
analysis of the relationship between brokers and customers. The general
public has a perception (often derived from television commercials and
other promotional material) of spokespersons proclaiming the integrity
and efficiency of a particular broker. The themes of such advertising
have led to popular understandings of what the shingle "stockbroker"
represents. At the very least, the shingle would seem to represent to the
public that the utmost in good faith, honesty, full disclosure and fair
dealing may be expected from the profession.

THE SUITABILITY DOCTRINE

Professor Loss describes the duty of a broker with respect to suitability
as, "an obligation on the part of the dealer to recommend only securities
that are suitable to the needs of a particular customer."[12] As an observer
and academician, Loss believes the suitability doctrine is in a process of
further evolution. Loss seems to believe that the following may be the
final standard.

> [T]he suitability doctrine has been well rationalized by Dean Mund-
> heim in terms of "risk threshold":
> "A suitability doctrine imposes a responsibility on the broker-
> dealer to take the risk threshold of his customers into account when he
> recommends or sells securities to them . . . The broker-dealer may
> discharge his responsibility under the suitability doctrine by informing
> the customer of the risk aspects of the transaction in a way which will
> enable the customer, in light of his individual capabilities, to relate
> these risks to his risk threshold and thus make his own determina-
> tion of suitability. If under these circumstances the customer wishes to

[10] Thropp v. Bache Halsey Stuart Shields, Inc., 650 F.2d 817, 820 (6th Cir. 1981).
[11] Loss, *Fundamentals of Securities Regulation* (Boston: Little, Brown & Co., 1983), 951;
Kahn v. S.E.C., 297 F.2d 112 (2d Cir. 1961).
[12] Loss, *Securities Regulation*, 969.

purchase the security, the broker-dealer can sell it to him even though he does not think it is within the customer's risk threshold. . . .

If the customer refuses to furnish the broker-dealer with information sufficient to determine the customer's risk threshold, the broker-dealer should not be required to prevent the customer from purchasing securities which are beyond his risk threshold.[13]

Whether the view of Professor Loss or the varying viewpoints reviewed in Chapter 6 on suitability are used, each has its own practical problems for brokers. Using Professor Loss' theoretical standard as an example, a broker should recognize the practical difficulties in meeting his duty to a customer.

According to the Loss/Mundheim standard, a broker should take the risk threshold of a customer into account. To meet this duty, what must a broker do? Is it enough for a broker to ask a customer what risks the customer wishes to take, or is he required to make an independent professional determination of what risks his customer can afford to take? Can he make that determination based upon the information he obtains from a customer? Must he take taxes into consideration? Perhaps a clearer problem is what does a broker say to relate the risks of a transaction to a customer in a way in which a customer can make her own determination of suitability? An argument can be made that when a broker determines that a transaction is unsuitable for a particular customer, the broker should unequivocally refuse to place an order unless a written statement is obtained from a customer acknowledging that her broker does not recommend the contemplated course of action. Isn't this the clearest way of communicating a negative recommendation to a customer? For his own protection the prudent broker would be advised at least to prepare a memorandum to the customer's file before entering an unsuitable transaction.

MISREPRESENTATIONS

Full disclosure is the duty of a broker. When disputes arise, nondisclosure is generally alleged to constitute a misrepresentation on the part of the broker and the breach of the duty of full disclosure constitutes negligence or worse.

What constitutes a misrepresentation? In discussing common law deceit, Loss states as follows:

[13] Loss, Securities Regulation, 976, quoting from Mundheim, *Professional Responsibilities of Broker-Dealers: The Suitability Doctrine,* Duke L.J. 445, 449–50 (1965).

In 1941, for example, the Supreme Court of the United States, applying Iowa law in a deceit case involving an allegedly misleading prospectus, approved the view of the American Law Institute to the effect (in the court's paraphrase) that "a statement of half truth is as much a misrepresentation as if the facts stated were untrue." A lay Englishman managed to capture the thought very well:

That a lie which is half a truth is ever the blackest of lies,
That a lie which is all a lie may be met and fought with outright.
That a lie which is part a truth is a harder matter to fight.

At the same time there is still no common law liability in deceit for complete nondisclosure as distinguished from a half truth, unless the one party to a business transaction "by concealment or other action intentionally prevents the other from acquiring material information," or the one party is under a duty to the other to exercise reasonable care to disclose the matter in question "because of a fiduciary or other similar relation of trust and confidence between them." So far as a fiduciary is concerned, however, the courts imposed an affirmative duty of "utmost good faith, and full and fair disclosure of all material facts," as well as an affirmative obligation "to employ reasonable care to avoid misleading" his clients.

Now, there are superimposed on this common law background the several antifraud provisions of the SEC statutes.[14]

Loss notes that salesmanship has application in the marketplace where the rule of *caveat emptor* (let the buyer beware) still is allowed to some extent. The sales tactic of "puffing" may be tolerated where tangible goods can be readily examined by the customer, but in the sales of securities, exaggerated claims have no rightful place.

Misrepresentations can be avoided by full disclosure of the risks and rewards of a particular transaction. Although making a sale might involve downplaying risk, the law indicates that a prudent broker would be better off losing the sale. If a broker cannot make a living without meeting the standard of full disclosure, then another line of work might be less dangerous for all concerned.

SOURCES OF SPECIFIC RULES—FEDERAL STATUTES

There are generally considered to be seven separate federal statutes which concern securities regulation; and other legislation, such as the

---

[14] Loss, Securities Regulation, 811–12.

Insider Trading and Sanctions Act of 1984[15] and the Commodity Exchange Act,[16] concerns specific types of investments. Each act contains specific rules related to the relationship of a broker and his customer in the purchase and sale of securities. However, our principal review will be of the Securities Act of 1933,[17] the Securities Exchange Act of 1934,[18] and the Investment Advisers Act of 1940.[19]

The other four statutes, the Public Utility Holding Company Act of 1935,[20] the Trust Indenture Act of 1939,[21] the complex Investment Company Act of 1940[22] (concerned primarily with face-amount certificate companies, unit investment trusts and mutual funds), and the Security Investors Protection Act of 1970[23] (which provides limited amounts of insurance in the event a broker becomes insolvent) relate to narrow subject areas which do not have common application. Regulation T of the Board of Governors of the Federal Reserve System may apply to narrow questions related to violations of security margin requirements.

The Securities Act of 1933

The Securities Act of 1933 (Securities Act) generally regulates the original distribution of securities to the public and meets two broad objectives of full disclosure, and prevention of fraud and misrepresentation in the distribution process. Much of the Securities Act deals with preparation of registration statements; sales activities during the prefiling period, during the waiting period, and during the period following registration.

Perhaps the most applicable portions of the Securities Act for most customers come under the sections related to private offering exemptions. These would encompass many of the real estate and oil and gas limited partnerships which were so popular prior to the Tax Reform Act of 1986.

Under both the registered and exempt securities sections, the focus is upon misrepresentations in the prospectus or oral communications.

[15] Insider Trading Sanctions Act of 1984, 15 U.S.C. §78 (1984).
[16] Commodity Exchange Act, 7 U.S.C. §§1–17 (1983).
[17] Securities Act of 1933, 15 U.S.C. §77 (1982).
[18] Securities Exchange Act of 1934, 15 U.S.C. §78 (1988).
[19] Investment Advisers Act of 1940, 15 U.S.C. §80(b) (1987).
[20] Public Utility Holding Company Act of 1935, 15 U.S.C. §79 (1987).
[21] Trust Indenture Act of 1939, 15 U.S.C. §77 (1987).
[22] Investment Company Act of 1940, 15 U.S.C. §80(a) (1987).
[23] Securities Investors Protection Act of 1970, 15 U.S.C. §78 (1982).

The Securities Exchange Act of 1934 and Rule 10(b)(5)

By and large, disputes arise with respect to the manner in which shares of securities are purchased and sold after an initial offering. Alleged violations of the Securities Exchange Act of 1934 and S.E.C. Rule 10(b)(5) have been the subject of many court cases. The specific statutory prohibitions, in some areas, supplement the common law duties of brokers and elevate specific violations to the status of fraud.

In an early decision, *Hughes v. Securities and Exchange Commission*,[24] the court analyzed the relationship between Rule 10(b)(5) and the common law duties of brokers. Arlene W. Hughes was registered as a broker-dealer and as an investment advisor with the S.E.C. Rule 10(b)(5) was recognized as an anti-fraud section of the Securities Exchange Act, and revocation of her registration to do business was upheld on the basis that Arlene Hughes had acted simultaneously in the dual capacity of investment advisor and broker-dealer. The court stated:

[T]he securities field, by its nature, requires specialized and unique legal treatment. This is recognized by the very statutes and regulations here under consideration as well as by recent Federal and State court decisions. Thus in the *Archer* case it was said:

"The business of trading in securities is one in which opportunities for dishonesty are of constant recurrence and ever present. It engages acute, active minds, trained to quick apprehension, decision and action. The Congress has seen fit to regulate this business. Though such regulation must be done in strict subordination to constitutional and lawful safeguards of individual rights, it is to be enforced notwithstanding the frauds to be suppressed may take on more subtle and involved forms than those in which dishonesty manifests itself in cruder and less specialized activities."

The acts of petitioner which constitute violations of the antifraud sections of statutes and of regulations thereunder are acts of omission in that petitioner failed to fully disclose the nature and extent of her adverse interest. The Commission found that petitioner failed to disclose to her clients (1) the best price at which the securities could be purchased for the clients in the open market in the exercise of due diligence and (2) the cost to petitioner of the securities sold by her to her clients. *In no less than three places in the above-quoted statutes and regulations we find that, "any omission to state a material fact necessary in order to make the statements made, in the light of the circumstances under*

[24] 174 F.2d 969 (D.C. Cir. 1949).

which they were made, not misleading," is expressly made unlawful. These quoted words as they appear in the statute can only mean that Congress forbid not only the telling of purposeful falsity but also the telling of half-truths and the failure to tell the "whole truth." These statutory words were obviously designed to protect the investing public as a whole whether the individual investors be suspicious or unsuspecting. The best price currently obtainable in the open market and the cost to registrant are both material facts within the meaning of the above-quoted language and they are both factors without which informed consent to a fiduciary's acting in a dual and conflicting role is impossible.

* * *

It is not enough that one who acts as an admitted fiduciary proclaim that he or she stands ever ready to divulge material facts to the ones whose interests she is being paid to protect. Some knowledge is prerequisite to intelligent questioning. This is particularly true in the securities field. Readiness and willingness to disclose are not equivalent to disclosure. The statutes and rules discussed above make it unlawful to omit to state material facts irrespective of alleged (or proven) willingness or readiness to supply that which has been omitted. [Citations omitted.][25]

The *Hughes* case could have been prosecuted for violations of the common law rules. Omitting to state material facts violates the broker's duty of full disclosure, and self-dealing violates the duties of honesty and fair dealing, for example. The provisions of Rule 10(b)(5) and the Securities Exchange Act of 1934 have in effect created new causes of action[26] to supplement the common law and, for that reason, a review of the securities statutes has become part of an attorney's analysis of customers' disputes with brokers. Whether a case should be prosecuted under the common law, under the securities laws, or both is a decision for the attorneys.

The Investment Advisers Act of 1940

Generally, the Investment Advisers Act of 1940 (Investment Advisers Act) provides for registration of investment advisers, regulation of their business, and setting forth prohibited transactions.

Broker-dealers are nominally exempt but may be regulated and may have to be registered under the Act. For example, section 202(a) states:

[25] Hughes v. S.E.C., 174 F.2d 969, 975–976 (Dept. of Commerce and Consumer Affairs, 1949).
[26] Loss, Securities Regulation, 1125.

(11) "Investment adviser" means any person who, for compensation, engages in the business of advising others, either directly or through publications or writings, as to the value of securities or as to the advisability of investing in, purchasing, or selling securities, or who, for compensation and as part of a regular business, issues or promulgates analyses or reports concerning securities; *but does not include . . . (C) any broker or dealer whose performance of such services is solely incidental to the conduct of his business as a broker or dealer and who receives no special compensation therefore;* . . . . [Emphasis added.]

Absent a new Supreme Court decision, the Investment Advisers Act offers little in terms of remedies for a customer. Although a customer's right to sue under the Act was approved in *Transamerica Mortgage Advisers, Inc. v. Lewis,*[27] it appears from note 14 of the decision that the remedies are restricted to declaring an investment advisory contract to be void, injunctions against the continuation of the contract, and restitution (presumably of advisory fees). Investment losses and other monetary relief were specifically found to be outside the customer's rights under the statute.

Special Federal Statutes

In the area of futures, other regulations should be consulted, such as the Commodity Exchange Act and regulations promoted by the Commodity Futures Trading Commission (CFTC) for the purpose of finding other duties of brokers in this specialized area. The Commodity Exchange Act established the (CFTC) with authority to promulgate new regulations as needed. It defines reporting requirements, registration requirements, prohibited activities, procedures related to revocation of licenses, and rules related to reparations proceedings. As an analogue to Rule 10(b)(5) of the Securities and Exchange Commission, the Commodity Exchange Act prohibits fraud in the connection with commodity contracts. Its general statement reads as follows:

Section 30.02 *Fraud in Connection With Transactions and Futures Contracts Other Than on Domestic Contract Market.*
    It shall be unlawful for any person, by use of the mails or by any means or instrumentality of interstate commerce, directly or indirectly, in or in connection with any account, agreement or transaction involving any contract of sale of a commodity for future delivery, traded or executed on any board of exchange, exchange or market other than a

[27] 444 U.S. 11 (1979).

contract market designated pursuant to Section 5 of the Act, as amended:
(a) to cheat or defraud or attempt to cheat or defraud any other person;
(b) to make or cause to be made to any other person any false report or
statement thereof or to enter or cause to be entered for any person any
false records thereof; (c) to deceive or attempt to deceive any other person by any means whatsoever in regard to any such account, agreement
or transaction or the disposition or execution of any such account, agreement or transaction or in regard to any act of agency performed with
respect to such account, agreement or transaction; or (d) to bucket any
order, or to fill any order by offset against the order or orders of any
other person or without the prior consent of any person to become the
buyer in respect to any selling order of such person, or to become the
seller in respect to any buying order of such person.

Besides its general regulations, special rules have been promulgated
by the CFTC. An example is Rule 1.55 of the CFTC which prohibits any
transactions in commodities prior to the delivery, signing, and dating of
a risk disclosure statement drafted by the commission. Without the risk
disclosure statement being signed and dated, the client may be entitled
to have all transactions set aside and any losses refunded.

The Commodity Exchange Act also provides for the establishment
of the National Futures Association (NFA), a self-regulating association,
to which the CFTC may delegate the responsibility for registration requirements, prohibited transactions, and for separate disciplinary and
reparations type proceedings. The NFA became operational on March
31, 1983 and has as its ostensible goals

1. The regulation of its members
2. Relieving the CFTC the burden of direct regulation and
3. Freeing the Commission to promote the growth of the industry.[28]

STATE REGULATIONS

In addition to the panoply of federal regulations, there are state regulations commonly known as *blue sky laws*. Review of the Uniform State
Securities Act[29] suggests that the state statutes generally attempt to accomplish the same goals as the Securities Act and the Securities Exchange Act. The states regulate the issuance of new securities and their

---

[28] National Futures Association, Articles of Incorporation, Art. III, Prentice-Hall (1986).
[29] Unif. Sec. Act, 7B U.L.A. 509 (1985).

distribution, and most state legislation contains provisions similar to Rule 10(b)(5) of the Securities Exchange Act.

SELF-REGULATION

Besides federal and state regulations, there are the rules of the self-regulatory organizations. The NASD, for example, was established as a self-regulatory body pursuant to the Securities Exchange Act. The various securities and futures exchanges have also established various exchange rules related to member broker-dealers. If broker-dealers are not members of any self-regulating exchange or the NASD, they may be subject to more stringent requirements which can be determined from a review of the Securities Exchange Act.

The self-regulating bodies have some rules and regulations which are more restrictive than the federal regulations and the common law, and should be consulted for that purpose. For example, although the Securities Exchange Act had a reference to a suitability doctrine, the clearest statements came from Article III, Section 2 of the NASD and exchange rules, such as NYSE Rule 405.

SPECIAL RULES RELATED TO SPECIALIZED PRODUCTS

Exchanges or self-regulatory bodies may have special rules particular to the product. Rule 9.8 of the CBOE, for example, requires brokerage houses to appoint a Senior Registered Options Principal (SROP) to establish policy and guidelines related to options transactions. These guidelines may establish the duty of brokers relative to net worth requirements, suitability requirements, and special risk disclosures for particular options strategies.

BROKERS' INTERNAL RULES

As will be examined at length in Chapter 15, brokers have their own policies and procedures which are contained in a variety of procedure manuals. These internal rules may define legal duties with respect to conduct of the firm's business. Whether their internal rules may be used in contested cases is the subject of legal controversy at the present time. Brokers have resisted the introduction of their internal rules into evidence, generally arguing that to do so penalizes the broker who adopts standards or procedures (i.e., duties) in excess of applicable legal standards. Yet the courts appear willing to consider the broker's internal rules for a number of different purposes. An account executive's handbook was admitted into evidence in *Mihara v. Dean Witter & Co.*[30] to establish the basis for finding a fiduciary relationship between the customer and the firm where Dean Witter, perhaps admirably, described its duty as a "sacred trust to protect our customers." In *Thropp v. Bache Halsey Stuart Shields, Inc.,*[31] a standard practice instruction manual was accepted into evidence. The court noted that such evidence did not automatically establish the appropriate standard of care, but that the trier of fact could consider such evidence in determining such a standard.

> The instant case involves evidence of *violations* of custom and *internal* rules. When a defendant has disregarded rules that it has established to govern the conduct of its own employees, evidence of those rules may be used against the defendant to establish the correct standard of care. The contents of such rules may also indicate knowledge of the risks involved and the precautions that may be necessary to prevent the risks . . . . The District Court correctly measured Bache's conduct by the standard of prudence it has established for its own employees. [Citations omitted.] [Court's emphasis.][32]

Examples of specific internal rules violations which have led to liability for brokers may involve failure of salespeople, branch managers, and other supervisory personnel to monitor accounts; failure to follow procedures which are designed to prevent losses to a customer from fraud or theft; violations of firm suitability standards, etc. Whether internal rules will be admitted into evidence or not, salespeople are encouraged to comply with firm policy and managers are encouraged to enforce those policies.

CONCLUSION

This brief overview of the general rules which may apply to the broker-customer relationship could not cover every rule. It is enough to know that there are many and where they may be found.

The most important generic rule which applies to brokers who are given the trust and confidence of a customer is that the broker owes the

[30] 619 F.2d 814 (9th Cir. 1980).
[31] 650 F.2d 817 (6th Cir. 1981).
[32] *Id.,* 819–20.

utmost in good faith, honesty, full disclosure, and fair dealing to the customer. This broad guideline should proscribe the conduct of a broker. Adherence to this general standard, and to the other rules, statutes, standards of the industry, and firm policy will tend to prevent disputes from arising in the first place. Yet, violations of rules occur and when disputes arise the last preventive measure takes place in front of a judge, jury, or panel of arbitrators. Not only are the potential penalties such as jail sentences, fines, license revocation, and money damages a deterrent; but the expense, loss of productive time, and loss of reputation are a natural result.

14

When Disputes Arise

This chapter describes generally what occurs when disputes arise and offers suggestions on dispute resolution prior to litigation or arbitration. If all attempts at adjusting a dispute fail, utilization of attorneys is almost inevitable. Thus, a description of the typical financial arrangements between attorneys and their clients for fees and expenses is included. An attempt has been made to contrast the expense of litigation and arbitration because there is generally a vast difference. Litigation is defined herein as court-related proceedings, as opposed to arbitration, which takes place before arbitrators outside of court. Last, a brief description of the various venues for arbitration has been included.

Arbitrations are stressed for two reasons. First, they are generally more economical than litigation, and second, given the Supreme Court's decision in *Shearson/American Express, Inc. v. McMahon,*[1] arbitrations will be the future forum for many disputes between brokers and their customers.

Finally, this overview attempts to forewarn all parties regarding the potentially large and sometimes wasteful expenditures of time and money related to disputes.

---

[1] 482 U.S. _____, 107 S. Ct. 2332 (1987). A further discussion of *McMahon* can be found in Chapter 16.

DISPUTE RESOLUTION BY THE BRANCH OFFICE MANAGER

A dispute has arisen and interrupted the professional relationship between a salesperson and a customer. The customer is angry and complains bitterly to the salesperson about a perceived wrongdoing. The salesperson does not believe that a wrong was committed and does not offer to accept responsibility for the alleged harm to the customer.

Given the above, a customer who wishes to pursue the matter has a number of different alternatives to consider. Most brokers have internal rules related to reporting customer complaints and which provide informal methods of handling disputes. These rules generally specify that when a customer complains to a salesperson, those complaints should be reported to the branch office manager and/or legal department of the brokerage house. For numerous reasons, salespersons do not always report customer's complaints and the customer cannot depend upon the salesperson to adjust any dispute.

The customer has the right to, and should register any complaints to the branch office manager of the brokerage house. The manager may be able to terminate the dispute at that time by explaining to the customer why no wrong was done or agreeing that a wrong was done and making the appropriate adjustment to the client's account. In some brokerage houses, disputes can be handled by the branch office manager up to a certain dollar amount, and there is an effort on the part of the brokerage houses to be solicitous of their clients' complaints. Reputable brokerage houses will attempt to resolve valid small complaints as soon as possible to preserve their good name and to prevent having disgruntled clients telling others of their shabby treatment. No one likes to have an unhappy client, and with respect to small disputes brokers may differ little from a supermarket or department store in attempting to satisfy the customer. In that regard, it is understandable that brokers tend to listen if a complaint comes from a longtime customer who has not complained often, whereas brokers may not be receptive if a complaint comes from a new customer who may have had a history of complaints with other brokers.

A customer is well advised to contact the branch office manager if the dispute involves a relatively small sum of money. This allows the branch office manager to supervise properly the brokers in the office and identify those who, perhaps, should not be salespersons. This is part of the system which prevents future abuses and identifies weaknesses or incompetent sales personnel. A number of complaints from different customers about a salesperson who is alleged to have entered unauthorized trades will soon result in a close review of that salesperson, and possibly lead to termination. Alternatively, a customer who complains that his salesperson is taking advantage of him, when the salesperson has few (if any) complaints by other customers, will probably be given a cold reception. The branch office manager is on the front lines and should be contacted for most small complaints and be given an opportunity to meet the broker's responsibility of dealing openly and honestly with a customer's complaints. If there is no satisfactory resolution from the branch office manager, then a complaint, in writing, should be made. Some brokerage houses will recognize both verbal and written complaints, but as a practical matter, the customer should file a written complaint with the brokerage house sent by certified mail, return receipt requested.

There are other regulatory bodies with which complaints can be filed, such as the Securities and Exchange Commission, the Commodity Futures Trading Commission, the National Futures Association, various state agencies related to securities, the exchanges upon which the trades were made, the NASD, offices of consumer protection, and the Better Business Bureau, to name a few. These organizations may be able to assist a customer in obtaining some relief.

LARGER DISPUTES

Assuming the dispute is of larger dimensions in terms of dollars (branch office managers may have authority to resolve disputes only up to $1,000 or so), there are various views on what a customer should do. If the customer has a long relationship with the firm and believes that she will get fair treatment from the company, then handling of her dispute without an attorney is a possible course of action, but it has some risk. If the customer views the company with distrust, it probably is a wise course of action to consult with an attorney.

A dispute which could cost the company a substantial amount of money may create a conflict within the system. If the company looks out for its own interests, then it may take protective action rather than honestly and fairly adjusting a dispute. Such protective action might involve delay tactics, or the possibility that the manager will solicit from the customer only that information which might help the company, but not necessarily help resolve the dispute fairly. The manager might tend to protect and believe the people that he works with every day and with whom he may socialize. Obviously, the branch office manager may have predetermined that he should have faith and confidence in the people he has hired and supervises. In an ideal world, brokers should be like the biblical Solomon and adjust disputes fairly as part of their duty to insure the proper functioning of the securities markets, but it may be a little bit too much to ask as a practical matter.

Customers tend to seek the aid of attorneys when significant dollar amounts have been lost because of perceived improper actions on the part of the broker. This is probably the preferred course of action in disputes involving amounts large enough to make it economically feasible to retain an attorney.

Predispute Negotiations

Once an attorney gets involved and has determined there is legal justification for a client's complaint, it usually is the practice for that attorney either to contact the branch office manager by telephone or by letter. Demand is usually made by the attorney for the amount of money which allegedly was lost due to the broker's actions. After a complaint has been filed with a brokerage house, the salesperson is generally requested to prepare a written report to the branch office manager. Once the facts are gathered, then there may be an effort on the part of the brokerage house to avoid litigation by working out a settlement of the differences. Typically, the complaint is referred to the legal department of the brokerage house and its typically overworked staff may eventually contact the customer's attorney and attempt to resolve the matter prior to litigation or arbitration.

Brokerage house responses to complaints vary. Some brokers will be amenable to resolving disputes, while others may adopt a uniformly hard line in dealing with customers' complaints or don't respond at all (the ultimate in stonewalling). The amount of time that it takes to go through the prelitigation period depends in part upon the timeliness of the parties in exchanging information and the good faith of the parties in their negotiations. Some disputes are resolved at this stage and may involve little of an attorney's time. Other cases involve long-term and costly litigation, or the less expensive alternative of arbitration. Because a case may be resolved within a short period of time or may be drawn out over a period of years, the client should carefully consider fee arrangements with an attorney.

Selecting an Attorney

Selection of attorneys for customers differs considerably from selection of attorneys for brokers and their salespersons. Customers usually do not have attorneys who are familiar with the legal duties and responsibilities of brokers. Customers may wish to ask their regular attorneys for recommendations of attorneys who are competent in this specialized area of law, or seek an attorney who may have the necessary qualifications through a referral service.

On the other hand, brokers generally have retained outside counsel or have attorneys at their corporate headquarters who are knowledgeable and experienced in brokerage law. The selection process, therefore, is generally not a difficult one for the broker. The brokerage house usually appoints a single attorney to represent the firm, the branch office manager, and the salesperson (the typical defendants in any dispute). In some cases, however, the same attorney may not represent all three parties because there is a conflict of interest among them. As an example, let's assume there is a case involving a salesperson who is accused of and is in fact guilty of churning. The brokerage house and the branch office manager may be unaware that the salesperson has churned the client's accounts. Without having made a determination of guilt or innocence, the brokerage house appoints an attorney to represent all three defendants. At a later date, close to trial or during trial, it may become apparent that the broker and the branch office manager had done all they could to supervise and prevent churning by any of their salespeople, but it also becomes clear that the salesperson did indeed churn the account. Like other conflicts of interest, this may provide an almost impossible situation relative to the respective legal rights of each party. Obviously an attorney representing all three parties cannot point the finger at the guilty salesperson in defense of his other clients.

A salesperson could find himself in the same predicament if the broker and branch office manager are guilty but he is not. Each defendant should give at least some consideration to the wisdom of independent counsel.

Fee Arrangements with Attorneys

There are three basic arrangements which attorneys customarily use in charging their clients for legal matters. Those arrangements are described as hourly, flat fee, and contingency fee arrangements.

Under an hourly rate arrangement, the attorney normally bills the client at a predetermined hourly rate (we will use as an example the rate of $100 per hour as a convenient round number). It is impossible to predict the exact amount of attorney's time that will be required in a matter which ultimately is resolved in the courtroom. Attorneys may be able to advise their clients of an estimate of the anticipated expense based upon fees charged in other similar cases. These estimates, however, can only serve as a rough guide of what the attorney's fees will ultimately be. Much of the uncertainty is caused by the impossibility of accurately anticipating what actions may be taken by other parties. The same case may cost $10,000 in fees or $100,000 in fees depending on the zeal of either the customer's attorney or the broker's attorney, or both.

Because it is virtually impossible to predict how much time a matter will take based on an hourly rate, there are few attorneys who will handle a lawsuit on a fixed or flat fee basis. Flat rates, for matters which may eventually end up in litigation, are especially rare. It is possible that an attorney will agree to represent a client in the prelitigation phase of a case for a fixed sum or flat rate, but it would be very unusual for an attorney to agree to a flat rate for litigation which might drastically exceed his prediction of the number of hours necessary to handle the legal matter. Arbitrated matters are perhaps a little easier to predict in terms of fees than a litigated matter, and it is possible that the client will be able to arrange with the attorney to do an arbitration on a flat rate. Generally, the attorney would quote a flat rate based upon the amount of time estimated to resolve a matter. Ethically, an attorney is obligated to represent his clients zealously and that principle may be in conflict with a flat rate fee where an attorney attempts to allocate only a certain amount of hours to be spent on a client's case. With the caveat that an attorney may only spend as much time as is mandated by the fixed fee, a fixed fee arrangement is a possibility in arbitrated matters.

Last, as far as the basic attorney's fee arrangements are concerned, there is the contingency fee arrangement. In some legal matters, notably personal injury cases, it has been the custom of lawyers to arrange with their clients for a contingency fee. These arrangements provide that the attorney shall receive a fixed percentage of the total recovery (usually one-third) as compensation for handling the case. No compensation for attorney's fees is payable in the event that the attorney is unsuccessful in obtaining a monetary recovery for the client. The justification for a contingency fee is commonly expressed as follows

> Contingency fee arrangements are justified on the basis that the contingency of recovery permits individuals otherwise unable to afford legal representation to obtain legal services by bartering a portion of the recovery. In essence, the attorney serves as an insurer of legal representation by demanding a sufficiently large percentage of sums recovered to finance cases to which little or no recovery is obtained.[2]

[2] R. Aronson, Attorney-Client Fee Arrangements: Regulation and Review 49 (The Federal Judicial Center, 1980).

It has been said that "[n]o form of attorney employment contract is subject to more discussion or controversy than the lawyer's contingent fee agreement. The topic has received exhaustive though inconclusive treatment by the courts, legal writers, and legislative bodies."[3] Perhaps the clearest situation in which a contingency fee arrangement would be necessary is one in which the total life savings of the customer has been lost due to a broker's actions. The customer may be able to obtain justice only if that person can find an attorney to take the case on a contingency fee basis. Although the following was written with a personal injury accident in mind, it equally applies to brokerage cases taken on a contingency fee basis.

> Because of the way the American system of accident compensation and protection of personal and property rights is structured, the average person usually cannot enforce his or her rights without the services of an attorney. Effective enforcement of these rights frequently calls for substantial expenditures of time, effort, and professional creativity and initiative on the part of the claimants or litigant's counsel. Since the complexity of accident cases varies so widely, it is impossible to standardize fees. Therefore, specific or fixed fee contracts are neither practical nor feasible. Moreover, inasmuch as a sizable number of accident compensation cases involves substantial investigation, analysis, research, discovery in litigation, payment of a lawyer's fee at an hourly rate is generally prohibitive for all but the very wealthy. . . . It is an appropriate device in almost any case where the success of the legal endeavor results in a monetary recovery or award for the client. In fact, there are only two types of cases where contingent fee agreements are either discouraged or condemned: Family law cases and criminal law cases.[4]

All of the advantages and disadvantages of the various fee arrangements are not discussed here. The customer or broker will have to review carefully the various fee agreements and their hybrids with the attorneys that they consult regarding their legal disputes. Contingency fees are subject to negotiation. Higher or lesser percentages may be set, or different percentages may be specified in the event a case is settled before trial (25 percent for example), during trial (33 1/3 percent) or after an appeal (40 to 50 percent). As an example of hybrids of the fee arrangements noted above, it should be observed that there are contingency fees not only for plaintiffs, but there are also contingency fee

[3] California Continuing Education of the Bar, Attorney's Fees Manual 13 (Berkeley, May 1976).
[4] Id., 14.

agreements for defense counsel, fixed fee and contingency combination agreements, combination hourly rate and contingency fee agreements, hourly rate following by contingency fee agreement, fixed fee on hourly basis followed by contingency fee agreements and agreements which provide a choice of hourly or contingent fees.[5]

LITIGATION EXPENSES

In addition to attorney's fees, the client is responsible for the expenses related to the litigation or arbitration. These expenses include court costs and expenses of litigation. Attorneys may not pay these expenses, under the American Bar Association Model Code of Professional Responsibility, Disciplinary Rule 5–103, and state bar association codes, but may advance them for future reimbursement.

Expenses incurred in litigation and arbitration are significant and must be carefully discussed with the attorney. For example, deposition transcripts can be quite costly. Usually several depositions of parties and witnesses are taken prior to trial. At the deposition, a court reporter records the testimony of the witness verbatim. The record is transcribed, typed, and loosely bound for use at trial. Depositions may used to impeach, or contradict, the testimony of a witness who changes his testimony at trial, and they are used to discover facts relevant to the lawsuit. In a court case involving allegations against a broker, there usually are at least three depositions taken by the customer's attorney. These are the depositions of the salesperson, the branch manager, and the defendants' expert witness (usually another registered representative or branch manager). The deposition of the salesperson might last for a few hours or several days, depending upon the complexity of the case. The cost for the deposition transcript varies, but a rough rule of thumb would be approximately $80 an hour (i.e., $800 for a ten-hour deposition transcript). This is in addition to any charges for the attorney's time.

Assuming that all three depositions are taken, each lasting ten hours, then the expense to the client would be approximately $2,400 for the transcripts. There is an additional expense when an expert witness is deposed, because such witnesses charge for their time. For example, an expert witness who charges $100 an hour will present a statement for $1,000 for a ten-hour deposition.

How much and what type of discovery to be utilized, how many

[5] American Law Institute, American Bar Association, The Practical Lawyer's Manual on Lawyer-Client Relations 163–197 (1983).

depositions to be taken, and the costs incurred in a given case will vary according to each attorney's style and strategy. Expenses will also be incurred for the research and preparation time of the customer's expert witness as well as the actual time spent in testifying at depositions and at trial. Assuming a stockbroker's expert testifies at trial for eight hours, again using an arbitrary rate of $100 per hour (although many experts charge a higher fee for court testimony), the expense of $800 is obvious. Less predictable, however, is the amount of time necessary for that expert to prepare for testimony in court. A rough rule of thumb would be approximately twice the amount of time that the expert is expected to testify in court, but much more time may be necessary if there are a lot of depositions or transactions in the account for the expert to review. Expenses can be substantial and should be carefully reviewed with the attorney prior to deciding whether to take the route of litigation or arbitration (which usually involves much less preparation time and expense).

Recovery of Attorney's Fees and Court Costs

In civil cases, it is sometimes possible to obtain attorney's fees and court costs as part of the recovery. Court costs are usually distinguished from the expenses enumerated above. Court costs such as filing fees and subpoena fees are typically awarded to the prevailing party, but are usually small in comparison to expenses. Expenses such as expert witness fees, copies of deposition transcripts, travel expenses, telephone charges, and duplicating costs are not typically recoverable, except in unusual circumstances.

Attorney's fees are generally recoverable in cases where a contract, statute, or public policy provides for their recovery. Some customer agreements between a brokerage house and a customer will provide a contractual basis for the recovery of attorney's fees by the prevailing party. Some legislation specifically provides for the recovery of attorney's fees (see Chapter 15).

Even if the recovery of attorney's fees is allowed, the entire amount of the fees may not be awarded. Whether recoverable by statute or by agreement, attorney's fees are usually limited by the court's view of what constitutes "reasonable" attorney's fees. The fee awarded may be less than the attorney has actually charged, because the court may not agree with the attorney concerning how much time and effort was reasonably required. In such cases, the client would remain liable to the attorney for the difference.

CONTRASTING THE EXPENSES OF COURT
VERSUS ARBITRATION

Litigation is generally the most expensive way to resolve a dispute between a broker and a client. One could argue that court cases may result in significantly higher judgments to justify the expense, but that is a trade-off which attorneys cannot guarantee. Due to the Supreme Court decision in *Shearson/American Express, Inc. v. McMahon,*[6] litigation will be a rare occurrence, but the Court left the door open for a few cases to be litigated.

If one were to contrast the high cost of litigation versus the lesser cost of arbitration, one would note that one apparent cause of the great expense involved in litigation is the amount of time during which discovery can occur. Discovery takes place between the filing of a complaint in court and the time of trial. Depending upon the efficiency of the state or federal courts in one's jurisdiction, the time between these two dates typically ranges between 18 months and five years. During that time, both parties have the opportunity to discover all facts reasonably calculated to lead to admissible evidence.[7] Modern litigation practice involves taking a number of depositions in preparation for trial which increases the expenses for deposition transcripts and time put in by the attorney. Time periods of 18 months to five years afford a long time, perhaps too much time, in which expensive discovery can take place.

On the other hand, arbitrations generally discourage extensive discovery. For example, between the time an arbitration claim is filed with the National Association of Securities Dealers (NASD) and the time of the hearing, there are no formal procedures allowing discovery. The NASD Code of Arbitration Procedure §32(b) merely states

> Prior to the first hearing session, the parties shall cooperate in the voluntary exchange of such documents and information as will serve to expedite the arbitration. . . .

There are exceptions, because applications can be made for extensive discovery in arbitration proceedings, and it is theoretically possible that an arbitration proceeding could involve as much discovery as a court matter. The amount of expense involved should be carefully discussed with the attorney in choosing between a court case and an arbitration.

[6] 482 U.S. _____, 107 S. Ct. 2332 (1987).
[7] Fed R. Civ. P. 24.

An Example of the Economics of Litigation

To illustrate the economics of litigation, assume a claim for $50,000 is being litigated. As a hypothetical example, we can approximate the types of fees, costs and expenses that might be incurred by a customer. This example assumes an attorney is compensated on an hourly rate basis at $100 per hour.

Preparation and investigation of a complaint involves some time before the complaint is filed with the court. Investigation, analysis, fact gathering and the drafting of the complaint that occurs in the prefiling period, could be estimated at 20 hours of time, or $2,000. The court filing fees for a complaint, if a jury trial is demanded, may range from $100 to $300, depending upon the jurisdiction in which the case is filed. Subsequent to the filing of the complaint, discovery begins. If we assume that the only depositions taken by the plaintiff's attorney are the depositions of the salesperson, the branch manager, and the defendant's expert witness, the transcription costs and expert's fees would be approximately $3,200, and attorney's fees for preparing for and taking the depositions could be estimated at an additional $8,000. The expense will be roughly the same amount for both the customer and the broker. In addition, the salesperson may also be subject to time-consuming and expensive depositions, document production, and other forms of discovery.

Case preparation also involves preparing for any discovery to be conducted by the defendants. The plaintiff has little control over the amount of discovery the defendants choose to undertake. If extensive discovery is entered into, then the expense of litigation can escalate rapidly. For example, the defendants may take the deposition of the plaintiff, possibly lasting for days, and perhaps the plaintiff's spouse or friends, prior business partners, or other people knowledgeable about the plaintiff thereby driving up the cost not only for the deposition transcripts but also for attorney's fees.

Because of the potentially great expense of litigation, it is appropriate for the attorney and the client to discuss the potential amount of a recovery which will justify the expense, risks, and stress of litigation.

Obviously, a contingency fee arrangement may assist in reducing the up-front cost for attorneys fees, but the expenses must be considered in relationship to the amount in controversy. It may not make economic sense to litigate a matter involving a loss of $50,000, where expenses and attorney's fees could reach $20,000 before trial. Arbitration might provide a more cost-effective forum.

An Example of the Economics of Arbitration

Presuming the same dispute for $50,000 is submitted to arbitration under the NASD procedures, the filing fee for claims above $20,000 but not exceeding $100,000 is $500. A claimant pays that amount to have the dispute heard by three to five arbitrators appointed by NASD. Because there is no express provision for discovery, arbitration generally proceeds with far less discovery and the expenses are usually significantly less. The arbitrators consist of a panel "at least a majority of whom shall not be from the securities industry, unless the public customer requests a panel consisting of at least a majority from the securities industry."[8]

Assuming that the controversy is over an alleged unauthorized trade and involves only one trade, the amount of attorney's fees to prepare a demand letter, followed by a request for arbitration, and for the hearing itself, would be much less than for a court-litigated matter. The principal savings in time would be the lack of full-scale discovery, which may work to a client's advantage or disadvantage.

On the other hand, a churning case may necessarily involve a considerable amount of documentation and preparation. Documents, such as order tickets, confirmation slips, broker's reports on unusual trading activity, internal memorandums, and inquiries to the salespeople by the broker's compliance department are often necessary to establish a client's case. Although the NASD code does not specifically provide for discovery, it has been interpreted to allow for requests for documents and other information necessary to prepare a claimant's case. To that end, extensive discovery may be allowed by the arbitration panel. The general rule, however, is that arbitrations are usually far less expensive than court matters because discovery devices such as depositions are discouraged.

The Choice Between Litigation and Arbitration

Assuming one can overcome the hurdles imposed by the Court in *Shearson/American Express v. McMahon* and litigate a claim, then one is truly presented with a choice between litigation and arbitration. In the example of a $50,000 dispute, arbitration is possibly the more suitable forum.

There may be significant reasons for litigating a case involving a small dollar amount, however, if there are substantial grounds to believe the damage award will exceed the amount of money lost by

---

[8] National Ass'n of Securities Dealers, NASD Manual—Code of Arbitration Procedure § 19 (CCH 1985).

the customer. A fair number of litigated cases have involved punitive damage judgments (involving many multiples of the amounts lost by a client) in instances of theft, churning, unauthorized trading, fraud, or other situations which would offend the fundamental instincts and values of society. Punitive damages are a possible offset to the cost of litigation in such cases. At the present time, arbitration panels differ in their approaches to punitive damage claims. There have been, however, few significant punitive damage claims awarded by arbitration panels. Thus, it is probable that arbitration panels will not award as much in punitive damages as a jury or a judge.

Another justification for pursuing costly litigation instead of arbitration was stated by Justice Blackmun, who disagreed with the Court's opinion in *McMahon* relative to section 10(b) claims being subject to arbitration. Part of his objection to the Court's decision concerned overturning a 1953 Supreme Court decision, *Wilko v. Swan,*[9] which was highly critical of the arbitration process. Justice Blackmun observed

> Even if I were to accept the court's narrow reading of *Wilko* as a case dealing only with the inadequacies of arbitration in 1953, I do not think that this case should be resolved differently today so long as the policy of investor protection is given proper consideration in the analysis. Despite improvements in the process of arbitration and changes in the judicial attitudes towards it, several aspects of arbitration that were seen by the *Wilko* court to be inimical to the policy of investor protection still remain. Moreover, I have serious reservations about the Commission's contention that its oversight of the SROs' arbitration procedures will ensure that the process is adequate to protect an investor's rights under the securities acts.[10]

Justice Blackmun notes that the Supreme Court in *Wilko* had cited the following inadequacies about arbitration of securities claims

1. Judicial review of the manner in which the arbitrators applied the securities laws to their decisions would be difficult since arbitrators are not required to give reasons for their decisions or to make a complete record of the arbitration hearings.

2. There are limited grounds upon which arbitration decisions could be overturned which are generally fraud in procuring the award, partiality or bias of the arbitrators, gross misconduct of arbitrators, and the failure to render a final decision.[11]

[9] 346 U.S. 427 (1953).
[10] 107 S. Ct. 2332, 2353 (1987).
[11] 107 S. Ct. 2332, 2353–54.

Justice Blackmun notes that today there is still no requirement of a complete record of the arbitration proceedings, and that arbitrators are "actually discouraged by their associations from giving reasons for a decision."[12] And he goes on to note the following

> As even the most ardent supporter of arbitration would recognize, the arbitral process *at best* places the investor on an equal footing with the securities-industry personnel against whom the claims are brought.
>
> Furthermore, there remains the danger that, *at worst,* compelling an investor to arbitrate securities claims puts him in a forum controlled by the securities industry. This result directly contradicts the goal of both securities acts to free the investor from the control of the market professional. The uniform code provides some safeguards but despite them, and indeed because of the background of the arbitrators, the investor has the impression, frequently justified, that his claims are being judged by a forum composed of individuals sympathetic to the securities industry and not drawn from the public. It is generally recognized that the codes do not define who falls into the category, "not from the securities industry." (citation omitted) Accordingly, it is often possible for the "public" arbitrators to be attorneys or consultants whose clients have been exchange members or SROs. The uniform opposition of investors to compelled arbitration and the overwhelming support of the securities industry for the process suggest that there must be *some* truth to the investors belief that the securities industry has an advantage in a forum under its own control. See *N.Y. Times,* Mar. 29, 1987, Section 3, p. 8, col. 1 (statement of Sheldon H. Elsen, Chairman, American Bar Association Task Force on Securities Arbitration: "The houses basically like the present system because they own the stacked deck").[13]

Despite the reservations of Justice Blackmun and others, it appears that arbitrations will be prevalent in financial cases where there is a written agreement between the broker and the customer providing for the arbitration of disputes. Although some disputes will still proceed in courts, the emphasis in the future will be upon arbitrations. The remainder of this chapter, therefore, will be devoted to the various alternatives available for arbitrations and similar proceedings.

ARBITRATIONS AND CFTC REPARATIONS

Under the heading of industry-wide organizations, the NASD and the National Futures Association (NFA), as well as a nonindustry organization,

[12] *Id.,* 2354.
[13] *Id.,* 2355.

the American Arbitration Association (AAA), hear disputes related to securities or futures transactions. There are other forums in which an arbitration could be held which are generally known as exchange organizations, such as the NYSE, the AMEX, and the CBOE to name a few. Generally, exchange procedures are more limited in scope and relate to transactions taking place on the exchange.

A number of these organizations are sponsoring organizations to the Securities Industry Conference on Arbitration (SICA), which publishes various pamphlets and guides related to arbitration procedures. These organizations have adopted a Uniform Code of Arbitration, and introduce their Uniform Code by stating

> Although most business in the securities industry is completed without a problem, disputes and controversies will occasionally arise. Such disputes and controversies can be resolved by impartial arbitration at one of the organizations listed on the last page of this pamphlet. The arbitration will be conducted in accordance with the Uniform Arbitration Code, as developed by the Securities Industry Conference on Arbitration, and the rules of the sponsoring organization which you choose. This pamphlet is designed to assist you or your attorney by explaining arbitration procedures and by answering some of your questions. Any additional questions you have regarding arbitration should be addressed to the Director of Arbitration where you file your claim.[14]

Information may be obtained by contacting the Director of Arbitration of the following organizations

American Stock Exchange, Inc.
86 Trinity Place
New York, New York 10006
(212) 306–1000

Boston Stock Exchange, Inc.
1 Boston Place
Boston, Massachusetts 02108
(617) 723–9500

Chicago Board Options Exchange, Inc.
LaSalle at Van Buren
Chicago, Illinois 60605
(312) 786–5600

[14] Securities Industry Conference on Arbitration, Uniform Code of Arbitration 2 (Sept. 1987).

Cincinnati Stock Exchange, Inc.
205 Dixie Terminal Building
Cincinnati, Ohio 45202
(513) 621–1410

Midwest Stock Exchange, Inc.
120 S. LaSalle Street
Chicago, Illinois 60603
(312) 368–2222

Municipal Securities Rulemaking Board
1150 Connecticut Avenue, N. W., Suite 507
Washington, D.C. 20036
(202) 223–9347

National Association of Securities Dealers, Inc.
2 World Trade Center, 98th Floor
New York, New York 10048
(212) 839–6251

New York Stock Exchange, Inc.
11 Wall Street
New York, New York 10006
(212) 623–3000

Pacific Stock Exchange, Inc.
233 Beaudry Avenue
Los Angeles, California 90014
(213) 614–8400

Philadelphia Stock Exchange, Inc.
1900 Market Street
Philadelphia, Pennsylvania 19103
(215) 496–5000

The sponsoring organizations listed above have adopted the Uniform Code of Arbitration, which describes arbitration as

Arbitration is a method of having a dispute between two or more parties resolved by impartial persons who are knowledgeable in the areas in controversy. Those persons are known as arbitrators. Disputes with broker-dealers often involve complicated issues which, in the interest of fairness, require a prompt and inexpensive means of resolution. Because of this, arbitration has long been used as an alternative to the courts. It must be noted, however, that there are certain laws governing the conduct of an arbitration proceeding which must be observed. Most importantly, perhaps, is the fact that an arbitration award is final; that is, the decision is subject to review by a court only on a very limited basis. It should be recognized, too, that in choosing arbitration as a means of resolving a dispute, the parties give up their right to pursue the matter through the courts.[15]

The sponsoring organizations begin arbitrations by what is called a claim letter. A claim letter should set forth the facts related to the dispute as clearly as possible with names, dates, and times. A specific amount of money requested should be specified, as well as any calculations used to arrive at the amount. The claim letter (and the response to the claim letter) should be as complete as possible, and have specific references to statutory law, the NASD Rules of Fair Practice (or the sponsoring organization's rules that might apply to the case). It is a time to put forward the best argument possible for relief because the claim letter and the response are the documents which give the arbitrators their first impression of the case.

A submission agreement must be filed along with the claim letter and fees. Fees are based on the following schedule, as set forth in the Code of Arbitration Procedure.[16]

Amount in Dispute (Exclusive of interest and expenses)	Deposit
$1,000 or less	$ 15
Above $1,000—but not exceeding $2,500	$ 25
Above $2,500—but not exceeding $5,000	$ 100
Above $5,000—but not exceeding $10,000	$ 200
Above $10,000—but not exceeding $20,000	$ 300
Above $20,000—but not exceeding $100,000	$ 500
Above $100,000—but not exceeding $500,000	$ 750
Above $500,000	$1,000

The location of the arbitration under the Uniform Code of Arbitration is in the discretion of the Director of Arbitration of the sponsoring organization. Consideration is generally given to "convenience of the parties, the availability of necessary records or witnesses, and the availability of qualified arbitrators."[17]

---

[15] *Id.*
[16] NASD, Code of Arbitration Procedure 18 (July 1987).
[17] *Id.,* 5.

After a claim us filed, the opposing party has 20 days to answer and may bring opposing claims into the arbitration (counterclaims). In addition, the opposing party may file a claim against a third person who may be responsible for all or part of the claims lost.

Subpoenas for witnesses and documents are generally allowed, but are subject to the discretion of the arbitrators. Requests for subpoenas must include a statement indicating what efforts have been made to obtain witnesses and documents without the subpoenas requested.

The arbitrators sometimes have "the power to direct the appearance of persons employed in the securities industry and the production of records in the possession or control of such persons. If you request the arbitrators to use this power, you should know that you may be required to bear all reasonable expenses in connection with such appearance or production."[18]

Generally, the parties will be notified well in advance of the hearing date. The procedure is much less formal than court, but the general outlines of a court procedure will be followed. Usually, the claimant begins presenting the case by testimony, documents, and other evidence to the arbitrators. Witnesses are sworn and subject to cross-examination and questioning by the arbitrators and the opposing party or his representatives. The usual procedure is patterned after litigated matters:

1. The claimant or his representative may make an opening statement
2. Respondent or his representative may make an opening statement
3. The claimant's case is presented
4. The respondent's case is presented
5. If no rebuttal evidence is appropriate, the parties may make final arguments.

The decision is in the form of an award mailed to all parties, usually within 30 days. The award, if not paid by the opposing party, may be filed with the court and registered as a judgment against the opposing side and is subject to a limited judicial review.

CONCLUSION

The system in which disputes are adjusted and attorneys are hired, and the costs of litigation and arbitration show that the economics of any

[18]*Id.*, 7.

dispute are unproductive. Our system chooses to use the most attorneys per capita of any other system in the world. Although attorneys may be blamed for the high cost of litigation or arbitration, their role in the system is one of prevention.

Given the incredible waste of productive energy, expense, and time related to litigation and arbitration, the proper view of our system is to prevent disputes from arising in the first place. Why disputes arise is subject to much speculation. The publicity associated with insider trading cases brought by the SEC and the Justice Department only point out the excesses which can lead people astray. Counterbalancing the capitalistic view of acquiring wealth are the regulatory schemes of the common law, the securities acts, the rules of the exchanges, the internal rules and regulations of the brokers' procedure manuals, and finally, the mandate and penalty resulting from litigation or arbitration. One could say that this chapter has been slanted in scope against the broker. This is not a bias on the part of the authors as much as it is a bias of the law. There are no direct statutory schemes related to customers. The SEC, in its promulgation of rules, the NASD, the CFTC, the NFA, the exchanges, and the self-regulatory procedures by the brokers are all designed to prevent the occurrence of disputes by specifying violations, penalties, and license revocations for brokers. On the other hand, customers' complaints are regulated by the economics of litigation and arbitration and the common law responsibilities of customers.

If anything, "Let the buyer beware" might now be rephrased to "Let the broker beware." The rules and the system related to the methods in which disputes are resolved are essentially for the protection of the customer.

15

Documents: An Attorney's Viewpoint

As will be discussed in Chapters 16 and 17, the Supreme Court's decision in *McMahon*[1] may force arbitration of customers' disputes when the customer has signed a standard form agreement containing an arbitration clause upon opening an account. Customers' attorneys who are unhappy with arbitration and prefer the courts as a forum may choose to attack these arbitration agreements and, if successful, may litigate their disputes.

A major advantage of litigation perceived by customers' attorneys has been the relative ease of obtaining documents and information. Rule 26(c) of the Federal Rules of Civil Procedure, for example, favors discovery where "the information sought appears to be reasonably calculated to lead to the discovery of admissible evidence."

Under the usual arbitration procedures, there are no express guidelines as to discovery, and it is more difficult to do discovery in arbitration. To obtain documents, the customer's attorney may have to persuade the arbitrators that certain documents which reside in the broker's control and possession are necessary. The need for such documents and justifying the need is difficult for an attorney who may be unfamiliar with

---

[1] Shearson/American Express, Inc. v. McMahon, 482 U.S. _____, 107 S. Ct. 2332 (1987).

the many different types of documents available. If arbitrations are truly going to meet their responsibility to render justice, then all involved will have to understand the necessity and importance of certain documents discussed in this chapter.

Since, as a practical matter many customers' disputes will be arbitrated, arbitration administrators or the arbitrators themselves will have the responsibility to determine which documents will be helpful for both sides to discover. Because a request for documents is one of the least expensive forms of discovery, it is hoped that this chapter will assist customers, brokers, attorneys, the courts, and arbitration panels to recognize the types of documents which may be necessary for a full presentation of any dispute.

An illustration of the wide variety of documents available and how they are used may be helpful. *Henricksen v. Henricksen*[2] illustrates how documents have been used in court cases.

In the *Henricksen* case, the husband was a salesman for a large national broker. His wife was a former school teacher but had given up teaching to be a housewife and mother. The husband had asked his wife to open three discretionary accounts in her name, a regular account, an options account, and a margin account, which she did. The wife's new account form was filled out by her husband, showing her investment goal as "long term growth of capital, income secondary."[3]

Because an option account was opened, an option client information form was prepared by the husband/salesman, showing that the account was a single (not joint) account, the investment goal was conservative growth, and only covered writing was anticipated. The branch manager approved the option account for covered writing only. Further, the document showed that the wife's income was less than $5,000 per year.

For almost four years, the wife's account was virtually inactive until $105,814 in stock and cash was received by the wife as trust proceeds from her family. Husband and wife agreed these funds would be for their child's future education and needs.

The problems started about a month later, when the husband changed the address for delivery of monthly statements and confirmation slips from their home address to his office address, in care of himself. Almost immediately, the husband began to sell off the account's blue chip stocks and began requesting checks, in the wife's name, totaling $55,356.91. These funds were never received by the wife, but appear to have been delivered to the husband. The majority of funds

---

[2] 640 F.2d 880 (7th Cir. 1981).
[3] *Id.,* 882.

apparently were deposited in the couple's joint bank account and withdrawn by the husband. Presumably, the husband kept records of the joint bank account secret from the wife. Other checks in the wife's name appeared to have had a facsimile of the wife's signature but were never cashed by the wife. Unsuitable speculative trading began in the options and margin accounts, resulting in a loss of $33,564.31 and $21,754.65 in commissions and margin account interest. About nine months later the couple separated as a result of the husband's drinking and gambling. The wife left her account with the husband and the firm. She explained she had total confidence in the firm which she thought would be supervising her accounts. In the process of obtaining a divorce, the husband fraudulently indicated the value of the wife's securities was $114,000 even though the account had been depleted. Only when the wife learned of their home being remortgaged did she suspect the true situation which was revealed over the next few months. A lawsuit was filed at that time.

BROKER'S PROCEDURES MANUALS

As our review of the *Henricksen* case will illustrate, the logical starting point for any request for documents is the broker's procedures manuals. The primary reason is that these manuals will lead to other documents which the attorney may or may not be aware of, and because these manuals will conveniently outline applicable federal and state laws or regulations, exchange rules, rules of self-regulating organizations, and firm policy. Further, broker procedures manuals will differentiate and specify the duties of the salespeople, branch office managers, regional managers, and of central management.

The basic procedures manuals will probably first express the firm's view of the nature of the relationship with a customer. The language may express a "sacred trust to protect" customers and maintain that "under no circumstances should we violate this confidence."[4] Procedures manuals will typically have provisions incorporating the suitability requirements of Article 3, Section 2 of the NASD and NYSE Rule 405, and refer to the latter as the "know your customer rule." With respect to the issue of suitability in the *Henricksen* case, the Court apparently found that the new account form and option account form were filled out in an attempt to comply with the "know your customer rule." The Court found that the options and margin trading were inconsistent with the account's stated

[4] Mihara v. Dean Witter & Co., Inc., 619 F.2d 814, 819 (9th Cir. 1980).

investment goals, and it concluded such trading was unsuitable for the account. It appeared helpful for the Court to note that "long-term growth of capital—income secondary" was "the second most conservative investment objective on the form."[5] Definitions of terminology related to investment goals are often contained in procedures manuals and may indicate the types of trading permitted consistent with the stated investment goals.

Relative to the option trading in the wife's account, various representatives of the firm testified that the transactions were unsuitable vis-a-vis the stated investment goals, but justified the suitability of the transactions by asserting that a customer's signature on the options and margin account documents made her a speculator by definition. This latter assertion was contradicted by reference to the firm's compliance manual.

Use of the firm's procedures manuals demonstrated that firm policy prohibited options trading when a person earned less than $20,000 annual income. By reference to the firm's compliance manual it was also clear that the spouse's income could not be considered since this was an individual account in the wife's name. Thus, the Court observed that options transactions should not have been approved for the wife's account because her annual income was less than $5,000.

Firm policy as expressed in the firm's compliance manual provided for daily, monthly, and periodic reviews of discretionary accounts. The branch manager was required by the firm's procedures to approve each order, but out of 40 order tickets, four had been approved by someone else, and 13 were not initialed at all. In cases where more than five trades were executed in any given month, the compliance department, the branch manager and salesman were to have reviewed the account for excessive activity, which apparently was not done. Under firm policy, the branch manager should have contacted the wife to verify that the activity in the account was consistent with her wishes. This had not been done.

Furthermore, firm policy prohibited the changing of the account address and delivery of checks. The firm's compliance manual required careful review and confirmation by letter (to the account's old address) of the client's request, which appears not to have occurred. As noted by the Court, errors in supervision may lead to liability to the firm under section 20(a) of the Securities Exchange Act of 1934. Also, prior court decisions had held the broker responsible if it did not have adequate internal controls or did not enforce its system of supervision with reasonable diligence.

[5] Henricksen v. Henricksen, 640 F.2d 880, 882 (7th Cir. 1981).

The *Henricksen* case merely illustrates the manner in which brokers' procedures manuals and other documents may be used. To present a full picture of the broker's responsibilities, customer's attorneys would generally want to review various brokers' procedures manuals, like the branch office procedures manuals, supervisor's manuals, legal and compliance manuals, operations manuals, and specific product manuals (e.g., options and futures). The titles of these procedures manuals may vary from firm to firm, but the manuals will usually be arranged on a similar functional basis.

Branch office procedures manuals (BOPM) are fairly comprehensive documents which central management disseminates to branch offices to help supervise, educate, and set forth firm policies and procedure. As a comprehensive management tool, the BOPM incorporates laws, regulations, trade practices, and firm policy relative to the opening, handling, and supervision of customers' accounts. General statements related to suitability standards, the importance of account opening papers relative to knowing one's client, and duties of the salesman and the branch office manager are typically contained in this type of manual.

Supervisors' procedures manuals are more specific relative to the duties of branch office managers, regional managers, and other supervisory personnel. Branch office managers' supervisory duties generally require the branch office manager (BOM) to review accounts on a daily, monthly, or periodic basis, or at the request of regional or central management. On a daily basis, the BOM usually is required to comply with the policies and procedures manuals relative to the opening of all accounts, the suitability of the contemplated transactions in the account, reviewing of all order tickets, reviewing the status of accounts from computer reports to determine if problems are developing, meeting with salespeople to see if clients' losses have exceeded company limits or suitability limits, etc. Monthly or periodic reviews would include meeting with the salesperson or customer and updating information on the customer's financial status. If churning is an issue, the BOM may have to respond to central management inquiries related to excessive trading or unusually high commissions. In cases like the *Henricksen* case, one would suspect a breakdown in the multitiered system of prevention, and the supervisor's duties would be subject to review. A supervisor's responsibilities would be delineated in the BOPM and/or supervisor's procedures manuals.

Legal and compliance manuals attempt to inform supervisors, BOMs, and salespersons of the constantly changing legal requirements and special procedures necessary to comply with the law, NASD rules, exchange rules, and firm policy. Interpretations of suitability standards, guidelines for qualifying clients for speculative trading, guidelines as specified by recent court cases, and detailed procedures relative to risk disclosure in specific products like futures and options is a partial listing of the subject matter of compliance manuals.

Operations manuals cover the details of how the company operates its business. The modern broker relies extensively on computers for record keeping and the operations manuals explain in detail the manner in which data are put into the computer and how the data are used. Reports generated by the firm's computers, such as unusual activity reports, will probably be described in the operations manual. Other reports may be described by the operations manuals such as commission runs which show the exact commissions earned by a salesperson and the split of commissions with the brokerage firm. Such reports are crucial if a significant number of principal transactions are involved, because they may be the only documents which reflect the principal credits earned by a salesperson. Confirmation slips do not show the amount of principal credits earned or the markups by the firm. In churning cases, significant amounts of compensation may be overlooked without the commission run. The operations manuals or commission runs themselves may reveal special incentives for salespeople, like more favorable commission splits for the salesperson on an escalating scale based upon levels of production. In a churning case this analysis may be helpful to show the total financial picture which may have caused the salesperson to seek $5,000 more in commission income to reach the next level of gross production, thereby entitling him to a greater piece of the pie. For example, the salesperson might qualify for 45 percent of the broker's gross commission instead of 35 percent.

Specific product manuals are manuals for individual products, like options, futures, and limited partnerships. If the dispute involves options, there would likely be an options procedures manual containing or supplementing the policies and procedures promulgated by the senior registered options principal (SROP) of the firm. These specific product manuals cover in greater detail the requirements of opening an account for the specific product, such as special risk disclosures, training requirements for brokers, suitability policies, and margin and credit policies. Some product manuals only allow salespeople who have the necessary training and experience in the specific product to open and handle accounts.

The length of this review of procedures manuals is merely a reflection of the amount of detail and substance in these important documents. With the knowledge that there are a number of different manuals to review, customers' attorneys will be prepared to seek these documents in any case.

Supervisors and salespeople who feel uncomfortable because a review of these procedures manuals might reveal some error on their part are encouraged to reread their firm's policies and to conform their activities to the policies and procedures specified by their firm. The policies and procedures are there for two broad purposes—to protect the firm and the customer. Compliance with the firm's procedures manuals will meet both goals.

NEW ACCOUNT DOCUMENTS

If a customer signs an agreement to arbitrate, the courts will continue to enforce such agreements in the absence of fraud, misrepresentation, or other reasons which would make the agreement invalid, unless the *McMahon* case is overturned.[6] Customers' attorneys have attempted to circumvent arbitration because of perceived advantages in discovery and/or a perception of obtaining higher awards. Some customers' attorneys have been successful in obtaining punitive damage verdicts in court cases, and are hesitant to submit to arbitration, where few punitive damage awards of any significance have been reported.

The agreement to arbitrate is usually contained in the customer's agreement which is the first document signed by the customer in opening an account. To circumvent arbitration a customer could attempt to delete the arbitration provision from the customer's agreement. The rules of the CFTC prohibit a broker from rejecting an account if a customer deletes an arbitration clause, but there is no corollary rule for securities transactions. The key factual issues surrounding the signing of the customer's agreement relative to the arbitration clause will revolve around the manner in which the agreement was presented. Was it presented like a form document necessary to open an account; i.e., sign here, sign here, and sign here; or, was it presented with an explanation of the importance of the document, the customer having adequate time to review it, and the broker having met his duty of full disclosure of its relevant provisions? These issues will be presented in greater detail in Chapter 17. For the moment, it is sufficient to note the importance of the customer's agreement being signed and whether it contains a valid arbitration clause.

In the process of opening an account various other new account documents are prepared or signed besides the customer's agreement. To meet the "know your customer" duties of the broker, information related to suitability is often obtained by way of multipurpose new

[6] Shearson/American Express, Inc. v. McMahon, 482 U.S. _____, 107 S. Ct. 2332 (1987).

account forms. Additional information may be needed for specific products (options, futures, limited partnerships) which may be on other client information forms. However, a typical multipurpose new account form used to open an account with a broker would ask for the following information:

1. Name(s), address, telephone numbers, social security numbers and other identifying data
2. Type of account—individual, joint, partnership, corporation, etc.
3. Referral sources, references, and general information
4. Educational background
5. Occupational background
6. Investment history
7. Investment objectives
8. Estimates of net worth
9. Liquid net worth
10. Tax bracket
11. Number of dependents
12. Employment status
13. Annual income
14. Amount of risk capital available for speculation

A careful review of this form or new account forms for specific products is necessary for any customer's attorney. In the *Henricksen*[7] case, the inconsistency between the stated investment goals on the new account and option account information forms and the actual trading apparently led the Court to a conclusion that the trading was unsuitable for the account. Errors on these forms related to net worth, income, investment goals, and past investments may be viewed negatively, especially if the broker has puffed the information to qualify the customer for a particular investment. Reference to the broker's procedures manuals will assist the attorney in determining how these forms should be filled out; for example, should liquid net worth include the equity in the customer's home. Custom and trade practice would say no.

[7] Henricksen v. Henricksen, 640 F.2d 880 (7th Cir. 1981).

MONTHLY STATEMENTS AND CONFIRMATIONS

Monthly statements and confirmation slips have been described in detail in Chapter 11. Customers' attorneys usually request copies of these documents if the customer has not maintained a complete file of all transactions. The usefulness of these documents is limited because reference to the actual order tickets and purchase and sale (p&s) statements yields more detailed information.

It is suggested that a complete set of these documents be obtained, numbered (as described in the next section), and placed in a binder or file for later review. Analysis of these documents may only be necessary for purposes of computing damages at a later date or in investigating the rare case of deceptive statements. The client should be interviewed carefully to determine if some statements were not received, because there is the possibility that certain documents (usually containing the bad news) were not sent.

ORDER TICKETS AND PURCHASE AND SALE SLIPS

Customers rarely see the order tickets by which their orders are placed. These orders are handwritten by the salesperson and submitted to the wire room of each branch office for execution. If there are any questions relative to the actual trade, for example, whether there was an unauthorized trade or even a question of whether an order was actually placed, the order tickets are important source documents.

In churning cases, the order tickets are the source documents which primarily assist in establishing who was in control of the account (one of the requirements of churning is that the broker had actual or de facto control). Analysis of the control issue relative to the order tickets presumes an understanding of the terms *solicited* and *unsolicited*. A clear example of an unsolicited trade is one in which the client has already made a decision, calls up and specifies a particular product, price, and quantity to purchase or sell. The salesperson merely acts as an order taker. A clearly solicited transaction takes place when a broker initiates the transaction by recommending a purchase or sale and the customer acts on the broker's advice. The spectrum of possibilities between these extremes is unlimited, and a key factual issue about whether the order was solicited or unsolicited may develop if there is an issue about the broker's control. The point about the order tickets is that there is usually an indication on the order tickets (in the salesperson's handwriting) as to whether it is a solicited or unsolicited transaction. If the order ticket is left blank relative to whether the order was solicited or unsolicited, company policies and procedures will generally presume such an order was solicited.

The order tickets should be obtained and some type of control system for managing these documents should be implemented. Order tickets may be placed in a separate file in chronological order and numbered. Summaries indicating whether the transaction was solicited or unsolicited can be made. If all the transactions were solicited, then de facto control by the broker may be reasonably inferred.

If the time an order was entered is important, the time of the order may also be included in a summary. On the order tickets there are generally two or more date-time stamps. Broker practices vary, but some use vertical time stamps to indicate when an order is submitted to the wireroom and horizontal date-time stamps to show when the order was filled or executed. In a dispute over an unauthorized transaction, the time the order was submitted to the wireroom can be important. If the order was placed at 9:10 A.M. and the customer was in the middle of brain surgery at that particular time, the unauthorized trade is easier to prove.

In futures cases which justify obtaining the order slips, a complete set of purchase and sale (p&s) documents should also be obtained, primarily to match the orders' opening and closing positions. If a client calls and purchases a contract of New York gold and then sells it at a later date, the p&s confirmations can be paired to determine the profit or loss. Purchase and sale documents which mismatch futures orders are highly suspicious. The custom and trade practice is to match the first purchase with the first sale of a like transaction. In some cases of outright fraud, transactions will be matched in violation of the first in first out (FIFO) standard to show profits when in fact there are losses, thereby misleading the customer as to the true status of the account.

POWERS OF ATTORNEY IN DISCRETIONARY ACCOUNTS

A general definition of a discretionary account is an account in which a customer gives the broker, or persons associated with the broker, authorization to trade the customer's account. In churning cases the attorney would normally request copies of any powers of attorney (and any revocations) signed by the customer. If a power of attorney was used, then the control requirement in proving churning will have been satisfied. It is important to note that the absence of a power of attorney does not eliminate churning as a possible cause of action. As explained in further detail in Chapter 17, the central question is who is in actual or defacto control of the account. If a salesperson trades the account as if she had a power of attorney, or the customer routinely follows the recommendations of the salesperson, de facto control of the account may be found.

In addition, firm policies should be reviewed relative to powers of attorney. Larger brokers may prohibit their use altogether. Other brokers may require specific approvals by regional or central management for discretionary accounts. Supervisors are required to approve all order tickets in light of the investment objectives and financial resources of a customer, as in the *Henricksen*[8] case. Principal transactions may not be made in a discretionary account without full disclosure to the client and the client's authorization in writing.

OFFERING STATEMENTS OF LIMITED PARTNERSHIPS

Assuming a dispute involves the purchase of a limited partnership interest, a determination should be made as to whether the broker properly fulfilled its obligations in soliciting the transaction. Brokers are required to comply with federal and state regulations concerning suitability requirements, furnishing a prospectus, and permissible promotional material and representations related to the offering. A tremendous amount of literature is available related to specific legal requirements. Suggested reading is delineated in Chapter 17.

General guidelines relative to a review of the offering statements would be to review all promotional material given to a customer, interview the client about the representations made by the salesperson, determine whether the customer was given a prospectus, ascertain whether the customer had a reasonable opportunity to review the prospectus, review the investment history of a customer to determine if similar investments were made in the past, and analyze the prospectus, concentrating on the differences, if any, between the salesperson's representations and the prospectus.

TELEPHONE RECORDS AND DAYTIMERS

Review of telephone records and daytimers (calendars) is not confined to disputes between customers and brokers, but may be useful in any dispute in which a determination must be made as to when certain

[8] Henricksen v. Henricksen, 640 F.2d 880 (7th Cir. 1981).

events occurred. Telephone records and calendars of both the customer and the broker are subject to review. From these records a chronology may be prepared which could be used to establish that a customer did not contact the salesperson when an unauthorized trade occurred, or to show that orders were routinely entered without obtaining the consent of a client (to establish the broker's control in churning cases). In a churning case, if a customer was on vacation during the relevant time period and there are no records showing contact with the salesperson, then there is at least circumstantial evidence that the salesperson acted as if he had a power of attorney in placing orders in a customer's account. Calendar notations of dental visits, hospitalization, golf games, and the like will tend to establish the fact that the customer did not contact the salesperson at a given time or date.

HAPPINESS LETTERS

As a matter of self-protection, brokers' written or unwritten policies sometimes mandate the preparation of happiness letters. A periodic happiness letter may be sent to the client thanking them for their business and asking whether there are any problems. Failure of a customer to bring *written* complaints to the attention of management may be used as evidence of the customer's satisfaction with the firm (and ratification of the firm's activities). Happiness letters also assist the firm in independently confirming the customer's understanding and assent to the salesperson's activities. A customer would be well advised to make any complaints known to the branch office manager directly, promptly, and in writing. The practical necessity for written complaints is explained in the next section.

Specific happiness letters may follow computer reports of an unusual volume of transactions or unusually large commissions in a customer's accounts. Given such a report, questions related to the unusual activity, suitability, and churning may be raised in a supervisor's mind. Ideally, a branch office manager will contact a customer, make sure the customer is aware of the transactions and amount of commissions and fairly document the client's happiness or complaints. Efforts to cover up a client's complaints by sending a happiness letter when the customer has legitimate concerns should be discouraged. Such letters may be a useful defense exhibit, if accurate, but do not fairly meet the obligations of the broker if the only objective is to protect the firm no matter what the facts really indicate.

COMPLAINT FILES

As a practical matter, complaints should be in writing. Although it may be argued that the law should require brokers to respond to verbal complaints, there is no assurance that brokers will record negative verbal complaints. In fact, industry rules require that complaints be in writing. Article III, Section 21 of the NASD, for example, states the following:

> *Record of written complaints*
> (d) Each member shall keep and preserve in each office of supervisory jurisdiction, as defined in Section 27 of these rules, either a separate file of all *written* complaints of customers and action taken by the member, if any, or a separate record of such complaints and a clear reference to the files containing the correspondence connected with such complaint as maintained in such office.

> *"Complaint" defined*
> (e) A "complaint" shall be deemed to mean any *written* statement of a customer or any person acting on behalf of a customer alleging a grievance involving the activities of those persons under the control of the member in connection with the solicitation or execution of any transaction or the disposition of securities or funds of that customer. [Emphasis added.]

Thus, according to the above definition, complaints must be written. A caveat for brokers is in order since the law may not excuse a broker's failure to respond to unwritten complaints. The complaint files may be useful for any number of reasons, but are generally used to review prior complaints against a specific salesperson and the action taken by the supervisors to prevent future errors by that salesperson.

PERTINENT INTERNAL WIRE TRAFFIC

A review of documents may include the internal wire traffic to and from central management, regional supervisors, departments, and the branch offices. The electronic wire system is used by management for immediate communication between the firm's offices. Legal and compliance departments may issue unusual activity reports, notices of violations of firm policy or legal requirements. When firm credit policies have been violated, the firms' credit departments will use the wire systems to issue margin calls, cancellations of orders, reversals of commissions, etc. As an example, internal wire documents can be useful in determining when margin calls were made. If a margin call arrived after a client had delivered the funds, but an early sell-out resulted in lost profits for the customer, then the liability of the broker may be established.

Management is constantly generating new supervisory tools. One of the ways it performs its duties is by sending inquiries to the branch offices. Thus, internal wires from departments handling options, futures, limited partnerships, or other products may be pertinent.

RISK DISCLOSURE STATEMENTS

For specific products, various risk disclosure procedures must be followed and/or signed documents must be obtained. Reference to procedures manuals will probably point out the relevant documents required by the firm and the law. Examples of specific products where risk disclosures are required would be futures (the CFTC risk disclosure document) and options (the OCC disclosure document). Risk disclosures relative to various investment strategies, investment funds, limited partnerships, and other investments are possible documents to review.

Although we have discussed the necessity for risk disclosure statements, some guidelines relative to their use may be in order. In *Sher v. Dean Witter Reynolds, Inc.,*[9] the CFTC decided that

> "[S]ection 1.55 basically prohibits *any* FCM from opening a commodity futures account for *any* customer" unless the FCM first provides the customer with a risk disclosure statement containing the prescribed language and receives a signed acknowledgment from the customer that he received and understood the statement. . . . We therefore are of the view that an FCM's opening of a customer account without previously having presented and received an acknowledgment of the risk disclosure statement constitutes a per se violation of regulation 1.55, and that the customer's actual awareness, if any, of the risks of commodities trading does not constitute a defense to such a violation.[10]

In deciding the *Sher* case, the CFTC was presented with what the defendants alleged was a sophisticated investor who full well knew the risks of commodities trading. However, the commission decided that without proper procedures being followed relative to the risk

[9] Comm. Fut. L. Rep. (CCH) ¶ 22,266 (June 13, 1984).
[10] *Id.,* at ¶ 29,370.

disclosure statement, the customer was entitled to a reversal of all transactions (and losses). The customer was awarded his money back.

Even if the superficial aspects of the risk disclosure are complied with, the broker is not exonerated. Many cases indicate that it is the obligation of the broker to present the risk disclosure statement in a fair manner and not make statements contrary to the risk disclosure document. Statements by a broker in derogation of the risk disclosure statement to the effect that the broker has a fair and conservative system of trading which does not constitute risk to the client would defeat the presentation of such a document. In any event, an examination must be made to determine whether the risk disclosure statements are present in the broker's files, and that all requirements of the law have been complied with.

CUSTOMERS' RECORDS

Depending on the issues in a given controversy, certain customers' records may be obtained. In tax shelter cases, as an example, the tax returns of customers and their financial affairs may be subject to analysis. In almost every case related to suitability, the broker's attorneys might request financial information as well as the past investment history of a customer, including all past and present accounts with other brokers and past investments in real estate, business, etc.

Telephone records, calendars, diaries, charge card records, and the like are all fair game, depending on the nature of the dispute. As a general matter, the customer must be prepared to lay financial and personal records open for scrutiny if it is deemed necessary by the customer's attorney, the courts, or an arbitration panel.

DOCUMENT CONTROL

Principally for attorneys, the following constitutes one method for organizing the amount of documentation which may result from discovery. Since every attorney would have a personal preference, the bias here is on a functional approach to broker-customer disputes. The following is a list of basic categories of information which might be obtained:

1. Account opening documents given to the customer
2. Monthly statements
3. Confirmation slips (including p&s statements)

4. Order slips

5. Prospectuses given to the client

6. Relevant procedures manuals

7. Chronological telephone records, calendars, memorandums and correspondence from the salesperson

8. Chronological records of the branch office manager and supervisors

9. All correspondence to and from the broker to a customer

10. All internal wire traffic

11. Other documents such as computer reports of commissions paid to salespeople, employment records, customer records, etc.

It is suggested that a numbering system be designed to reveal the source of the data (e.g., from the customer's records, from the broker, or from other sources). Often records will come to the attorney piecemeal and the numbering system should be flexible enough to reveal, for example, the date the documents were received, the exact source (customer's records from his accountant, records from the broker's operations department, etc.). Any records obtained from a client should be copied immediately and the source documents should be put away for safekeeping.

Once some basic control is achieved over these documents a true analysis of what happened to who and when will be possible. Typically a chronology of events will be prepared using the documents. Control over the documents using a numbering system allows the attorney to retrace where the documents came from in order to lay the proper foundation for their admission into evidence.

CONCLUSION

The variety of documents, as we have seen, is almost endless. Given all of these documents, the paper trail of evidence will generally reveal the truth. The question is how much of the paper trail will be discovered or revealed. In court cases, the bias is towards the production of those documents which may lead to the discovery of admissible evidence. In arbitration, which appears to be the future forum for many disputes, the ability of attorneys for both customers and brokers to obtain documents is limited by the tendency of arbitration panels to provide an economical method of handling disputes. Yet the obligation of both forums is to render a fair decision.

This chapter has been devoted to the dull subject of documents, in the hopes that the litigants, their attorneys, the courts, and arbitration panels will have a broader perspective on the necessity of certain documents. In reviewing the high cost of litigation in Chapter 14, it was noted that the cost of document production is relatively low compared to depositions, interrogatories, and other forms of discovery. Despite their relatively low cost, it must be recognized that the more documents there are, the greater the expense to the litigants of having attorneys and experts review the documents. What will be permissible to arbitration panels remains to be seen.

16

Frequent Allegations, Defenses and Remedies: A Case Study

A review of court cases indicates customers most frequently allege breaches of fiduciary duty (usually regarding suitability), churning, and fraud. The typical defendants are the salesperson, the branch office manager, and the firm. Firms may be responsible simply by virtue of the employer-employee relationship, by accepting or condoning the acts of the employee, failure of the firm to have adequate internal controls, or failure of the firm in enforcing its policies and procedures. Damages for lost profits, trading losses sustained by the customer, commissions, and punitive damages are usually alleged.

When a dispute arises, the defense commonly maintains that the customer is exhibiting "sour grapes." The usual theme is that the customers wish to have their cake and eat it too: They accept the profits from risky transactions, but complain that they did not know what the risks were when losses occur. Why, the defendants ask, didn't the customer complain after the receipt of confirmation slips and monthly statements? If something was not clear why were not questions asked?

Occasionally happiness letters have been sent to the customer soliciting the customer's comments about any problems related to the transactions. Why didn't the customer object at that time? There may be many reasons why the customer did not complain of the transactions immediately, but the defendants view any delay in making complaints as evidence the customer waited to see how the transactions turned out before complaining.

Disputes have the nasty habit of skewing the presentation of the facts. Defendants reviewing complaints filed by their customers often become offended when they learn they were the avaricious, unscrupulous promoters of the financial ruin of a sweet, trusting widow. Customers are equally offended when the defense answers that the customer was a well-seasoned, greedy, sophisticated investor, who traded with full knowledge of all the risks involved in the transactions. From this presentation of the "facts," the bewildered person(s) who make the ultimate decision must believe themselves to be prospectors for the few grains of truth that may or may not be present.

To provide an overview of disputes, a specific legal case has been selected for in-depth review. The illustrative case is *Hecht v. Harris, Upham & Co.*[1] Before beginning a review of the *Hecht* case, it should be pointed out that the case involved many years out of the lives of the participants, presumably years which both the customer and the defendants could have devoted to more productive pursuits. Beginning in 1957, Mrs. Hecht's accounts were transferred to the defendants. In March of 1964, Mrs. Hecht's tax accountants informed her that the accounts had been substantially depleted. The *Hecht* case was filed in 1965 when the plaintiff customer was approximately 74 years old. A decision was reached by the trial court in 1968. The decision was appealed and ultimately reversed in part and affirmed in part by the Court of Appeals for the Ninth Circuit in 1970 when the plaintiff was approximately 80 years old. From the beginning of the account to the final resolution, approximately 13 years passed. Although many cases are resolved in shorter time frames, all should be mindful of the toll on both sides in expense, the stress of litigation, as well as in the most precious commodity, time.

To benefit from the experience of others, perhaps the questions to keep in mind while reviewing the *Hecht* case are what could have been done to prevent the losses sustained by Mrs. Hecht, or what could have been done to minimize her losses.

[1] 283 F. Supp. 417 (N.D. Cal. 1968), *modified*, 430 F.2d 1202 (9th Cir. 1970).

THE BASIC FACTS OF THE DISPUTE

Mrs. Hecht sued her salesman, the branch office manager, and the firm for alleged violations of various federal regulations (the Securities Act of 1933, section 10(b) of the Securities Act of 1934, SEC Rule 10b-5, the Commodity Exchange Act); article 3, section 2 of the rules of the NASD, and the common law of the State of California. Essentially, she proceeded upon the most common allegations: breach of fiduciary duty for lack of suitability; fraud under the common law and federal statutes; and churning.

Mrs. Hecht had been born and educated in England, where she attended a teacher's college for two years before starting her teaching career. She moved to Canada at age 23, then to New York, Salt Lake City, and ultimately to San Francisco. She worked in retail sales and then as a private tutor for about forty years. Her last employment was as a housekeeper and a tutor for the daughter of a wealthy San Francisco businessman. She did so for 14 years before she married her employer. Upon his death two years later, she inherited one-half of his substantial estate comprised mainly of securities with a net value of about $500,000.

Shortly after her husband's death, an acquaintance of her husband and his wife befriended Mrs. Hecht, and the relationship thereafter was both social as well as business. The acquaintance was a stockbroker who took over the widow's accounts. Blue chip stocks were liquidated in favor of less conservative issues, the salesman engaged in fraudulent transactions related to two specific issues, and relative to the churning claim, the court observed

> During the 6 year and 10 month period over 10,000 transactions occurred with a gross dollar volume of about $100,000,000. About 1200–1400 of these transactions (with a dollar volume of 9 and one-half million) involved transactions in 200 different corporate stocks. About 9,000 transactions (with a gross dollar volume of about 90 million) involved transactions in various commodities.[2]

Of course, the case appeared to involve a bad situation for the defendants. The customer's view of the case could be summarized as involving a naive trusting widow who was manipulated by a deceitful salesman, with the knowledge of the branch office manager and the firm.

The defense, however, presented Mrs. Hecht's lengthy prior involvement in the stock market. For over 16 years prior to her experience with

[2]*Id.*, 425.

the defendants, the widow had small stock and margin accounts with various firms. Although her accounts showed only 72 transactions (an average of less than five per year), from an initial investment of $2,000 in 1931 her accounts had grown to $65,000 by 1955.

During the life of the account with defendants, she received confirmation slips, which requested "immediate notice of any error."[3] She also was in contact with the salesman almost daily by telephone and he would visit her home at least once a week. During these weekly visits, the widow would separate the week's worth of confirmation slips into buys and sells to discuss them with the salesman, after which he would gather them up and take them, despite having duplicates at the office.

Mrs. Hecht was periodically represented by tax accountants to whom the salesman provided information. The court noted Mrs. Hecht was represented by competent counsel, but did not explain what they did during the life of the account.

Thus, defendants' position was that the widow was an experienced and sophisticated trader in securities, having gained her knowledge from frequent discussions with other brokers for many years prior to engaging the defendants. It was alleged she discussed business, stocks, and commodities almost daily with Mr. Hecht for over 16 years. Mrs. Hecht apparently read the financial pages of the newspaper regularly.

Prior to engaging in the allegedly improper transactions, there was some evidence that the salesman had suggested a portion of the assets be placed in trust or in a bank, which the widow refused. The defense posture was that Mrs. Hecht was a "veteran gambler"[4] who was well aware of risks, who understood the nature of the transactions, and who thoroughly understood the extent of the trading and the nature of the markets. They further alleged that Mrs. Hecht was "estopped by her conduct and barred by laches from asserting any such breach or violation."[5] The nature of the waiver, estoppel, and laches defense was that she had waited too long to complain about the transactions which had been occurring for six years and ten months. After all, the defense contended, she received confirmation slips which asked her for immediate notification of errors, and her monthly statements summarized all the transactions. The defense believed her claims would also be barred legally by the statute of limitations (the time limit specified by law within which a party must sue unless otherwise excused).

[3] *Id.*, 426.
[4] *Id.*, 428.
[5] *Id.*

One of the key considerations in the court's decision was the extent to which Mrs. Hecht understood what was happening relative to the transactions taking place in her accounts. Was she a widow who had mistakenly entrusted her accounts to defendants as a result of a nervous breakdown following the death of her husband, as alleged by her counsel, or was she the highly sophisticated "veteran gambler" as alleged by the defense? The court's observation was thus:

> A question of fact is involved concerning the extent to which plaintiff was able to comprehend what was going on. This case is a classic example of the trial process wherein able counsel for the respective parties have polarized the issues by their extreme and undiscriminating contentions concerning plaintiff's alleged competence or her alleged ignorance with respect to brokerage accounts and the securities and commodities markets.
>
> Actually, plaintiff was neither as "dumb" in matters of brokerage accounts as plaintiff's counsel contends or as plaintiff, herself, made herself appear to be on the stand, nor was she as smart, experienced, or informed as defendants' counsel would make her out to be.
>
> The truth concerning this issue lies in between and it is the function of the court to try and find it from the evidence. For the reasons hereinafter set forth, this case cannot be and will not be resolved on a simplistic formula under which either side can "take all."[6]

Based upon the claims for breach of fiduciary duty, churning, and fraud, plaintiff's attorney requested loss of bargain and compensatory damages in the amount of $1,109,000 as listed below, along with punitive damages.

1. Commissions, markups and interest paid on the customer's margin account—$232,000
2. $64,520 because of two transactions in which the salesman bought stock from Mrs. Hecht at less than its fair market value
3. The difference between the projected value of the customer's account if the account had not been traded inappropriately and the value of the account at the time in which it was closed and litigation begun—$776,000
4. The difference between the projected amount of income in dividends and interest if the account had been left intact versus the actual amount of dividends and interest received—$69,898

[6] *Id.*, 429.

5. Income taxes paid resulting from capital gains—$64,730
6. An unspecified amount of punitive damages

Of the damages alleged, the trial court awarded Mrs. Hecht the following:

1. The $232,000 in commissions, markups and interest charged to her on her margin account on a finding of churning
2. $64,520 in damages from the two fraudulent stock transactions
3. $143,000 in other damages due to churning (comprised of $78,000 in losses in her commodities account and $65,000 in lost dividend income)
4. Prejudgment interest in the approximate amount of $64,871.02 on item 1

On appeal to the ninth circuit, the "other damages due to churning" was reversed; thus her judgment was reduced by $143,000. The remainder of the judgment amount appears to have been left undisturbed by the court of appeals.

THE COURT'S DECISION ON WAIVER, ESTOPPEL, AND LACHES

The court found after a more extensive review of the facts than noted herein that as to the allegations of breaches of fiduciary duty, the widow would not be allowed to recover under those claims based upon the legal principles of waiver, estoppel, and laches. The court stated

It has also been held that investors who repeatedly accept confirmations and statements disclosing the essentials of transactions with salesmen of a brokerage partnership, thereby indicate an election not to rely on any breach of duty imposed by the [Federal Securities] Act and that such investors, failing seasonably to make complaints concerning reasonably discoverable facts, are barred by waiver, estoppel and laches from later assertion of wrongdoing. [citations omitted][7]

This should not be construed as insulating salesmen and brokers from liability in each case where confirmation slips and monthly statements are present. In fact the multitude of cases in which brokers have

[7] Id., 428.

been found liable presumably involve the almost universal use of confirmations of trades and monthly statements. This case is merely an illustration of why waiver, estoppel, and laches are common defenses for brokers and provides a guideline for customers to make their complaints known in writing as soon as reasonably possible. Such complaints should be made directly to the branch office manager or through one's attorney.

Based upon the widow's prior experience with brokers, the court found the widow had the ability to understand the confirmation slips and monthly statements, to note the transfers of monies from one account to another, to understand those securities which she thought had not been sold were in fact sold, that the transactions taking place might have been contrary to her understanding or instructions, that the account was not being maintained but actively traded, that commodities were being traded and that commissions were being charged. The court noted

> Having, with this knowledge and understanding, permitted [the salesman] and his firm to continue handling the account on this basis in reliance upon her apparent acquiescence for nearly seven years, the Court finds that plaintiff's conduct is such that she is barred by estoppel, laches and waiver from suddenly taking the position that such trading of the account in securities and commodities was unsuitable for her needs and objectives, contrary to her instructions and should never have occurred. [citation omitted]
>
> * * *
>
> It is, therefore, unnecessary in our view of the facts of this case to determine whether a broker, even considered as a fiduciary holding himself out as skilled in matters of the market (the so-called "shingle theory"), can be held liable under the Security Acts for what has been described as "unsuitability" of the account for the needs and objectives of the customer—as plaintiff contends in this case.[8]

A finding of estoppel, laches, and waiver will generally apply to all causes of action, but interestingly enough, the case did not end there but continued on to a finding of liability on the part of the salesman and brokerage house for churning and fraud.

Although the court found that Mrs. Hecht could appreciate the nature of the transactions in her account and was somewhat knowledgeable, it expressly found that she was unable to appreciate the excessive trading in her account by observing

---

[8] *Id.*, 429–30.

After hearing the testimony of doctors, psychiatrists and others who observed and dealt with plaintiff, this Court is satisfied that, although her experience and competence were such that she knew her account was being actively traded by [the salesman] in both securities and commodities, contrary to her claimed instructions and her claimed needs and objectives, her comprehension of market operations and business affairs beyond that was so meagre that she still had to rely upon [the salesman] concerning whether trading in any particular volume or with any particular frequency was reasonably suitable or, on the contrary, whether it was excessive under the circumstances.[9]

The court went on to note the widow, despite her earlier experience, exhibited a "superficial"[10] comprehension of the markets. Her use of the jargon of the industry tended to establish that she was a "woman trying to appear smarter than she really was."[11] It was the court's conclusion that the gains in her own account had resulted mainly from advice from her former stockbroker and husband rather than from her own dealings.

In a way the *Hecht* decision is schizophrenic in terms of the widow's degree of sophistication. On the one hand the court prevented Mrs. Hecht from complaining about breaches of fiduciary duty and the suitability of the transactions because she was sophisticated enough to understand the transactions. On the other hand, the court found her superficial knowledge of the transactions did not allow her to recognize the excessive nature of the transactions sufficient to bar her claim of churning.

Perhaps our illustrative case reveals more of the judicial process than meets the eye. The decision of the court could be justified by the hair-splitting distinctions made by the court, or by simply noting that the facts of the case relative to the churning and fraud were so bad, the court was compelled to do something. If the latter theory is correct, we return to the fundamental instincts of society being expressed in the decisions of judges, juries, and arbitrators. Review of cases involving customer-broker relationships can be bewildering in the contradictions between cases of almost identical facts. The result, however, of the *Hecht* case can be explained by the nature of the misdeeds, as fully observed by the court in its decision.

[9] *Id.*, 433.
[10] *Id.*
[11] *Id.*

THE COURT'S DECISION ON CHURNING

Similar to our discussion of churning in Chapter 10, the court looked at three factors:

1. Practical control over the account by the broker as to the volume and frequency
2. Whether an excessive number of transactions was present
3. Whether the commissions and profits appeared to benefit the salesman and broker without regard to the needs and objectives of the customer

The court found the requisite control by noting that the widow invariably followed the broker's advice except for a few instances where she had entered transactions after reading something about a specific company. The question of excessive trading presented no problem based upon the following.

> The evidence is to the effect that of a total of 644 security transactions, 296 or 45% were held for less than 6 months; 434, or 67% were held less than 9 months; and 529, or 82% were held less than a year.
>
> The securities account, according to plaintiff's theory of computing turnover rate, was turned over 11.5 times during the 6 year, 10 month period. According to defendants' theory, the turnover rate was 8.04 times.
>
> The commodities account, assuming an average investment of about $35,000, and a gross volume of purchases and sales of 89 million, was turned over about 2,500 times during the period.
>
> On an account of about $500,000, plaintiff paid commissions and markups of $189,000 on security and commodity transactions, and interest of $43,000—a total of $232,000, or about 40% of the size of the account without considering plaintiff's capital gain taxes which further affected the possibilities for net gain.
>
> Commissions earned by [the firm] on plaintiff's account on security transactions—$76,000—were more than any other of the firm's 8,000–9,000 security accounts in the San Francisco Office—except 11–14 other accounts—and amounted to 39% of all security commissions generated by [the salesman].
>
> Commissions earned by [the firm] from plaintiff's account on commodity transactions—$98,333—were more than any other commodity account at its San Francisco Office, 31%—38% of all commodity commissions at that office and 59% of all commodity commissions generated by [the salesman].

Although plaintiff's account represented less than ¹/10 of 1% of the accounts in the San Francisco Office, the commissions ($174,000) and the interest ($43,000) charged plaintiff represented at least 4.7% of the total income of the San Francisco Office—about 50 times the average charged a customer during the period.

In the course of 1200–1400 security transactions and 4457 closed commodity transactions [the salesman] generated 51% of the total commissions earned by him for [the firm].[12]

As noted earlier, the court found the damages to consist of commissions and interest of $232,000 and $143,000 in other damages due to churning (losses in her commodities account and lost dividend income). These other damages were reversed on appeal by the Court of Appeals for the Ninth Circuit. What is confusing is that other courts of equal stature have endorsed legal standards which could have supported an award of trading losses and lost dividend income. In *Fey v. Walston & Co.*,[13] the Court of Appeals for the Seventh Circuit expressed the possibility of awarding greater damages than commissions and interest by stating in a note to its decision

By this we do not mean to indicate that some other measure of damages should not be considered by trial courts in appropriate cases—loss-of-bargain recovery, for example.

See *'Churning by Securities Dealers'* 80 Harvard Law Review, 869, 884 (1967), *supra*. We think there may be merit to the view that the traditional discretion left to trial courts should be heavily relied upon while the law in this area remains largely uncharted. *Ibid* at p. 885. And it seems unlikely that a rule can be designed to cover all combinations of fact and their complications beyond the generalization that damages should compensate the customer by fair approximation for the losses sustained as a proximate result of unlawful churning.[14]

Customers and brokers are not expected to know the details of the uncharted seas of damages. It is enough to know that given the facts of a churning case, the amount of damages may be the amount of commissions and interest caused by the churning; all losses proximately caused by the

---

[12] *Id.*, 436.

[13] 493 F.2d 1036 (7th Cir. 1974).

[14] *Id.*, 1054, n.26. A close reading of the appellate court decision in *Hecht v. Harris, Upham & Co.*, 430 F.2d 1202 (9th Cir. 1970) does not necessarily limit damages due to churning to commissions and interest. The appeals court merely found it inconsistent to award 'other damages' due to estoppel, yet award the same damages as an adjunct to a churning claim.

churning, such as loss of bargain damages; or anything in between. Each should also be aware that questions of law related to "uncharted" areas may necessarily have to be resolved in lengthy appeals.

FRAUD

In *Hecht,* the salesman was found to have committed fraud in buying shares of stock from Mrs. Hecht for an amount far less than their true market value. The actual value of the securities was approximately $64,520 more than the broker had paid Mrs. Hecht, which the court found to be the measure of damages. In addition, churning was found to be a violation of the antifraud provisions of the Securities Act and Securities Exchange Act.

These are clear examples of fraud but at the other end of the spectrum, and a little bit more difficult for all to understand, are misrepresentations or concealments of material facts which may constitute fraud under the securities acts and common law. Fraudulent misrepresentations can be defined as those representations which

1. When made were false
2. Were made by the broker with the knowledge that the facts were false (or without a care as to whether the facts were true or false)
3. Were made with the expectation that the plaintiff would rely upon said misrepresentations in acting
4. The plaintiff reasonably relied upon

As part of its discussion of churning, the court in *Hecht* noted that the usefulness of the confirmation slips and monthly statements was limited by the salesman's practice of taking the confirmation slips from the widow after each of his weekly visits and his practice of preparing annual summaries. The last summary misrepresented the status of the account by the use of misleading statements to the effect that "the account still has a greater value than the original amount."[15] This in fact was contrary to the true status of the account which had been substantially diminished, and the court found that the broker expected Mrs. Hecht to rely on the misleading statement, and that it was reasonable for Mrs. Hecht to rely upon the broker's representations. The court discussed what the proper disclosure should have been related to the trading.

[15] 283 F. Supp. 417, 439 (N.D. Cal. 1968).

We are of the opinion that, when the extent, volume and frequency of the trading to which plaintiff was apparently assenting, or to which at least she was not objecting, began to impair the net value of her capital and its potential for real income, it became [the salesman's] duty to frankly and fairly explain these basic considerations to her.[16]

The obligation on the part of the broker to make full disclosure is especially acute with decisions like *Leib v. Merrill, Lynch, Pierce, Fenner & Smith, Inc.,*[17] where the court stated

[W]here the customer is uneducated or generally unsophisticated with regard to financial matters, the broker will have to define the potential risks of a particular transaction carefully and cautiously. Conversely, where a customer fully understands the dynamics of the market or is personally familiar with a security, the broker's explanation of such risks may be merely perfunctory.

*   *   *

Where a broker engages in a more active trading, particularly where such trading deviates from the customer's stated investment goals or *is more risky than the average customer would prefer, he has an affirmative duty to explain the possible consequences of this action to his customer. This explanation should include a discussion of the effect of active trading upon broker commissions and customer profits.* (emphasis added)[18]

Close analysis of the facts in individual cases and general statements of law only confuse the issues even more. *Hecht,* for example, presumably involved an educated woman who had over 23 years of experience in the stock market before her salesman was found liable for fraudulent churning of her account, which involved the nondisclosure of a material fact, i.e., the impairment of her capital due to trading losses and commissions. The court seems to have glossed over the fact that her accountants presumably were given accurate summaries of the transactions for purposes of computing her capital gains and losses each year of the six years and ten months of trading. It may also seem improbable that she could not ascertain her losses from the monthly statement she received.

Given the court's decision and perception of broker's duties, it would appear that to avoid fraud, brokers must be careful when dealing with unsophisticated and even "sophisticated" clients like Mrs.

[16] *Id.,* 434.
[17] 461 F. Supp. 951 (E.D. Mich. 1978).
[18] *Id.,* 953–4.

Hecht, especially when varying from stated investment goals. Given the possibility of later fraud claims for not disclosing the material risks of the transaction when such transactions are more risky than the average customer (notably left undefined by the court) would prefer, the prudent broker might well be advised not to enter the unsuitable transactions.

THE RESPONSIBILITY OF THE FIRM

Brokerage firms are often tied to the acts of their salespeople by principles of agency (the salesperson's status as an employee or agent of the firm), by accepting and defending the conduct of the salesman, or by participating in prohibited conduct, among other things. More often, however, the firm's system of supervision or its enforcement is called into question. As noted in the *Hecht* case, where the court reviewed publications from various organizations which the firm was a member of

> These publications indicate that good standard practice in the brokerage business requires that a "partner" is obliged to know the "essential facts" relative to each customer and to "supervise diligently" all accounts handled by registered representatives to obtain the appropriate facts concerning each customer prior to opening the account; that each time a new account is opened new information should be obtained directly from the customer; that the investigation performed by the registered representative should be a continuing one; that note of any changes in the customer's financial status should be kept; that the registered representative should ascertain whether the customer understands the basic mechanics of purchasing securities; that representatives must know and keep themselves informed of circumstances relating to their clients' interest which may have a bearing on the clients' interests as investors, and that a firm should not rely exclusively on a registered representative to obtain the essential facts but should have a series of checks to determine that the full facts are being obtained sufficiently to satisfy the firm's responsibilities.
>
> It might be noted that a [firm] supervisory memorandum required a partner to approve commodity transactions for a woman's account before it was effected (Plaintiff's Exhibit 13) and that its Commodity Manual made commodity accounts for women unacceptable unless approved by a partner who has determined that the woman has "sufficient experience and knowledge of commodity trading."[19]

[19] 283 F. Supp. 417, 438 (N.D. Cal. 1968).

The evidence in the *Hecht* case indicated that the brokerage firm knew or should have known that Mrs. Hecht was a retired person who was living off the dividend income from her account. Additionally, the account documents were deemed to be insufficient because they did not provide a space to determine the age, financial circumstances, previous securities experience, the investment objectives or needs of the client or other information which would allow the broker to know his client. The branch office manager for the firm had never met or talked to the customer and had relied solely upon the salesman to inform him as to her situation. Before entering high risk commodity futures and other speculative transactions no additional inquiries had been made by the firm. The branch office manager admitted that he "knew very little about the Hecht account—notwithstanding the fact that the firm's daily records clearly indicated that her account was among the most actively traded and most lucrative (in terms of commissions and interest earned by the firm) in the San Francisco office."[20] As stated by the court

> The Court finds and concludes from the evidence that [the] defendant [firm] did not maintain a reasonably adequate system of internal supervision and control; that it did not enforce with any reasonable diligence such system as it did maintain and that in this respect [the] defendant [firm] cannot be said to have acted in good faith within the meaning of Section 20(a) of the Securities Exchange Act (15 U.S.C. Sec. 78t(a)) but did, on the contrary, indirectly induce, participate in, approve and accept the benefits of what we have found to be the excessive trading of the account by [the salesman].[21]

On those transactions where the salesman had defrauded the widow by buying her securities for $64,520 less than their true value, the firm was also found to be responsible even though the salesman acted contrary to firm policy. It appears the salesman was also a manager for the firm and by virtue of his role as an employee and manager, his acts were deemed to be the acts of the firm. This finding was probably supported by the firm's failure to exercise appropriate supervision. Thus, the firm was found liable for something it probably knew nothing about and would surely have objected to.

The importance of tying a firm to the acts of its salespeople may be strictly a practical consideration. Few salespeople have the financial resources to pay a judgment of any magnitude. If a salesperson is the only defendant found liable, but is unable to pay, a judgment may only be

---

[20] *Id.*, 439.
[21] *Id.*

useful to paper one's bathroom (along with stock certificates from one's latest hot tip). Firms often view themselves as defendants only because they have "deep pockets," but it should be noted the firm will only be found liable if they meet the criteria of having somehow participated in or ratified the acts complained of, or failed in their supervisory duties. Avoiding such responsibility depends upon strict supervision, prudent hiring practices, and termination or censure of employees engaged in prohibited acts.

PUNITIVE DAMAGES

Along with the actual losses sustained by a customer, certain conduct exposes the salesperson and the broker to punitive damages.[22] The court in *Hecht* found such damages were not allowed under the federal securities act claims, but could be awarded under the state law claims. Although the churning and fraud findings would lead to punitive damages in most cases (based upon review of other cases where less egregious offenses have led to substantial punitive damages), the court in *Hecht* declined to award such damages due to its award of prejudgment interest and the fact that the defendants were subject to disciplinary proceedings before the NASD.

Punitive damages are often called exemplary damages. To customers and their attorneys, punitive damages result in additional compensation for their efforts. Defendants may view this as unjust compensation, since such damages exceed the customer's actual damages. In theory, punitive damages are justified as having a deterrent effect in cases involving "circumstances of aggravation or outrage, such as spite or 'malice,' or a fraudulent or evil motive on the part of the defendant, or such conscious and deliberate disregard of the interests of others that his conduct may be called willful or wanton."[23]

In practice, juries who are asked to decide punitive damage claims are instructed on the law by judges. An example of such an instruction is

> If you find that plaintiff suffered actual damage as a proximate result of the conduct of the defendant on which you base a finding of liability, you may then consider whether you should award additional damages against defendant, for the sake of example and by way of

[22] Other potential claims of a punitive nature, such as causes of action under special federal or state statutes which may lead to a trebling of actual damages and an award of attorney's fees and costs are not discussed for the sake of clarity.

[23] W. Prosser, *Handbook of the Law of Torts*, 9–10 (4th ed. 1971).

punishment. You may in your discretion award such additional damages, known as punitive or exemplary damages, if, but only if, you find a preponderance of the evidence that said defendant was guilty of oppression, fraud, or actual malice in the conduct on which you base your finding of liability.

"Malice" means a motive and willingness to vex, harass, annoy, or injure another person. Malice may be shown by direct evidence of declarations of hatred or ill-will or it may be inferred from acts and conduct, such as by showing that the defendant's conduct was wilful, intentional, and done in reckless disregard of its possible results.

"Oppression" means subjecting a person to cruel and unjust hardship in conscious disregard of his rights.

"Fraud" as used in this instruction means an act of trickery or deceit, intentional misrepresentation, concealment or nondisclosure committed for the purpose of causing injury or depriving a person of his property or his legal rights.

The law provides no fixed standard as to the amount of such punitive damages, but leave the amount to the jury's sound discretion, exercised without passion or prejudice.[24]

It is the lack of fixed standards related to punitive damages which causes concern to the defense, especially where oppression, fraud, or malice can effectively be argued. This overview does not purport to champion or condemn punitive damages, but merely to recognize such damages as a risk in disputes of a substantial nature. All concerned may minimize the exposure to such damages by adhering to the rules and weeding out substandard personnel as quickly as possible.

STATUTES OF LIMITATIONS

Waiver, estoppel, and laches are legal defenses which may require a customer to bring a lawsuit within a reasonable time after notification of an error. A statutory or common law time limit within which a lawsuit or claim must be filed provides the outer limit of the time within which someone has a right to sue. After that legal time period runs, the statute of limitations bars even the most meritorious of lawsuits. As noted in the *Hecht* case, causes of action under section 10b-5 and Rule 19b-5 rely upon state statutes of limitations related to fraud, which was three years in Mrs. Hecht's case. Given the fact that Mrs. Hecht's claim for churning arose over the course of six years and ten months, why

---

[24] California Jury Instructions (Civil) 635–36 (P. Richards 6th ed. 1977).

was she allowed to recover all of the commissions and interest due to churning?

The court noted in its decision that the state statute did not begin to run until Mrs. Hecht discovered the fraud, and set the date of discovery as the date when Mrs. Hecht's accountants advised her the account had been substantially impaired.

> The applicable California statute is, therefore, Cal.C.C.P. Sec. 338(4) providing a three year limitation for actions for relief on the ground of fraud provided, however, *that the cause of action is not deemed to accrue until the discovery by the aggrieved party of the facts constituting the fraud.*
>
> We have held that Rule 10b-5 does condemn churning and we have also found that so far as "excessive" trading is concerned, i.e., churning, the information on hand to plaintiff at any one time, considered in the light of the limitations upon her competence and the circumstances already reviewed, was not sufficient to put her on notice that the trading of her account was excessive—until she was so advised by her income tax accountants in March, 1964—the date we find to be the date of discovery so far as "excessive" trading is concerned. (Emphasis added)[25]

Caution would be advised relative to statutes of limitation. First, the defense would be entitled to argue that the date of discovery of the facts should have been earlier since she was receiving confirmation slips, monthly statements, the salesman met with her weekly, and the accountants were provided with annual summaries. Second, the applicable statutes of limitation may be as short as one year relative to certain types of transactions.

> It will be observed, therefore, that the limitations contained in Section 29 (providing a 1 year statute of limitations after discovery) would be applicable only (1) to excessive transactions in the "over-the-counter" markets, (2) to transactions in which the broker or his agent is vested with a "discretionary power," and (3) to actions in reliance upon Section 29 (15 U.S.C. § 78cc) to declare contracts void for violation of a rule prescribed by Section 15(c)(1).[26]

In Mrs. Hecht's case, the one year statute of limitations was found not to be applicable, but it may apply in other types of transactions. Thus, it is advisable to seek legal assistance as soon as possible after a problem occurs.

[25] 283 F. Supp. 417, 441 (N.D. Cal. 1968).
[26] *Id.,* 441–42.

THE BATTLE TO GET INTO OR OUT OF COURT

There will be one issue which should be common to all cases which post-date the *Hecht* case. As we have discussed, based upon the Supreme Court's decision in *McMahon*, disputes will generally be heard before arbitration panels, because of the arbitration clauses which have become standard provisions in customers' agreements. Some customers' attorneys will routinely resist arbitration believing that

> The brokerage firms would love to see all disputes between them and their customers arbitrated. For one thing arbitration is quicker than litigation. More important, critics of the arbitration system say, the amount of money a client can expect to get in an arbitration proceeding in which he prevails is less—often far less—than what a court might award.[27]

Or, as noted by Justice Blackmun in his dissent in *McMahon*

> Furthermore, there remains the danger that, *at worst*, compelling an investor to arbitrate securities claims puts him in a forum controlled by the securities industry. This result directly contradicts the goal of both securities acts to free the investor from the control of the market professional. The Uniform Code provides some safeguards but despite them, and indeed because of the background of the arbitrators, the investor has the impression, frequently justified, that his claims are being judged by a forum composed of individuals sympathetic to the securities industry and not drawn from the public. It is generally recognized that the codes do not define who falls into the category "not from the securities industry." (citation omitted) Accordingly, it is often possible for the "public" arbitrators to be attorneys or consultants whose clients have been exchange members or SROs. See Panel of Arbitrators 1987–1988, CCH American Stock Exchange Guide pp. 159–160 (1987) (53 out of 70 "public" arbitrators are lawyers). The uniform opposition of investors to compelled arbitration and the overwhelming support of the securities industry for the process suggest that there must be *some* truth to the investors' belief that the securities industry has an advantage in a forum under its own control. See N.Y. Times, Mar. 29, 1987, section 3, p. 8, col. 1 (statement of Sheldon H. Elsen, Chairman, American Bar Association Task Force on Securities Arbitration: "The houses basically like the present system because they own the stacked deck").[28]

---

[27] Barrons, Mar. 2, 1987, at 16. This statement was made the day prior to oral arguments before the Supreme Court in *McMahon*.

[28] Shearson/American Express, Inc. v. McMahon, 482 U.S. _____, 107 S. Ct. 2332 (1987).

Obviously, the brokerage industry denies there is a "stacked deck" and takes the position that arbitration is quicker, cheaper, and fairer to all concerned. The authors decline to jump into the middle of this debate, other than to observe that great effort is often expended by customer's attorneys to avoid arbitration whereas brokers' attorneys usually exert equally great effort to avoid the courts. This battle to get into court appears to be especially frequent in the larger cases or cases involving punitive damages.

Despite the concerns of customers, it is likely disputes will generally be heard before arbitration panels. If customers do not want their cases arbitrated they should consider striking arbitration clauses if possible from customer agreements. The alternative will be to prove some reason to void the arbitration clause, such as fraud in the procurement of the agreement to arbitrate. The clear preference would be the right to avoid signing an arbitration agreement if one does not wish to do so.[29]

CONCLUSION

The aim of this chapter has been to illustrate, educate, and warn both customers and brokers of the risks of litigation and arbitration. Customers must be concerned about delays in bringing errors to the attention of brokers through informal complaints or court cases. If moneys are lost, the customer's road to the recovery of such losses is covered with pitfalls, delays, and further expense.

Brokers must be concerned with the problems created by salespersons who act out of greed rather than fulfilling professional responsibilities. The possibility of losses in productivity, reputation, and judgments must be a consideration.

As the *Hecht* case illustrates, disputes are to be avoided. If we assume the widow in *Hecht* was as much the victim as her attorneys advocated, and she was in fact a widow in her late 60s when the trading began, who was systematically defrauded over almost seven years. Her inability to recognize what was happening to her was based upon her trust and confidence in the salesman, but resulted in losses of over $1,109,000 in the amount of equity she would have had if the account had been maintained. The result of the litigation was the return of the commissions paid and margin interest of $232,000, plus interest of about $65,000, and $64,520 related to two fraudulent transactions.

---

[29] In futures, brokers may not reject an account if a customer refuses to sign an arbitration agreement, but they can reject a securities account.

Thus, at the end of the litigation Mrs. Hecht was 80 years old, with less than one-third of the equity she should have had. Assuming she paid her attorneys on a contingency fee basis of one-third of the recovery, and if she had expenses of $20,000 resulting from the litigation, she would have received as a net amount about $222,000, or about 20 percent of the equity she should have had.

On the other hand, let us assume the salesman and broker were totally blameless and that Mrs. Hecht was a canny, sophisticated investor who called her broker every morning to direct a myriad of investments in which she had nearly a quarter century of experience. Let us further assume that each transaction was in fact ordered by the widow who was in every respect the "veteran gambler" which the defense observed. The results for the broker are even less satisfactory. Years of litigation, loss of reputation, a finding of churning and fraud, a significant monetary award, and the possibility of censure or license revocations. Was the dispute worth it for either side?

Prevention of disputes is a far better scenario. Many problems could be avoided in the first place by employing common sense, which tells us that situations which seem too good to be true probably are. Recognize that some stockbrokers are overly aggressive salespeople and if they claim to have a foolproof system or one which increases reward while minimizing risks, either run as fast as possible or get it in writing—preferably, the former.

Salespeople should be mindful of their basic conflict of interest. Do not solicit business just to generate commissions. If salespersons cannot make an honest living by selling respectable products in an honest way, another line of work might be best for them, their firms, and certainly for their customers.

17

The Lawyer's Bookshelf

AN APPROACH TO BROKER-CUSTOMER DISPUTES

Let us assume you are an experienced litigation attorney. Your firm has been approached by a brokerage house or by a customer concerning a dispute and has accepted the case. You have little or no training in such disputes or in securities law. How do you prepare to handle the case?

Obviously, consideration should be given to associating counsel familiar with such disputes or with securities law. If the economics of the case allow for co-counsel, then the respective roles of the attorneys must be coordinated. If the economics do not justify co-counsel, then a significant amount of research time should be spent in educating oneself. This chapter provides an approach towards such self-education in the law, just as this book as a whole has attempted to give brokers, customers, and attorneys a general overview of disputes.

One approach would be to consult with expert witnesses as soon as possible. They can be a tremendous source of information related to the specific technical and legal problems in your case. Expert witnesses are often familiar with the statutory framework, regulations, exchange rules, and customs and trade practices within the industry. Pleadings, briefs, discovery material, and legal citations may be available from such experts and can form the starting point for drafting, research, and analysis.

In educating oneself on the legal and technical aspects of a case, a large number of publications are available. Some of the publications which may be helpful are listed here.

Securities

American Bar Association, Litigation Section, Broker/Dealers Subcommittee of the Securities Litigation Committee, *Model Jury Instructions in Broker/Customer Litigation.* October 1986. (Usually quoted in brokers' briefs.)

Federal Securities Law Reports. Chicago: Commerce Clearing House.

Goldberg, Stuart C. *Fraudulent Broker-Dealer Practices.* New York: American Institute for Securities Regulation, 1978.

Jacobs, Arnold S. *Litigation and Practice Under Rule 10b-5.* New York: Clark Boardman Company, LTD., 1982.

Jaffee, Sheldon M. *Broker-Dealers and Securities Markets: A Guide to the Regulatory Process.* Colorado Springs: Shepard's, Inc., 1977.

Loss, Louis. *Fundamentals of Securities Regulation.* Boston and Toronto: Little, Brown & Co., 1983.

Meyer, Charles H. *The Law of Stockbrokers and Stock Exchanges.* New York: Baker, Voorhis & Co., 1931. (Out of print, but may be available in larger law libraries.)

NASD Manual. Chicago: Commerce Clearing House, 1985.

New York Stock Exchange Guide. Chicago: Commerce Clearing House. (Or consult the exchange rules related to the case.)

Teweles, Richard & Bradley, Edward. *The Stock Market.* 5th ed. New York: John Wiley & Sons, Inc., 1987.

Commodities

Chicago Board of Trade, *Commodity Trading Manual.* 1985.

Commodity Futures Law Reports. Chicago: Commerce Clearing House.

Fishman. *Commodities Futures: An Introduction for Lawyers.* 65 Chicago Bar Record 306 (1984).

Johnson, Philip & McBride. *Commodities Regulation.* Boston and Toronto: Little, Brown & Co., 1982.

Labuszewski, John & Sinquefield, Jeanne. *Inside the Commodity Option Markets.* New York: John Wiley & Sons, Inc., 1985.

Markham, Jerry W. *Commodities Regulation: Fraud, Manipulation & Other Claims.* New York: Clark Boardman Company, Ltd., 1988.

Teweles, Richard J. & Jones, Frank J. *The Futures Game: Who Wins? Who Loses? Why?* 2d ed. New York: McGraw-Hill, 1987.
Russo, Thomas A. *Regulation of the Commodities Futures and Options Markets.* Colorado Springs: Shepard's/McGraw-Hill, 1983.

Options

Chicago Board Options Exchange Guide. Chicago: Commerce Clearing House.
Gastineau, Gary L. *The Stock Options Manual.* 3rd ed. New York: McGraw-Hill, 1988.

These publications are listed only as a starting point. If a regular diet of broker-customer disputes is anticipated, then additional publications should be gathered over time, such as other exchange manuals, product manuals, Option Clearing Corporation manuals, and policy and procedure manuals from major brokerage houses.

All of the above represent sources for legal and technical issues. Publications like the *Chicago Board Options Exchange Guide* offer sources for brokers' duties in options cases. Rule 9.8(a), for example, covers supervision, which includes the appointment of a senior registered options principal (SROP) who "shall develop and implement a written program for the review of the organization's non-member accounts and all orders in such accounts, and Rule 9.8(b) specifies the appointment of a compliance registered options principal (CROP) (which may be the SROP) who "shall be responsible to review and propose appropriate action to secure the member organization's compliance with securities laws and regulations and Exchange rules in respect of its options business." Obviously, in any case involving options, the manner in which such supervision was implemented or conducted is important.

CASES YOU SHOULD KNOW

The methodology by which the following cases were selected is important. Theoretical disputes over esoteric areas of the law were avoided in favor of a more practical approach. The cases were selected in recognition of their almost routine appearance in court or arbitration briefs. The cases are reviewed relative to their most common usage, but many cases, like

[1] 619 F.2d 814 (9th Cir. 1980).
[2] 262 Cal. App. 2d 690, 69 Cal. Rptr. 222 (1968).

Mihara v. Dean Witter & Co.,[1] and *Twomey v. Mitchum, Jones & Templeton, Inc.*[2] are cited for many different reasons. Where cases or issues have been highlighted in other chapters, they may not be referred to again.

To begin, an issue in each case will involve the decision of whether to file for litigation or arbitration. The economic impact of the decision has been discussed in Chapter 14, and the legal analysis is covered herein.

The Battle to Get into or out of Court

The validity of arbitration clauses in customers' agreements is a crucial issue in determining whether a case may proceed in court. Prior to and for a period of time after *Dean Witter, Reynolds, Inc. v. Byrd,*[3] there was a split among the courts of appeals related to whether arbitration clauses in customers' agreements would be enforced and, if so, what causes of action would be susceptible to arbitration. Practitioners, the district courts, and the courts of appeals were confused by the holding in *Wilko v. Swann,*[4] which looked with disfavor on the arbitration process and appeared to make it a violation of federal securities statutes even to attempt to force arbitration of federal securities claims.

Some brokerage houses did not have arbitration clauses in their customers' agreements, presumably because of the Supreme Court's decision in *Wilko,* various decisions of the circuits, and later, SEC Rule 15c 2-2 (adopted on November 28, 1983 and discussed *infra*), which prohibited arbitration clauses seeking to compel arbitration of federal securities law claims. However, the vast majority of brokerage houses have arbitration clauses in their customers' or margin agreements.

In *Byrd,* the brokerage firm had filed a motion to sever state law claims from a pending federal court lawsuit and to compel arbitration of these state claims. The broker further asked for a stay of the arbitration of the state law claims pending the resolution of the federal claims in the litigation. Under the facts in *Byrd,* the Supreme Court's decision was limited to enforcing the arbitrability of the state law causes of action, and the arbitrability of federal law claims was left up in the air.

We now come to the Court's decision in *Shearson/American Express, Inc. v. McMahon,*[5] which appears to enforce arbitration clauses for both state and federal law claims unless they are clearly nonarbitrable by statute or "absent a well-founded claim that an arbitration agreement resulted from the sort of fraud or excessive economic power that 'would

[3] 470 U.S. 213 (1985).
[4] 346 U.S. 427 (1953).
[5] 107 S. Ct. 2332 (1987).

provide grounds for the revocation of any contract.'"[6] Before turning to the issue of how arbitration clauses might be voided, some observations about *McMahon* are necessary.

McMahon involved causes of action under section 10(b) of the Securities Exchange Act of 1934 (including claims under SEC Rule 10b-5), the Racketeer Influenced and Corrupt Organizations Act (RICO), and state law fraud and breach of fiduciary duty claims. The district court held that the Securities Exchange Act and state law claims were arbitrable, but the RICO claim was not. The Court of Appeals for the Second Circuit affirmed on the state law claims, but decided that the Securities Exchange Act and RICO claims were not subject to arbitration.

The facts of the case involved an arbitration provision which read as follows

> Unless unenforceable due to federal or state law, any controversy arising out of or relating to my accounts, to transactions with you for me or to this agreement or the breach thereof, shall be settled by arbitration in accordance with the rules, then in effect, of the National Association of Securities Dealers, Inc. or the Boards of Directors of the New York Stock Exchange, Inc. and/or the American Stock Exchange, Inc. as I may elect.[7]

Before the Supreme Court, the McMahons complained that arbitration of section 10(b) claims would be destructive to their rights under the Securities Exchange Act, as had been pointed out in the *Wilko* decision. *Wilko* had raised serious questions as to whether arbitrators would apply federal securities law correctly, since arbitrators did not generally state how they interpreted the law in arriving at their decision. *Wilko* pointed out that judicial bodies reviewing arbitrators' decisions would not be able to find a ground for reversal without written decisions and in the absence of a record of the proceedings. The Court in *McMahon* indicated that the significant issues raised in *Wilko* about arbitration were no longer material when it stated

> In 1953, when *Wilko* was decided, the Commission had only limited authority over the rules governing self-regulatory organizations (SROs)—the national securities exchanges and registered securities associations—and this authority appears not to have included any authority at all over their arbitration rules. (Citation omitted.) Since the 1975 amendments to § 19 of the Exchange Act, however, the

[6] Id., 2337.
[7] Id., 2335–36.

Commission has had expansive power to insure the adequacy of the arbitration procedures employed by the SROs. No proposed rule change may take effect unless the SEC finds that the proposed rule is consistent with the requirements of the Exchange Act, 15 U.S.C. § 78s(b)(2); and the Commission has the power, on its own initiative, to "abrogate, add to, and delete from" any SRO rule if it finds such changes necessary or appropriate to further the objectives of the Act, 15 U.S.C. § 78s(c). In short, the Commission has broad authority to oversee and to regulate the rules adopted by the SROs relating to customer disputes, including the power to mandate the adoption of any rules it deems necessary to insure that arbitration procedures adequately protect statutory rights. (Footnote omitted).

In the exercise of its regulatory authority, the SEC has specifically approved the arbitration procedures of the New York Stock Exchange, the American Stock Exchange, and the National Association of Securities Dealers, the organizations mentioned in the arbitration agreement at issue in this case. We conclude that where, as in this case, the prescribed procedures are subject to the Commission's § 19 authority, an arbitration agreement does not effect a waiver of the protections of the Act. While *stare decisis* concerns may council against upsetting *Wilko*'s contrary conclusion under the Securities Act, we refuse to extend *Wilko*'s reasoning to the Exchange Act in light of these intervening regulatory developments.[8]

In dissent, relative to whether section 10(b) claims should be arbitrable, Justice Blackmun criticized the majority's view of the adequacy of existing arbitration procedures by observing

> Even those who favor the arbitration of securities claims do not contend, however, that arbitration has changed so significantly as to eliminate the essential characteristics noted by the *Wilko* court. Indeed, proponents of arbitration would not see these characteristics as "problems," because, in their view, the characteristics permit the unique "streamlined" nature of the arbitral process. As at the time of *Wilko*, preparation of a record of arbitration proceedings is not invariably required today. Moreover arbitrators are not bound by precedent and are actually discouraged by their associations for giving reasons for a decision. See R. Coulson, *Business Arbitrations—What You Need to Know*, 29 (3d Ed. 1986) ("Written opinions can be dangerous because they identify targets for the losing party to attack"); see also Duke Note, at 553; Fletcher, 71 Minn.L.Rev., at 456–457. Judicial review is still substantially limited to the four grounds listed in § 10 of

[8] Id., 2341.

the arbitration act and to the concept of "manifest disregard" of the law.[9]

The SEC's position in its amicus briefs and the reliance of the Court on the SEC's position was severely criticized by Justice Blackmun.

> More surprising than the Court's acceptance of the present adequacy of arbitration for the resolution of securities claims is its confidence in the Commission's oversight of the arbitration procedures of the SROs to ensure this adequacy. Such confidence amounts to a wholesale acceptance of the Commission's *present* position that this oversight undermines the force of *Wilko* and that arbitration therefore should be compelled because the Commission has supervisory authority over the SROs' arbitration procedures. The Court, however, fails to acknowledge that, until it filed an *amicus* brief in this case, the Commission consistently took the position that § 10(b) claims, like those under § 12(2), should not be sent to arbitration, that predispute arbitration agreements, where the investor was not advised of his right to a judicial forum, were misleading, and that the very regulatory oversight upon which the Commission now relies could not alone make securities-industry arbitration adequate. (Footnote omitted.) It is most questionable, then, whether the Commission's recently adopted position is entitled to the deference that the Court accords it.
>
> The Court is swayed by the power given to the Commission by the 1975 amendments to the Exchange Act in order to permit the Commission to oversee the rules and procedures of the SROs, including those dealing with arbitration. See *ante*, at _____ (slip op.12). Subsequent to the passage of these amendments, however, the Commission has taken the *consistent* position that the predispute arbitration agreements, which did not disclose to an investor that he has a right to a judicial forum, were misleading and possibly actionable under the securities laws. (Footnote omitted.) The Commission remained dissatisfied with the continued use of these arbitration agreements and eventually it proposed a rule to prohibit them, explaining that such a prohibition was not inconsistent with its support of arbitration for resolving securities disputes, particularly existing ones. See Disclosure Regarding Recourse to the Federal Courts Notwithstanding Arbitration Clauses in Broker-Dealer Customer Agreements, SEC Exchange Act Rel. No. 19813 (May 26, 1983), [1982–1983 Transfer Binder] CCH (Fed. Sec. L. Rep., para. 83,356, p. 85,967, while emphasizing the Court's *Wilko* decision as a basis for its proposed rule, the Commission noted that its proposal also was in line with its own understanding of the problems with such agreements and with the "[c]ongressional determination that public investors

---

[9] *Id.*, 2354–55.

should also have available the special protection of the Federal Courts for resolution of disputes arising under the Federal Securities Laws." *Id.*, at 85,968. Although the rule met with some opposition, (Footnote omitted) it was adopted and *remains in force today.* (Footnote omitted) (Court's emphasis.)[10]

The rule referred to by Justice Blackmun is Commission Rule 15c 2-2 adopted on November 28, 1983, which provided that it was a fraudulent, manipulative or deceptive act or practice for brokers to have agreements binding customers to arbitration of future disputes arising under federal securities laws. Accounts operating under agreements containing such arbitration clauses at the time the Commission adopted the rule were to have been sent notices with the following disclosure

> Although you have signed a customer agreement form with [FIRM NAME] that states that you are required to arbitrate any future dispute or controversy that may arise between us, you are not required to arbitrate any dispute or controversy that arises under the Federal securities laws but instead can resolve any such dispute or controversy through litigation in the courts.[11]

Following the Court's decision in *McMahon*, the Commission rescinded the rule by Exchange Act Release No. 2503 (October 15, 1987), but an argument may be made that those persons who were sent the notice between November 28, 1983 and the effective date of its rescission have the right to litigate. This argument apparently could not be made on behalf of the McMahons, since the term of their accounts was between 1980 and 1982.

The effect of the *McMahon* decision may result in creating two trials in the event a customer's attorney decides to attack the arbitration clause in an attempt to get into court. The first could involve a jury trial under the Federal Arbitration Statute to determine whether or not any reason exists to declare the arbitration clause or the customer's agreement void. If the arbitration clause is declared void, then litigation on the merits would proceed.

One approach to voiding the arbitration clause can be seen in a case predating *Byrd* and *McMahon*. In *Main v. Merrill, Lynch, Pierce, Fenner & Smith*,[12] an arbitration clause was voided and the court stated

[10] *Id.*, 2356.
[11] 17 C.F.R. § 240.15c2-2.
[12] 67 Cal. App. 3d 19, 136 Cal. Rptr. 378 (1977).

A question before us is whether it may be inferred that defendants gained an advantage over plaintiff by inclusion, in the lending agreement, of the provision to arbitrate.

It is said on high authority that the right to select a judicial forum, vis a vis arbitration, is a "substantial right," not likely to be deemed waived. (See *Wilko v. Swan,* (1953) 346 U.S. 427, 438, 74 S.Ct. 182, 98 L.Ed 168; *Boyd v. Grand Trunk Western R. Co.,* (1949) 338 U.S. 263, 266, 70 S.Ct. 26, 94 L.Ed 55.) In a factual context somewhat similar to that before us, the federal Court of Appeals has decried the practice of securities dealers "using their superior bargaining position to require arbitration clauses in contracts with members of the investing public." (*Laupheimer v. McDonnell & Co., Inc.,* (2 Cir. 1974) 500 F.2d 21, 26.) And it is notable that the defendants and plaintiff, respectively, of the instant proceeding treat the subject arbitration clause as an advantage to be held, and as a disadvantage to be invalidated.[13]

The court in *Main* went on to find that relationships involving trust and confidence require the duty of full disclosure of all material facts and any concealment would be fraudulent. In effect, the court found that the defendant brokers were under an obligation to disclose to the customer that important legal rights were being waived by virtue of the arbitration provision.

Many other methods of attack on arbitration clauses will be tried using successful arguments in other types of cases where an agreement has been found void, such as fraudulent inducement, adhesion contracts, etc. Perhaps, to alleviate some concerns about the unequal economic position of the parties, the securities statutes should make it improper to refuse an account if a customer does not want arbitration.[14] In any event, it would seem important for brokers to give a fair presentation of the arbitration provision to a customer and to allow a free and informed decision to be made.

Fiduciary Relationships

A difficult point to establish is when a fiduciary relationship arises between a broker and the customer. Fiduciary relationships may be

---

[13] *Id.*, 32.

[14] As suggested by Justice Blackmun, a legislative answer may be necessary. At the time *McMahon* was decided Representative Dingell, Chairman of the House Subcommittee on Oversight and Investigations, was conducting hearings on the adequacy of the SRO's arbitration procedures. Given the *McMahon* decision customers may have to lobby for legislation if the adequacy of the arbitration procedures is still a perceived problem in the future. This effort is likely if the SEC does not mandate changes to the present arbitration procedures.

established by the nature of the agency, contractual duties, custom and trade practice, or even firm policy, which might recognize the relationship to be one involving a "sacred trust to protect" the firm's customers.[15]

Customers' attorneys often refer to *Twomey v. Mitchum, Jones & Templeton, Inc.*,[16] or analogous cases to indicate that a fiduciary relationship exists whenever the broker-client relationship is entered into.[17]

> "The relationship between broker and principal is fiduciary in nature and imposes upon the broker the duty of acting in the highest good faith towards the principal." (Citations omitted.) With respect to stockbrokers it is recognized, "The duties of the broker, being fiduciary in character, must be exercised with the utmost good faith and integrity. (Citations omitted.)[18]

On the other hand, brokers' attorneys do not agree that every broker-customer relationship is a fiduciary relationship, and point to cases like *Robinson v. Merrill, Lynch, Pierce, Fenner & Smith*,[19]

> A broker's office, without special circumstances not present here, is simply to buy and sell. The office commences when the order is placed and ends when the transaction is complete.[20]

Other facts and circumstances which tend to establish a fiduciary relationship are social and business relationships, placing one's confidence and trust in a broker, or some dependence of the customer upon the recommendations of the broker. As noted by Professor Loss: "Unfortunately there is no touchstone for determining when a dealer assumes the obligation of a fiduciary . . . ."[21]

Other variant themes related to fiduciary duties are exemplified by decisions like *Leboce, S. A. v. Merrill, Lynch, Pierce, Fenner & Smith, Inc.*,[22] where the court stated: "It is where the agent 'for all practical purposes' controls the account that California law imposes fiduciary obligations."[23]

---

[15] Mihara v. Dean Witter & Co., Inc., 619 F.2d 814 (9th Cir. 1980).

[16] 262 Cal. App. 2d 690, 69 Cal. Rptr. 222, 236 (1968).

[17] *See also*, Charles H. Meyer, *The Law of Stockbrokers and Stock Exchanges* (New York: Baker, Voorhis & Co., 1931), 251–252, which describes virtually every transaction as involving a fiduciary relationship.

[18] 69 Cal. Rptr. 222, 236 (1968).

[19] 337 F. Supp. 107 (N.D. Ala. 1971), *aff'd per curiam*, 453 F.2d 417 (5th Cir. 1972).

[20] *Id.*, 111.

[21] L. Loss, *Fundamentals of Securities Regulation* (Boston and Toronto: Little, Brown & Co., 1983), 966.

[22] 709 F.2d 605 (9th Cir. 1983).

[23] *Id.*, 607.

Establishing a fiduciary responsibility may depend upon a case by case analysis of the nature of the customer's relationship to the broker. The court in *Leboce* would apparently concur that stockbrokers who advise widows who have no previous experience in securities are fiduciaries, as opposed to the situation in *Leboce* where the customer was a Luxembourg investment holding company for which the broker was a mere order taker.

Suitability

The suitability doctrine has been thoroughly discussed in Chapters 6 and 13 relative to the duty of a broker to recommend the purchase or sale of securities suitable to the investment objectives and financial resources of a customer. In *Twomey v. Mitchum, Jones & Templeton, Inc.*, the court stated

> If, as appears from the evidence and as found by the court, it was improper for her to carry out the speculative objectives which defendants attribute to her (but which her testimony does not admit), there was a further obligation to make this known to her, and refrain from acting except on express orders.[24]

As such, *Twomey* stands for the proposition that no solicited orders (orders based upon the broker's recommendation) may be entered for an unsuitable investment.

The Issue of Control in Churning Cases

Many of the arguments in churning cases appear to revolve around the issue of control. The three common elements of churning are excessive trading in light of the investment objectives of the account, actual or de facto control over the account by the broker, and subservience of the customer's investment objectives to the interests of the broker in generating commissions or sales credits. The mainstream seems to be that where the customer typically follows the recommendations of a broker, the control element is satisfied by this de facto control of the account by the broker.[25]

Brokers' attorneys often quote from decisions like *Follansbee v. Davis, Scaggs & Co.*,[26] which they assert for the proposition that if the

[24] 262 Cal. App. 2d 690, 719 (1968).
[25] Mihara v. Dean Witter & Co., 619 F.2d 814, 821 (9th Cir. 1980).
[26] 681 F.2d 673 (9th Cir. 1982).

customer had the *capacity* to say no, then the customer is in control of the account and not the broker. The usual citation is

> As long as the customer has the capacity to exercise a final right to say "yes" or "no", the customer controls the account.[27]

Theoretically, applying the *Follansbee* standard, any person with a normal intelligence quotient is in control of her account and cannot claim churning as a cause of action. It may be that *Follansbee* can be distinguished on the basis that the customer kept accounting records, followed his transactions carefully, participated in discussions of investment strategies at his investment club, and was a very sophisticated investor.

The court in *Follansbee* was attempting to distinguish between Mrs. Hecht, who it described as an unsophisticated investor,[28] and Mr. Follansbee, who had a bachelors of art degree in economics and who apparently kept close watch on his investments. The actual standard enunciated in *Follansbee* is

> If a broker is formally given discretionary authority to buy and sell for the account of his customer, he clearly controls it. *Short of that, the account may be in the broker's control if his customer is unable to evaluate his recommendations and to exercise an independent judgment.* (Citations omitted.)
>
> In *Hecht*, the customer was a widow. She spent most of her adult life working as a housekeeper and as a tutor of children. Finally, she married a man in whose home she had worked as a housekeeper and, a few years later inherited a small fortune from him. Her account was very actively handled in securities and commodities markets. The District Judge found that she knew nothing whatever of commodity trading and that her understanding of securities transactions was minimal.

* * *

> The touchstone is whether or not the customer has sufficient intelligence and understanding to evaluate the broker's recommendations and to reject one when he thinks it's unsuitable. Mrs. Hecht was found to lack that capacity. Lacking that capacity, Mrs. Hecht necessarily relied on her broker's expertise. (Emphasis added.)[29]

---

[27] *Id.,* 677.

[28] Apparently, the court overlooked Mrs. Hecht's 20-plus years of prior securities experience which estopped her from complaining about breaches of fiduciary obligations and the suitability of the transactions. Hecht v. Harris, Upham & Co., 430 F.2d 1202 (9th Cir. 1970).

[29] 681 F.2d 673, 676 (9th Cir. 1982).

The law may eventually turn to a middle ground as exemplified by decisions like *Costello v. Oppenheimer & Co.*,[30] which held

> A few courts have suggested, as a third element, that the customer must also have been relatively unsophisticated about the market. (Citations omitted.)
>
> But while it is true that most successful churning plaintiffs have fit within this category, (citation omitted) imposing lack of sophistication as an absolute requirement would appear to go too far. Even a savvy investor may choose, for various reasons, to entrust the handling of his account to the broker and there is no reason to immunize that broker if he exercises control and intentionally trades the account excessively. The better view would seem to be that business sophistication is simply another consideration bearing upon the issue of control.[31]

As an additional consideration, churning claims are also subject to attack relative to how the excessiveness of the trading was computed. In securities, a ready reference to methods of computations and authorities may be found in *Hecht v. Harris, Upham & Co.*,[32] and Note, *Churning by Securities Dealers*, 80 Harv. L. Rev. 869 (1967). *Looper and Co.*,[33] is a case involving one of the first expressions by the SEC of turnover ratios, and is often quoted.

Special problems exist in the computation of excessive trading in options and commodities which may be explored in greater detail by reviewing articles such as Poser, *Options Account Fraud: Securities Churning in a New Context*, 39 Bus. Law. 571 (1983) and Teweles, *Excessive Trading and the Expert Consultant*, Commodity Futures Law Letter, vol. IV, no. 2 (April 1984).

Damages in Churning Cases

A definitive statement of how damages should be computed in churning cases has been virtually impossible for the courts to fashion. As seen in Chapter 16, *Hecht* is a good starting point for any analysis of churning damages.

Brokers' counsel tend to cite the appellate court's decision in *Hecht* for the proposition that the measure of damages in churning cases is the

---

[30] 711 F.2d 1361 (7th Cir. 1983).
[31] *Id.*, 1369 n.8.
[32] 283 F. Supp. 417, 435–36 (N.D. Cal. 1968).
[33] 38 S.E.C. 291 (1958).

amount of commissions generated. However, customers' attorneys are quick to point out that the appellate court's decision is restricted to the particular facts of the case, which limited the amount of damages based upon the trial court's findings on estoppel, waiver, and laches.[34]

Given the "uncharted" seas of damages, the cases and articles which could be reviewed as a start would include the trial and appellate court's decisions in *Hecht; Fey v. Walston & Co.;*[35] *Churning by Securities Dealers,* 80 Harv. L. R. 869 (1967); and *Miley v. Oppenheimer & Co.*[36]

In *Miley,* after an extensive review on the issue of churning damages, Justice Goldberg expressed the Fifth Circuit's view of damages as follows

> First, and perhaps foremost, the investor is harmed by having had to pay the excessive commissions to the broker—the "skimmed milk" of the churning violation. The broker's wrongful collection of commissions generated by the intentional, excessive trading of the account constitutes a compensable violation of both the federal securities laws and the broker's common law fiduciary duty, regardless of whether the investor's portfolio increased or decreased in value as a result of such trading. Second, the investor is harmed by the decline in the value of his portfolio—the "spilt milk" of the churning violation—as a result of the broker's having intentionally and deceptively concluded transactions, aimed at generating fees, which were unsuitable for the investor. The intentional and deceptive mismanagement of a client's account, resulting in a decline in the value of that portfolio, constitutes a compensable violation of both the federal securities laws and the broker's common law fiduciary duty, regardless of the amount of the commissions paid to the broker. In sum, once a jury finds that the broker has churned an investor's account, it may also find that the investor would have paid less commissions and that his portfolio would have had a greater value had the broker not committed the churning violation. See Nichols, *The Broker's Duty to His Customer Under Federal Fiduciary and Suitability Standards,* 26 Buff.L.Rev. 435, 445 (1977) ("Where there is excessive trading in an account ("churning"), the customer can be damaged in many ways. He must pay the brokerage commissions on both purchases and sales, he may miss dividends, incur unnecessary capital gain or ordinary income taxes depending on the holding period, and, most difficult to measure, he may lose the benefits that a well-managed portfolio in long-term holdings might have brought him"); Brodsky, *Measuring Damages in Churning and Suitability Cases,* 6 Sec.Reg. Law J. 157,

---

[34] *See* discussion of the court's decision on churning in Chapter 16.
[35] 493 F.2d 1036 (7th Cir. 1974).
[36] 637 F.2d 318 (5th Cir. 1981).

159–160 (1978). ("Most often, the customer complains that the broker churned unsuitable securities. Then, both causes of action are appropriate and both damage theories [excess commissions and excess decline in portfolio value] should be considered.")[37]

Review of the legal theories on churning damages must be supplemented by a command of the facts of each case. Where a customer, for example, has ordered unsolicited trades, losses and commissions related to such transactions would appear inappropriate to include in one's damage calculations.

Estoppel, Ratification, Waiver and Laches

Common defenses for brokers revolve around customer's delays in objecting to transactions. A few cases which appear popular from defense briefs would be *Ocrant v. Dean Witter & Co.,*[38] *Merrill, Lynch, Pierce, Fenner & Smith, Inc. v. Bocock,*[39] *Royal Air Properties, Inc. v. Smith.*[40]

Ocrant and *Bocock* are cited for the proposition that delays may be found to bar the customer's claims. *Ocrant* involved imputing to a wife the knowledge of the husband at the time of the transactions that sales of the wife's "nest egg" were taking place. When the wife objected nine months later the husband's knowledge and failure to object precluded recovery. *Bocock* involved a short sale which the plaintiff (a successful businessman) knew about, but did not object to until some eleven months later. *Royal Air* is often quoted as follows

> The purpose of the Securities Exchange Act is to protect the innocent investor, not one who loses his innocence and then waits to see how his investment turns out before he decides to invoke the provisions of the Act.[41]

Often unsophisticated customers are excused from acting.[42] As the court stated in *Karlen v. Ray F. Friedman & Co.*

---

[37] *Id.,* 326.
[38] 502 F.2d 584 (10th Cir. 1974).
[39] 247 F. Supp. 373 (S.D. Tex. 1965).
[40] 312 F.2d 210 (9th Cir. 1962).
[41] *Id.,* 213.
[42] Karlen v. Ray F. Friedman & Co., 688 F.2d 1193 (8th Cir. 1982); Hecht v. Harris, Upham & Co., 430 F.2d 1202, 1208–09, 1211 (9th Cir. 1970); Kravitz v. Pressman, Frolich, & Frost, Inc., 447 F. Supp. 203, 211 (Mass. 1978).

The defendant next contends that even if the trades were unauthorized, the plaintiff's actions are barred by the doctrine of ratification, waiver and estoppel. Although these doctrines are distinct, (footnote omitted) the defendant—by relying on the same underlying facts—has essentially treated them as one defense. Its theory is, in essence, that the Karlens' claim must fail as a matter of law because even if the plaintiffs did not authorize the trades, they knowingly and voluntarily assented to them after they occurred.

* * *

We reject the defendant's arguments. The question is not simply whether Karlen assented to the trades; rather it is whether his apparent assent was given voluntarily and intelligently with full knowledge of the facts . . . .
Several factors support the jury's finding that the plaintiffs did not knowledgeably and voluntarily consent to the trades. First, we must consider the factual setting in which this controversy arose. Commodities futures trading is an arcane and complicated field in which specialized knowledge is generally required to participate intelligently and successfully. (Citations omitted.) *The plaintiffs lacked sophistication and experience as commodities futures traders. (Emphasis added.)*[43]

The court further stated that

It has been recognized that confirmation slips and monthly statements *do not* enable a customer to determine his or her overall position or the total amount of real profit or loss occurring, *unless the customer is sufficiently skilled to elaborate upon them to make that determination.* (Citations omitted.) *When a customer lacks the skill or experience to interpret confirmation slips, monthly statements or such other documents, courts have generally refused to find that they relieve a broker of liability for its misconduct. (Citations omitted.) (Emphasis added.)*[44]

In *Fey v. Walston & Co., Inc.,*[45] the court likewise stated that

To create an estoppel some reliant change in position by the one claiming the estoppel is essential, and waiver presupposes knowledge of one's rights and intent to relinquish them. Royal Air Properties, Inc. v. Smith, 333 F.2d 568 (9th Cir. 1964), *supra. Mere failure to read statements and confirmations, or to object to actions revealed therein, could not be deemed sufficient as a matter of law to establish waiver or to raise an estoppel in view of plaintiff's theory of fiduciary relationship and related impositions by defendants.*

[43] Karlen v. Ray F. Friedman & Co., 688 F.2d 1193, 1197–98 (8th Cir. 1982).
[44] *Id.,* 1200.
[45] 493 F.2d 1036 (7th Cir. 1974).

> *Express consent to churning transactions would not necessarily raise these defenses if such consent were induced by the undue influence of a fiduciary. Indeed, it has been said that transactions initiated by the customer themselves may be indicative of churning where the trust and confidence of the customer vest control in the broker. Moscarelli v. Stamm, 288 F.Supp. 453 (E.D.N.Y. 1968). (Emphasis added.)*[46]

An extension of the defenses of ratification, waiver, and estoppel relates to proposed standards of customer due diligence as exhibited in cases and articles like *Eichen v. E. F. Hutton,*[47] *Thompsen v. Smith, Barney, Harris, Upham & Co.,*[48] and *Customer Sophistication and a Plaintiff's Duty of Due Diligence: A Proposed Framework for Churning Actions in Nondiscretionary Accounts Under SEC Rule 10b-5,* 54 Fordham L. Rev. 1101 (1986).

Computations of Portfolio Damages Due to Unsuitability or Fraud

Damages in the context of broker-customer disputes are complex, but should be ascertained as soon as practical. Some issues related to damage calculations have been resolved. In tax shelter cases, for example, where rescission is the remedy sought, there should be no offset for tax benefits. *Austin v. Loftsgaarden.*[49] However, how are damages computed where there is a wholesale loss in portfolio value due to alleged breaches of fiduciary duties and fraud? The legal question has been susceptible to many different analyses, but the decisions in *Rolf v. Blyth, Eastman Dillon & Co.,*[50] (Rolf I) which did not award net trading losses; *Rolf v. Blyth, Eastman Dillon & Co.*[51] (Rolf II) directing that trading losses be awarded upon suggested methods of computation; and *Rolf v. Blyth, Eastman Dillon & Co.*[52] (Rolf III) applying damage calculations to the case on remand; and the second circuit's review of these decisions in *Rolf v. Blyth, Eastman Dillon & Co.*[53] are often quoted.

It appears from the multiple decisions in *Rolf* that once the beginning and end dates for the relevant time period are established, the following may be one standard to follow in computing damages

[46] *Id.,* 1050.
[47] 402 F. Supp. 823 (S.D. Cal. 1975).
[48] 709 F.2d 1413 (11th Cir. 1983).
[49] 106 S. Ct. 3143 (1986).
[50] 424 F. Supp. 1021 (S.D.N.Y. 1977).
[51] 570 F.2d 38 (2d Cir. 1978).
[52] [1979 Transfer Binder] Fed. Sec. L. Rep. (CCH) ¶ 96,919 (S.D.N.Y. 1979).
[53] 637 F.2d 77 (2d Cir. 1980).

The proper method of determining damages is to take the initial value of the portfolio, adjust it by the percentage change in an appropriate index during the aiding and abetting period, and subtract the value of the portfolio at the end of the period.[54]

The facts of individual cases will likely influence the selection of an appropriate index. It is unlikely that effective settlement negotiations may be entered into unless there is some common ground for damage calculations.

Mitigation of Damages

Mitigation of damages is only briefly mentioned here. As a general principle of law, there is little to add to the existing body of knowledge. Consideration should be given to the effects of the market on the calculation of damages.

Markets are not static and an unauthorized purchase of stock on October 10, 1987 may have resulted in a tremendous loss for a customer on Black Monday, October 19, 1987. Standards related to mitigation of damages may have required the customer to liquidate his positions and the failure to mitigate damages may impact settlement negotiations or limit damages.

Use of Internal Rules as Standards of Care

Under a negligence theory, custom and practice within an industry may be introduced as evidence of the appropriate standard of care.

Section 295 A. Custom

In determining whether conduct is negligent, the customs of the community, or of others under like circumstances, are factors to be taken into account, but are not controlling where a reasonable man would not follow them.[55]

The introduction of these standards of care in broker-customer disputes has been made in cases like *Mihara*,[56] where an employee's handbook was admitted to establish a fiduciary relationship.

The court in *Thropp v. Bache, Halsey, Stuart, Shield, Inc.*[57] stated

---

[54] *Id.*, 84.
[55] Restatement (Second) of Torts § 295A (1965).
[56] Mihara v. Dean Witter & Co., 619 F.2d 814 (9th Cir. 1980).
[57] 650 F.2d 817 (6th Cir. 1981).

The instant case involves evidence of *violations* of custom and *internal* rules. When a defendant has disregarded rules that it has established to govern the conduct of its own employees, evidence or those rules may be used against the defendant to establish the correct standard of care. The contents of such rules may also indicate knowledge of the risks involved and the precautions that may be necessary to prevent the risks. . . . The District Court correctly measured Bache's conduct by the standard of prudence it has established for its own employees. [Citations omitted.] (Court's emphasis.)[58]

An example of the full use of internal procedures and policy manuals would be *Henricksen v. Henricksen*,[59] as described in Chapter 15.

Regarding admission of testimony about NYSE and NASD rules the court in *Mihara* found

Appellants' second point, that the Court should not have permitted testimony regarding the rules and regulations of the New York Stock Exchange, is without merit. New York Stock Exchange Rule 405 requiring that each securities broker "know [his] customer" has been recognized as a standard to which all brokers using the Exchange must be held, the violation of which is tantamount to fraud. *Rolf v. Blyth, Eastman Dillon, supra,* 424 F.Supp., at 1041. The Court in *Rolf* went so far as to permit a private cause of action for violation of NYSE Rule 405. *Id.* Appellants contend that the admission of testimony regarding New York Stock Exchange and NASD rules served to "dignify those rules and regulations to some sort of standard." The admission of testimony relating to those rules was proper precisely because the rules reflect the standard to which all brokers are held.[60]

Caution should be observed in attempting to establish any private right of action based upon NASD or exchange rules under sections 15A(b)(6) and 6(b) of the SEA, respectively. *Jablon v. Dean Witter & Co.,*[61] for example, is consistent with those cases which refuse to recognize violations of NYSE and NASD rules as a private right of action. An example of a contrary view would be the Second Circuit's decision in *Leist v. Simplot.*[62]

[58] *Id.,* 820.
[59] 640 F.2d 880 (7th Cir. 1981).
[60] Mihara v. Dean Witter & Co., 619 F.2d 814, 824 (9th Cir. 1980).
[61] 614 F.2d 677 (9th Cir. 1980).
[62] 638 F.2d 283 (2d Cir. 1980).

Private Rights of Action

Frequent arguments occur over the question of whether there are implied private rights of action for violations of particular federal statutes. Such a private right of action under the fraud provisions of the Commodity Exchange Act was found in *Merrill, Lynch, Pierce, Fenner & Smith v. Curran*, [63] which provides a historical review of the Court's standards in analyzing the issue. In note 51 to the *Curran* decision the Court reviewed the four-part test enunciated in *Cort v. Ash*, [64] as involving

1. Whether the plaintiff is in the class whom the statute was intended to benefit
2. Expressions of legislative intent to create or not to create a remedy
3. Whether a private cause of action would be consistent with the underlying purposes of the legislative scheme
4. If it involves an area traditionally relegated to state law so that it would be inappropriate to imply a private cause of action

The holding in *Curran* basically finds that at the time the Commodity Exchange Act was passed, the courts had already recognized that private remedies were available under existing commodities statutes. Thus the court found that "The inference that Congress intended to preserve the preexisting remedy is compelling."[65]

It was in this light that the Court found that it need not go through the four-part *Cort* test in order to find an implied right of action. See also, *Transamerica Mortgage Advisors, Inc. v. Lewis*, [66] establishing a limited private right of action under the Investment Advisors Act.

CONCLUSION

The selection of the foregoing topics and the suggested publications has been aimed toward giving the nonspecialist an introduction to some of the common issues involved in broker-customer disputes. It is hoped that this chapter provides a convenient point of reference in beginning

[63] 456 U.S. 353 (1982).
[64] 422 U.S. 66 (1975).
[65] 456 U.S. 353, 387 (1982).
[66] 444 U.S. 11 (1979).

a study of the law related to such disputes. Nothing will substitute for substantial research and preparation.

Although much time has been spent on the battle to get into or out of court, it should be remembered that the decision is one involving a substantial economic decision as discussed in Chapter 14. Smaller cases should probably be arbitrated. Cases involving significant losses, perhaps in amounts exceeding $100,000; and for cases involving some clearly fraudulent or reprehensible conduct, litigation should be initiated as soon as possible. The time spent on the issue of arbitration versus litigation simply reflects one of the significant legal battles which has gone on in the last decade. That battle is likely to continue until some resolution is reached which is acceptable to all.

18

Keeping the Peace

The increased volatility of many financial instruments in recent years has resulted in greater than usual opportunities for profit. As is usually true, these opportunities are accompanied by greater than usual risks. So long as those who sell financial instruments tell those who buy them that risks can be tightly controlled or even eliminated through the use of technical devices or trading strategies, and those who buy are willing to believe such representations, there will be disputes. Increased volume and scale of trading results in more and larger disputes concerning what was said or what should have been said and these disputes cannot be casually brushed aside.

No book can ever eliminate disputes between brokerage houses and their customers. So long as brokers are paid commissions based on trading activity and most customers would be wiser to follow a strategy of buy and hold or not to invest at all, there will be conflicts. So long as brokerage house personnel offer naive or unreasonable projections about markets which are practically, if not entirely efficient, thereby precluding the value of most predictions, there will be conflicts. So long as new arcane and complex financial instruments and complex strategies are introduced and accompanied by esoteric jargon, there will be conflicts. So long as some brokerage house personnel and some customers are dishonest, there will be conflicts.

This book was not conceived as a how to manual for either customers or brokers. It does not provide a set of guidelines for customers to sue brokers in an effort to recover money lost as a result of a customer's own acts, or by uncontrollable and unpredictable circumstances. It also does not purport to help brokers escape their liability for wrongdoing by providing advice on how best to delay proceedings, inflate a customer's legal costs, or harass or browbeat customers to the point where even when they are in the right, they give up because of monetary expense or mental and emotional stress. It is not designed to teach attorneys how to encourage lawsuits and arbitrations bordering on the frivolous merely to gain a nuisance settlement offer or to incur costs for discovery if the costs greatly exceed the value of what is discovered.

If this book could accomplish the mission contemplated by its authors, the number of disputes would be materially reduced. Costs and losses associated with disputes that remain would also be reduced. It should be helpful to end this book with some reminders of the most constructive actions that can be taken by our cast of characters to make the financial world a better place.

EDUCATION

Many problems are caused by simple misunderstanding of terminology and concepts. An investment program can provide a stimulating as well as a financially rewarding activity for all persons involved. Spending a reasonable time learning about investments may prove to be quite valuable both intellectually and financially. The student of finance, of course, like the students of other complex fields, always faces the problem of learning which approaches and sources are accurate or, at least, logical.

Customers can read books or shorter publications about the securities and futures markets on almost any level desired, but must take a little time to distinguish between scholarly publications and self-serving works which offer advice that springs full-blown from the imaginations of their authors but has never been validated or yielded long-term successful results, even for the authors. Cynics have long questioned why winning trading systems would be sold for a few dollars a year by someone who must know that widespread use of such systems would render them worthless. Active or potential investors can also consider interesting and inexpensive short courses offered by the extension arms of local universities and probably acquire knowledge of far more value than that acquired at "seminars" offered by those with something to sell. Some of the printed material offered by brokerage houses is well written, evenhanded, and of real value. Such materials may cite risks which a salesperson may have glossed over or omitted to mention. If so, further inquiry may suggest a wiser approach to investing or, perhaps, to one's choice of a broker.

All too many customers maintain that they did not have time to read material that could easily be absorbed in an hour, or allege that they did not understand the material. It is worth spending some time understanding something as important as the acquisition and preservation of one's wealth. If any terms or concepts are not understood, questions can be asked or references can be consulted. Salespersons should take care not to convince customers that reading and asking questions are unnecessary because they will be ever watchful of the client's best interests.

Brokerage house sales personnel would be well advised to know more about their business than they learned in their training classes, or acquire from reading the morning gossip, by watching a quotation machine, or by updating their dog-eared charts. Dealing in financial products should be a professional activity and, as is true in all professions, there is always more to learn. Although any brokerage house personnel worth their salt will read a basic financial newspaper and a financial magazine or two, this is not nearly enough. The financial world is broad and deep and is constantly changing.

Salespersons who conclude that the financial world is too complex to absorb and that it is wiser to specialize than make the attempt to learn more are all too often dangerous to their clients. Unlike professionals in other fields, salespersons are reluctant to refer clients to other specialists. Not only are they paid on commission, but they must always seek new customers as old ones are lost because they die, move away, or, most likely, withdraw their accounts because of results deemed to be unsatisfactory. Salespersons who specialize are only too likely to recommend that their clients buy whatever item that has been chosen by the salesperson as his specialty. This leads to potentially serious problems of unsuitability and solicitation without reasonable basis. It would be far healthier for salespersons to learn enough about all of their firms' merchandise to be able to handle the varying needs of different clients.

Salespersons who refuse to learn anything about futures, options, bonds, investment companies, or other products commonly offered by many financial firms are more likely to be mentally lazy than truly professional specialists. Salespeople who believe that a product or strategy is beyond their capacity to understand are better advised to refer the customer to a qualified person than to risk errors or to use the customer's trading as a learning experience. Giving up or splitting commission revenues may prove to be the most economical approach in the long run.

Firms can provide really valuable education through their own internal training programs. This should go beyond providing advice about sales techniques or information about the mere mechanics of the business. A thorough understanding of finance should be imparted by experienced internal personnel. If such people are not available, competent outside instructors should be utilized. Instructors should not only be informed about their areas but should know how to teach. Proper training will return its cost many times over not only in increased revenue, but in reduced problems. A serious dispute can easily cost a firm its profit from a branch office for an entire year or more. Presentations to a firm's training classes, sales forces, or management personnel about compliance can be of great value but are seldom stressed or absorbed by the students because there is no quick and clear translation of such presentations into revenue.

For lawyers, the education process is more evident. Their basic function is maintaining their professionalism as advisors and litigators. Some litigation is unsuitable simply in terms of its potential risks, costs, or the chance of prevailing. Beyond this, however, individual attorneys cannot possibly know everything there is to know about the wide variety of cases that may come their way. If a case is beyond their experience, they should acquire a more knowledgeable co-counsel or engage consultants who can educate them quickly and relatively economically. If a case is not settled, such consultants may later effectively be used to assist at trial or arbitration or to testify as expert witnesses if technical testimony is needed. Considering that brokerage firms are usually represented by house counsel or by law firms which specialize in financial disputes, attorneys who do not acquire some help may find themselves at a serious disadvantage in financial cases even though they have a high degree of skill in litigation.

Attorneys who are especially interested in financial disputes should certainly acquire and read some basic literature. In addition to respected law books emphasizing financial disputes there are services that provide current information about securities and futures. Attorneys should also absorb at least one basic general text on stocks, one on futures, and one on options. In addition, the rule books of the various exchanges and regulatory bodies can be of great value. As attorneys acquire experience, they will also acquire files containing much of value such as the internal operations, policy, compliance, and sales manuals of various brokerage firms, internal memoranda, and samples of the documents typically used in the finance industry.

SUPERVISION

A surprising amount of trouble is caused by inadequate supervision either by a brokerage firm's local management, central management, or both. The fact that all too many salespersons are more interested in selling than learning is well known. In fact, some firms maintain that a salesperson's primary job is to acquire and service a clientele and they should not be concerned with basic research which is best left to the research department.

It is only natural for such sales personnel to be interested primarily in the number of accounts they open, the size of the pool of capital that can be utilized for investment, and the sales revenue generated therefrom. Although a firm needs revenue to pay its bills, sales personnel who try too hard to produce revenue may cause problems that can substantially exceed all the revenue generated. Eventually the firm may be left with nothing but a loss if the salesperson's customers lose too much or lose as a result of misrepresentations, churning, or other abuses. In addition to out-of-pocket losses and the costs of financing disputes, the firm may also lose both salespersons and the clientele who choose to erase their unpleasant pasts and seek their fortunes elsewhere.

Local management should review new account documents carefully for completeness, accuracy, and determination of customers' suitability. Orders, daily blotters, and statements should be studied logically and carefully and management should not regard this task as merely undesirable red tape interrupting more important activities. Early detection of abuses may save substantial amounts of money for a firm.

Central management should have well-designed controls to make certain that effective local supervision is taking place. The various manuals that firms prepare dealing with such topics as policies, compliance, operations, management, and sales should be kept updated and efficiently distributed. Some effort should be made to make certain that recipients are made aware of important changes and do not merely place the manuals unread on a shelf.

Margin policies should be clear and compliance should be rigid. Local managers are all too often caught between central managers who want money collected promptly and fully, and local star salespeople who want to please important clients by giving them more time to meet margin calls or avoid forced liquidations. If a firm threatens to sell a customer's position and fails to do so, the customer can then complain about losses that occur if the market for his position worsens. If a firm liquidates a position which then improves, the customer can allege that he fully intended to deposit sufficient funds to support the position but was not given a reasonable time to do so.

Activity letters designed to confirm customers' satisfaction with frequent trading or relatively high commission generation in their accounts should be carefully followed up and not just mailed. It is far better to get a written or a documented oral response directly from a customer than to merely rely upon a salesperson's assurance that all is well.

THE PAPER TRAIL

As is true with most disputes, especially where there may be real misunderstandings concerning what was said or what was meant, clear and timely documentation can be of vital importance if fair resolutions of such misunderstandings are to be accomplished. If both sides are reasonable it is even possible sometimes to retain mutual good will when events are clarified.

Customers should read all documents signed when an account is opened and ask questions if anything is unclear. They should obtain copies of whatever is signed and retain them. Confirmations should be checked for accuracy when received and kept at least until the monthly statement reflecting the same trades has also been received and checked. Inaccuracies and unexplained or unclear transactions should be questioned promptly. If the salesperson does not offer a satisfactory explanation, the manager should be called or sent a certified letter.

Salespeople should complete documents accurately and fully. They should not base information upon mere observation or conjecture. This is especially true of information gathered to evaluate initially or update customers' suitability. Customers should not be hurried or lulled into signing anything which they do not thoroughly understand. They should be encouraged to ask questions and should be given copies of any documents signed.

It is wise for a salesperson to arrange a personal meeting with new clients at an early stage of their relationship rather than relying entirely on telephone or mail contact. If a customer is relying upon a broker's suggestions, personal meetings allow the use of illustrations, charts, or diagrams which may result in a greater understanding than is otherwise possible. Although a broker may be reluctant to foist advice on a customer, it might be wise to require a customer to provide something in writing indicating that he wishes to pursue a road that the broker believes will lead to ruin. Some people are inclined to accept the blame for problems which they cause for themselves, but others tend to take credit for successes and blame others for failures. The latter may be inclined to attempt to change history to justify their innocence. If a customer's proposed actions are unreasonably risky or foolish a broker would be well advised to reject the business or not maintain an account for that customer at all.

With or without the aid of ubiquitous computer output it is still wise for salespeople to maintain two basic records that are traditional in the brokerage business. One is a holding record for every customer indicating the activity in the account and a summary of each customer's objectives and any special kinds of service that have been requested and agreed to. Second is a cross-file of customers' holdings enabling appropriate follow-up service to be rendered.

The local manager should be certain that account information is accurate, updated, and utilized properly, and not merely filed. All correspondence to and from customers should be carefully monitored and filed in order to anticipate problems or, if this fails, to solve them as early and economically as possible.

If a dispute arises, salespersons and management should deal with them promptly in a forthright manner and not fan the flames by delaying responses or not responding at all. If exposure is serious, senior management should be notified, and clear internal documentation of the facts should be made as early and completely as possible.

If all of this is done well and conscientiously, it might be possible to avoid one of life's least pleasant documents—the one that begins with "Now Comes the Plaintiff . . . ."

Index

Order(s) *(Continued)*
  verbal instruction, 92
  writing buy instead of sell, 93
Over-the-counter (OTC) stocks:
  fees, 168, 169
  market(s), 27
  markups, 97–98
  participation, membership, 28
  specialty firms, 17–18

P

Pacific Stock Exchange, 27, 219
Partnerships:
  See also Limited partnerships
  opening accounts, 69
Passive:
  income, 87
  investors, 25
Payment rule, 50, 107
Penny stocks, 18, 91, 99, 109, 123
Performance guarantee, 177
Petroleum, 28
Philadelphia Stock Exchange, Inc., 219
Pink Sheets, 99
Pools, 41–42
  disputes in, 41
  limited partnerships, 42
  profits, 42
  vulnerability to legal action, 41
Post office box, 154
Powers-of-attorney, 69–70, 119
  cautions in granting, 165, 180
  discretionary accounts, 163, 165,
    232–233
  limited power, 163
  sample form, 164
Predictions, 281
Preferred stock, 34–35
  provisions, problems, 35
  risk, 34
Prices:
  efficient markets hypothesis, 6, 7
  markups, 98–99
Principles, 186–188

Private offerings, 196
Private rights of action, 279
Problems, customer responsibilities,
  183–185
Procedure manuals, 201, 225–229
  branch office manuals, 227
  compliance manuals, 227–228
  definitions in, 226
  operations manuals, 228
  options procedures, 228
  supervisors manuals, 227
Professional ethics, 20, 77, 85,
  192–193, 202–203
Profit(s):
  brokerage firms, 96–97
  futures accounts/margins, 113, 175
  pool operators, 42
Property, transfer of, 67
Prospectus, 97, 233
Prudential Insurance, 19
Public Utility Holding Company Act
  of 1935, 196
Puffing, 195
Punitive damage verdicts, 229,
  254–255
Puts and calls, 37, 38
Pyramid clubs, 99

R

Racketeer Influenced and Corrupt
  Organizations Act (RICO), 264
Real estate, partnerships, 42
Real estate investment trusts (REITs),
  43
Recommendation(s), by salespersons,
  192
Records, *See* Documents
Referrals, 57
Registered representatives:
  See also Brokers, Salespersons
  brokerage sales personnel, 130–131
  broker selection, 58–61
  earnings, 97
  investment advisers, 30